S

SOVIET and RUSSIAN NEWSPAPERS at the HOOVER INSTITUTION

HOOVER
INSTITUTION
BIBLIOGRAPHICAL
SERIES: XXIV

SOVIET and RUSSIAN NEWSPAPERS at the HOOVER INSTITUTION:

A CATALOG COMPILED BY KAROL MAICHEL

THE HOOVER INSTITUTION
ON WAR, REVOLUTION, AND PEACE
STANFORD UNIVERSITY 1966

FOREWORD

Frequently, American as well as foreign students and scholars who lack direct access to the Stanford campus request printed catalogs listing the various holdings of the libraries here. As a result, the Hoover Institution has in past years published "collection surveys" of its holdings on Russia,[1] Germany,[2] and Japan[3] thereby giving these interested persons at least the basic information on its collections. Since the last of these surveys was published in 1958, the extensive acquisitions made during the intervening years have made them obsolete.

This fact coupled with the growing worldwide demand for a more comprehensive presentation of the holdings of the Hoover Institution library made it obvious that the publication of detailed catalogs was of utmost importance. As a start, the Hoover Institution in 1963 published *A Checklist of Serials for African Studies, Based on the Libraries of the Hoover Institution and Stanford University*[4] prepared by Peter Duignan and Kenneth M. Glazier. Because of the ever-growing interest in African affairs, this publication became an immediate success both here and abroad. The extensive listing contained in this catalog resulted in its serving as a basic bibliographic tool for the development of African collections in many other libraries, including libraries in Africa.

The present checklist of Russian newspapers, prepared by Mr. Karol Maichel, the Curator of the East European Collection at the Hoover Institution, goes one step further: In addition to listing the complete holdings at the Hoover Institution, it contains references to the holdings of the Columbia University Library and the Library of Congress as well. A second publication, listing the Russian periodicals held here, is in preparation.

Other checklists of holdings of both the Stanford University and Hoover Institution libraries are approaching completion and will appear in the near future. Among these are a catalog of German language serials, a list of Polish periodicals and newspapers, holdings of statistical yearbooks, etc.

This and the other catalogs are prepared by the Hoover Institution staff as outside projects. It is to these dedicated and tireless workers that we are all indebted.

WITOLD S. SWORAKOWSKI
Assistant Director
Hoover Institution

Stanford, May 1966

---

[1] Sworakowski, Witold S. *The Hoover Library Collection on Russia.* Stanford, Stanford University Press, 1954. 42 p. (Collection Survey, No. 1.)

[2] Boeninger, Hildegard R. *The Hoover Library Collection on Germany.* Stanford, The Hoover Institution on War, Revolution, and Peace, 1955. 56 p. (Collection Survey, No. 2.)

[3] Ike, Nobutaka. *The Hoover Institution Collection on Japan.* Stanford, The Hoover Institution on War, Revolution, and Peace, 1958. 63 p. (Collection Survey, No. 3.)

[4] Duignan, Peter and Glazier, Kenneth M. *A Checklist of Serials for African Studies; Based on the Libraries of the Hoover Institution and Stanford University.* Stanford, The Hoover Institution on War, Revolution, and Peace, 1963. 104 p. (Bibliographical Series, No. XIII.)

v

INTRODUCTION

Newspapers are often one of the primary sources for scholarly investigation. They are of special importance to the student of the Soviet world since, in many instances, they are the only source dealing with a particular event in Soviet history. Equally important is the availability of ready information as to where these newspapers can be located in various American libraries. This catalog is an attempt to provide that information.

It is generally recognized that the four largest holdings in the Western Hemisphere of twentieth-century Russian language newspaper collections are to be found at the Hoover Institution at Stanford University, the Columbia University Library, the Library of Congress, and the New York Public Library. Most of the above libraries have already made their holdings in this field readily known by the issuance of catalogs.[1] The Hoover Institution, which is considered to have the largest collection of Russian newspapers, is now listing its holdings for the first time in catalog form. It is hoped this handy reference tool will enable the scholar to save many precious hours in his search for source materials.

The current catalog lists 1,108 titles of Russian language newspapers—Imperial Russian, Soviet, and émigré—held at the Hoover Institution as of January 1966. In addition to the obvious value of listing all holdings in a particular subject field under one cover, this catalog offers the further advantage of providing the following information: (1) References are given to catalogs of the Columbia University Library and the Library of Congress:[2] (2) References, whenever feasible, are given to other bibliographical works where specific and detailed bibliographical information on a particular title can be located.[3]

The newspapers listed here are arranged alphabetically by title. Different newspapers having the same title are listed alphabetically according to place of publication. Those newspapers still being received on a subscription basis are indicated by the wording "up to present" placed after the last year listed.

All titles are transliterated according to the Library of Congress system, with the exception that diacritical marks are omitted.

Translations are given of subtitles and names of publishing organizations when it is apparent that they indicate the nature and scope of the newspaper. These translations follow the Russian title or subtitle in square brackets.

Whenever available and deemed necessary, additional information on particular titles is given. Changes in titles are indicated whenever possible as are issues which have been

---

[1] New York Public Library. Reference Department. *Dictionary Catalog of the Slavonic Collection.* Boston, G. K. Hall and Co., 1959. 26 vols., folio.

For other catalogs see footnote 2.

[2] Horecky, Paul L. *Russian, Ukrainian, and Belorussian Newspapers, 1917–1953: A Union List.* Washington, Library of Congress, 1953. 218 p. (Referred to in text as *LC.*)

Maichel, Karol and Schatoff, M. V. *A List of Russian Newspapers in the Columbia University Libraries.* New York, Columbia University Libraries, 1959. 130 p. (Referred to in text as *Columbia.*)

[3] Lisovskii, Nikolai M. *Bibliografiia russkoi periodicheskoi pechati, 1703–1900 gg.* (Materialy dlia istorii russkoi zhurnalistiki). P., 1915. 1067 p. (Referred to in text as *Lisovskii.*)

Beliaeva, L. N. (and others). *Bibliografiia periodicheskikh izdanii Rossii, 1901–1916.* Pod obshch. red. V. M. Barashenkova. L., 1958–1961. Vols. 1–4. (Referred to in text as *Beliaeva.*)

suppressed or misnumbered. Cross references are provided if alternate spellings occur. In many instances, however, supplementary information was not available—usually for newspapers published irregularly in mimeographed form by émigré groups or by various short-lived political organizations.

Holdings are itemized and identified by date and/or number. Newspapers published during the period when the new style of dating was adopted for the Russian calendar often are given two dates, one to indicate the new style and the other, the old. Also, two numberings often appear for the same issue: the lower number represents the number of the issue within that particular year; the higher number, the number calculated from the original date of publication. For the sake of brevity, in some cases the identification of missing issues replaces the usual indication of holdings.

It should be called to the reader's attention that the present list represents only about 85 per cent of the Hoover Institution holdings of Russian newspapers. This discrepancy is due to technical problems with which all librarians are familiar and with which they will, no doubt, be sympathetic. For example, many of the titles which comprise the estimated missing 15 per cent were "one day's newspapers," or publications which started as newspapers and later became journals. It is our aim to remedy this gap in the forthcoming catalog of Russian language journals held at the Institution.

At this point, it is well to remind the reader that there are constant changes and new acquisitions in any library. Thus, it is possible that some of the titles or issues listed as missing in this catalog may have been acquired by the time the researcher has occasion to consult it.

In conclusion, I would like to express my gratitude to Mrs. Helena Sworakowski and Mrs. Maria Kolesnikoff for their very able assistance in compiling this catalog.

K. M.

ABBREVIATIONS

Amerik. Khris. o-vo molod. liudei	Amerikanskoe Khristianskoe Obshchestvo Molodykh liudei (YMCA)
ASSR	Azerbaidzhanskaia Sovetskaia Sotsialisticheskaia Respublika
b.	byvshikh
Beliaeva	Beliaeva, L. N. (and others) Bibliografiia periodiches-kikh izdanii Rossii, 1901-1916. Pod obshch. red. V. M. Barashenkova. L. 1958-1961. Vols. 1-4
Blag.	Blagoveshchensk
bw.	biweekly
Columbia	Maichel, Karol and Schatoff, M. V. A list of Russian Newspapers in the Columbia University Libraries. New York, Columbia University Libraries, 1959. 130 p.
dr.	drugie
D. V.	Dal'nii Vostok
Ekstr. prilozh.	ekstrennoe prilozhenie
Est.	established
f-ki	fabriki
g.	gorod(a)
gr.	graf
GSSR	Gruzinskaia Sovetskaia Sotsialisticheskaia Respublika
Gub.	Guberniia, gubernskii
H. I.	Hoover Institution
im.	imeni
inc., incomp.	incomplete
irreg.	irregular
ispolnit., ispolnitel'n.	ispolnitel'nyi
kaz.	kazach'i
KH. S. M. L.	Khristianskii Soiuz Molodykh Liudei (Y. M. C. A.)
KPA	Kommunisticheskaia partiia Armenii
KP(b)	Kommunisticheskaia partiia (bol'shevikov)
KP(b)U	Kommunisticheskaia Partiia (bol'shevikov) Ukrainy
KPSS	Kommunisticheskaia Partiia Sovetskogo Soiuza
K-t	komitet
Lisovskii	Lisovskii, Nikolai M. Bibliografiia russkoi periodi-cheskoi pechati, 1703-1900 gg. (Materialy dlia istorii russkoi zhurnalistiki). P., 1915. 1067 p.
m.	monthly
MGSPS	Moskovskii gorodskoi sovet professional'nykh soiuzov
MK i MGK	Moskovskii komitet i Moskovskii gorodskoi komitet

MK VKP(b)	Moskovskii komitet Vsesoiuznoi Kommunisticheskoi partii (bol'shevikov)
NKP	Narodnyi komissariat prosveshcheniia
No.	number
n. p.	no place
oblastn., obl.	oblastnoi
Obshch.	Obshchestvennyi
OIK	Oblastnoi Ispolnitel'nyi Komitet
OK	Oblastnoi komitet
org.	organizatsionnyi
OSPS	Oblastnoi sovet professional'nykh soiuzov
otd.	otdel
O-vo	Obshchestvo
p.	pages
P.	partiia
Petrogr.	Petrograd
p-lei	potrebitelei
PRIVO	Privolzhskii voennyi okrug
prof.	professional'nyi
pr-vo	pravitel'stvo
P. S. R.	Partiia sotsialistov-revoliutsionerov
red.	redaktsiei
Ref.	Reference
revol.	revoliutsionnyi
r., k., k. d.	rabochikh, krest'ianskikh i krasnoarmeiskikh deputatov
RKP	Rossiiskaia Kommunisticheskaia partiia
RKP(b), RKPB	Rossiiskaia Kommunisticheskaia partiia (bol'shevikov)
ROND	Rossiiskoe natsional-sotsialisticheskoe dvizhenie
ROOVA	Russkoe ob"edinennoe o-vo vzaimopomoshchi v Amerike
ROSTA	Rossiiskoe telegrafnoe agentstvo
R. O. V. S.	Russkii obshche-voinskii soiuz
RS-DRP	Rossiiskaia sotsial-demokraticheskaia rabochaia partiia
Serpukh.	Serpukhovsk
sm.	semimonthly
SNK	Sovet Narodnykh Komissarov
Soed.	Soedinennye
sold.	soldatskie
sots.-dem.	sotsial-demokraticheskaia
Sov. r., kr. i kr. dep.	Sovet rabochikh, krest'ianskikh i krasnoarmeiskikh deputatov
SPB	St. Peterburg
s.-r.	sotsialist-revoliutsioner
S. SH.	Soedinennye Shtaty
sw.	semiweekly
trud.	trudiashchikhsia
TSIK	TSentral'nyi Ispolnitel'nyi Komitet

TSK	TSentral'nyi komitet
T-vo(a)	Tovarishchestvo
u. , uezdn.	uezd(nyi)
UKRKP	Uezdnyi komitet Russkoi Kommunisticheskoi Partii
USSR	Ukrainskaia Sovetskaia Sotsialisticheskaia Respublika
VKP(b)	Vsesoiuznaia (Vserossiiskaia) Kommunisticheskaia partiia (bol'shevikov)
Vladiv.	Vladivostok
VLKSM	Vsesoiuznyi Leninskii Kommunisticheskii soiuz molodezhi
V. S. R. M.	Vserossiiskii soiuz rabochikh-metallistov
VTSIK	Vserossiiskii TSentral'nyi Ispolnitel'nyi Komitet
V TS SPS	Vsesoiuznyi TSentral'nyi Sovet professional'nykh soiuzov
w.	weekly
zh. -d.	zhelezno-dorozhnyi

A

ALEKSINSKII VESTNIK
Organ Aleksinsk. Uezdn. k-ta RKP(b) i uezdn. ispolnit. k-ta sovetov. Upolitprosvet Agenstva Gosizdata. [Organ of the Aleksin District Committee of the Russian Communist Party and of the District Executive Committee of Soviets.]
Aleksin, 1918

1921:   Nov. 7 (No. 35[280])

Ref: LC, p. 2

AMERICAN-RUSSIAN FALCON
Amerikanskii russkii sokol soedineniia.
Absorbed by Amerikansky Russky Vestnik.
Homestead, Pa., 1932-36, weekly

1932:   Dec. 27 (No. 51)
1933:   Jan. 3 - Dec. 26 (Nos. 1-52)
1934:   Jan. 2 - Dec. 25 (Nos. 1-52)
1935:   Jan. 1 - Dec. 31 (Nos. 1-53)
1936:   Jan. 7 - Aug. 4 (Nos. 1-30)

AMERIKANSKIE IZVESTIIA
Ezhednevnaia gazeta russkikh kul'turno-prosvetitel'nykh organizatsii Soedinennykh Shtatov i Kanady. [Weekly newspaper of Russian cultural-educational organizations of the United States and Canada.]
Detroit, Mich., 1937-38, weekly

1937:   Nov. 26 - Dec. 31 (1-6)
1938:   Jan. 7 - Oct. 7 (1-32)

AMERIKANSKIIA IZVESTIIA
Organ rossiiskikh professional'nykh soiuzov. [Organ of Russian Trade Unions.]
Issued by the Rossiiskie rabochie organizatsii Soedinennykh Shtatov i Kanady.
New York, 1920-24, daily; later weekly

(Continued on next page)

AMERIKANSKIIA IZVESTIIA (Continued)

1920:   Feb. 3, 5, 9-12; May 1, 5, 8, 10, 19, 22; June 10 (Nos. 5, 7, 10-12, 13, 81, 84-86, 94, 97, 112)

1921:   Mar. 19; Apr. 11, 21; Dec. 21, 28 (Nos. 61, 80, 89, 1, 2)

1922:   Jan. 4 - Dec. 27 (Nos. 3-54)

1923:   Jan. 3 - Dec. 26 (Nos. 55-106)

1924:   Jan. 2 - Dec. 3 (Nos. 107-155)

Ref: Columbia 3

AMERIKANSKY RUSSKY VIESTNIK

Organ greko-kaftoliceskaho sojedinenija v S. S. A. cerkovnykh i narodnych sprav. [Organ of the Greek-Catholic Union in the U. S. A. and of the churches and the people's rights.]

Continuation of the American-Russian Falcon and supplemented by Svet Detei.

Homestead, Pa., weekly

1932:   Dec. 22, No. 50 - 1945, Dec. 27, No. 52

AMURSKAIA GAZETA

Politicheskii, obshchestvennyi i literaturnyi organ. [Political, social and literary organ.]

Blagoveshchensk, 1895, three times a week

1902:   Jan. 4; June 16 (Nos. 2, 66) [Illustrated supplement: Jan. 1; June 16 (Nos. 1, 25)]

Ref: Beliaeva 78; Lisovskii 2395

AMURSKAIA PRAVDA

Organ Amurskogo narodnogo upravleniia. [Organ of the Amur Regional People's Administration.]

Blagoveshchensk, 1920, daily

1921:   Nov. 6; Dec. 6 (Nos. 500, 524)

AMURSKAIA PRAVDA

Organ Amurskogo Okruzhkoma VKP(b), Okrispolkoma VKP(b), Okrispolkoma i Akrprofsoveta. [Organ of the Amur Provincial Committee of the All-Russian Communist Party (of Bolsheviks) and of the Provincial Soviet of Toilers' Deputies.]

Blagoveshchensk, 1921, daily

1928:   Nov. 20, 23, 24 (Nos. 268, 271, 272)

1929:   Mar. 10 (No. 57)

Ref: LC, p. 12

ANARKHIST

Organ Donskoi federatsii anarkhistov-kommunistov. [Organ of the Don Federation of Anarchists-Communists.]
Rostov, daily

1907: Oct. 22 (No. 11)

ARGUS SAKHALINA

1920: June 4 (No. 1)

ARMIIA I FLOT RABOCHEI I KREST'IANSKOI ROSSII

[Organ of the People's Commissars for the Army and the Navy.]
Continued as Rabochaia i Krest'ianskaia krasnaia armiia i flot.
Petrograd, 1917, daily

1917: Dec. 5-21, 24 (Nos. 12-26, 29)
Ref: LC, p. 45

ARMIIA I FLOT SVOBODNOI ROSSII

Gazeta voennaia, politicheskaia i literaturnaia. [The Military, Political, and Literary Newspaper published by the Council on Military and Naval Affairs.]
Continuation of Russkii Invalid.
Petrograd, 1917, daily

1917: Aug. 18(31), 19(Sept. 1), 23(Sept. 5) - 29(Sept. 11), Sept. 1(14), 2(15), 5(18), 6(19), 13(26), 14(27) (Nos. 191, 192, 194-199, 201, 202 incomp., 205, 210 incomp., 211 incomp.)
Ref: LC, p. 45

AVTONOMNAIA IAKUTIIA

Ezhednevnaia gazeta IAkutskogo oblastnogo komiteta VKP(b), IAkutskogo tsentral'nogo ispolnitel'nogo komiteta i IAkutskogo obl. sov. profsoiuzov. [Daily newspaper of the Yakutsk Regional Comm. of the All-Union Communist Party, of the Yakutsk Central Executive Comm. and of the Yakutsk Trade Unions.]
Yakutsk, 1922, daily

1930: June 16 (No. 137)

AZOVSKII KRAI

Ezhednevnaia obshchestvenno-politicheskaia i literaturnaia gazeta. [The Daily, Socio-political and Literary Newspaper.]
Azov, 1919, daily

1919: Dec. 11, 13-15, 20 (Nos. 5, 7-9, 13)

B

BAIKAL

        Ezhenedel'naia gazeta.
        Kiachta, 1897, weekly (from 1905, three times a week)

    1897:   June 1-July 27; Aug. 10, 24-Nov. 30; Dec. 14-28 (Nos. 1-9,
               11, 13-27, 29-31)
    1898:   Jan. 4-May 24; June 14-July 12; Aug. 2-Dec. 20 (Nos. 1-21,
               23-25, 27-46)
    1905:   Mar. 9 (No. 25)

                      Ref: Lisovskii 2542; Beliaeva 184

BAKINSKII PROFESSIONAL'NYI VESTNIK

        Baku, 1909, daily

    1909:   Nos. 3-4; 12 (microfilm)

                      Ref: Beliaeva 210

BAKINSKII RABOCHII

        Organ TSentral'nogo i Bakinskogo komitetov KP(b) Azerbaidzhana.
[Organ of the Central and Baku Committees of the Communist Party and
of Azerbaijan.]
        Baku, 1908, daily

    1908:   Nos. 1-18 (microfilm)
    1922:   March 12 (No. 57)
    1927:   Sept. 20 (No. 220)
    1945:   July 20; Dec. 8 (Nos. 144, 244)
    1946:   Feb. 7, 8 (Nos. 28, 29)

                      Ref: Beliaeva 211; Columbia 7;
                      LC, p. 7

BEDNOTA

        [Published by the Central Committee of the Russian Communist
Party (of Bolsheviks).]
        Moscow, 1918, daily

    1918:   Nov. 24-Nov. 29 (Nos. 197-201)
    1919:   Sept. 4; Oct. 2; Dec. 23 (Nos. 423, 447, 517)

(Continued on next page)

BEDNOTA (continued)

1920: March 9; Apr. 15-22; May 26, 28-June 30; July 2-9, 14, 16-18,
23, 24, 27, 29; Aug. 6, 12, 13, 15-19, 22-25; Sept. 11, 16, 18-
26, 30-Oct. 6, 8-16, 19-24, 27, 29; Nov. 2-17 (Nos. 577, 603-
609, 636, 638-665, 667-673, 677, 679-681, 685, 686, 688, 689,
698, 701, 702, 704-707, 709-711, 725, 729, 731-738, 741-746,
748-755, 757-762, 764, 766, 769-782
1921: Aug. 2, 27-31 (Nos. 987, 1008-1011)
1927: Jan. 7, 15 (Nos. 2606, 2613)

Ref: Columbia 14; LC, p. 86

BELEVSKII PROLETARII
[Published by the Belev-District Executive Committee and by the
District Committee of the Russian Communist Party (of Bolsheviks).]
Belev, 1918

1921: Nov. 7 (No. 44)

Ref: LC, p. 10

BELGORODSKAIA PRAVDA
Organ OK VKP(b), OIK i OSPS. [Organ of the OK of the Com-
munist Party, the OIK and the OSPS.]
Belgorod, 1928, daily

1928: Oct. 7 (No. 36)

BESSARABSKAIA POCHTA
Kishenev, 1915

1929: Jan. 6, 7, 10-25, 26-Feb. 25, 27-Mar. 22-26, 28-30; Apr. 2, 3,
5-7, 11-13, 16-21 (Nos. 2240, 2241, 2244-2259, 2262-2287, 2289-
2312, 2314-2316, 2318-2320, 2323, 2324, 2326-2328, 2332-2334,
2337-2342)

Ref: Beliaeva 327

BESSARABSKOE SLOVO
Gazeta obshchestvenno-politicheskaia, literaturnaia i ekonomi-
cheskaia. [The Socio-political, Literary and Economic Newspaper.]
Kishenev, 1922, daily

1927: March 25-27 (Nos. 801-803)

BEZBOZHNIK
> [Organ of the Central Soviet and the Executive Bureau of the League of Atheists.]
> Moscow, weekly

1923: Feb. 4 (No. 8)
1925: Jan. 4-Dec. 20 (No. 1-51 and 52)
1926: Jan. 5-Sept. 19 (No. 1-36)
> Ref: LC, p. 86

BEZVLASTIE
> Organ anarkhistov g. Luga. [Organ of the Anarchists of Luga.]
> Luga, 1921

1921: Sept. 1 (No. 8)

BIROBIDZHANSKAIA ZVEZDA
> [Organ of the Provincial Committee of the All-Union Communist Party (of Bolsheviks), of the Provincial Soviet of Toilers' Deputies of the Jewish Autonomous Region and of the Birabidzhan City Committee of the All-Union Communist Party (of Bolsheviks).]
> Birobijan, daily

1945: Oct. 10 (No. 203)
> Ref: Columbia 23; LC, p. 11

BIRZHEVYIA IZVESTIIA
> Gazeta finansovo-ekonomicheskaia, politicheskaia i obshchest-vennaia. [The Political, Literary and Financial Newspaper.]
> St. Petersburg, 1906, weekly

1914: July 21 (No. 2123)
> Ref: Beliaeva 327

BIRZHEVYIA VEDOMOSTI
> Politicheskaia, obshchestvennaia i literaturnaia gazeta. [The Political, Social and Literary Newspaper founded by S.M. Propper.]
> Continued as Vecherniia Vedomosti, Vedomosti, Nashi Vedomosti, Novyia Vedomosti.
> Petrograd, 1880, twice daily

Morning editions:
1914: July 23 (extra), Dec. 15 (Nos. 14266, 14566)
1915: Jan. 1-8, 10, 11, 29; Feb. 4-6, 8-13; Mar. 22; Apr. 1, 7, 20;
> Oct. 27, 29; Nov. 2; Dec. 2-5, 7-10 (even nos. from 14586-14598,

(Continued on next page)

BI RZHEVYIA VEDOMOSTI (continued)

        14602, 14604, 14640, 14650, 14652, 14654, 14658-14668, 14741,
        14758, 14769, 14795, 15173, 15177, 15185, 15245, 15247, 15249,
        15251, 15255, 15257, 15259, 15261)

1916:   Jan. 1, 4, 23, 24, 31; May 21, Oct. 13, Nov. 29, Dec. 8 (Nos.
        15356, 15571, 15859, 15953, 15971)

1917:   Jan. 1-Feb. 24, Mar. 5-Apr. 23, 25, 27, 30, May 2-7, 9-11,
        13, 14, 16-July 9, 11-Aug. 10, 13-Sept. 2, 5-10, 12-17, 19-24,
        26-30, Oct. 1, 3-8, 10, 11, 14, 15, 17-22, 24 (Nos. 16014-16118,
        16120-16198, 16200, 16204, 16210-16222, 16224, 16226, 16228,
        16230, 16232, 16234, 16236-16318, 16320, 16322, 16324-16326,
        16328-16380, 16386-16400, 16402-16406, 16406, 16410, 16411,
        16413, 16415, 16417, 16419, 16421, 16423, 16425, 16427, 16429,
        16431, 16433, 16435, 16437, 16439-16447, 16449-16459, 16461-
        16469, 16471, 16473-16481, 16483-16487, 16493, 16495, 16497-
        16503, 16505, 16507, 16509 [some nos. on microfilm])

Evening editions:

1914:   July 19, 21, 21 (extra)-24, 25 (extra), 26-29, 29 (extra), 31,
        Aug. 1, 2, 6, 8, 9, 11-14, 19, 20, 22, 30, Sept. 3, Oct. 9
        (Nos. 14260, 14263, 14263 (extra-14269, 14271 (extra), 14273-
        14279 (odd nos. only), 14283-14287 (odd nos. only), 14295, 14299,
        14301, 14305-14311, 14321, 14323, 14327, 14343, 14351, 14423)

1916:   Jan. 24, 31, June 16, Oct. 9 (Nos. 15343, 15357, 15622, 15852)

1917:   Jan. 14, Mar. 6-10, 13, 15-17, 20, 22, 27, 31, Apr. 4-16, 20-
        22, 24-29, May 1-5, 8, 10, 12, 13, 16, 17, 20, 24-27, 29-31,
        June 1, July 1, 3, 4, 6-8, 10-12, 19-22, 24, 26, 27, 31, Aug. 1-5,
        7, 9-12, 15-19, 21-22, 24, 26, 28, 30 31, Sept. 1, 4, 5, 7-9, 11-
        16, 18-23, 25-29, Oct. 5, 7, 10-14, 16-18, 21; Nov. 17, 20 (Nos.
        16039, 16121-16129, 16133, 16137-16141, 16145, 16149, 16155,
        16163-16187, 16193-16209, 16211-16219, 16223, 16227, 16229-
        16231, 16235, 16237, 16243, 16247, 16249-16253, 16255-16259,
        16261, 16265, 16267-16269, 16237-16277, 16287, 16299, 16303-
        16309, 16313-16317, 16321-16325, 16327-16331, 16343-16349,
        16351, 16355, 16357, 16363, 16365-16369, 16371, 16373, 16375,
        16379-16385, 16389-16397, 16399, 16401, 16405, 16409, 16412,
        16416, 16418, 16420, 16424, 16430, 16430-16434, 16436-16446,
        16448-16458, 16460-16468, 16478-16482, 16486-16494, 16496-
        16500 [some nos. on microfilm])

                                Ref: Beliaeva 389-391; Columbia 26;
                                  Lisovskii 1455; LC, p. 46

BIULLETEN' MOSKOVSKAGO GORODSKOGO PRODOVOL'STVENNAGO
KOMITETA
[Published by the Moscow City Food Committee of the Soviet of
Workers' Deputies.]
Moscow, 1918, daily

1918:   Apr. 7, 9 (Nos. 63, 64)
Ref: LC, p. 87

BIULLETEN' MOSKOVSKOGO POTREBITEL'SKOGO OBSHCHESTVA
Moscow, 1919, daily

1920:   Nov. 13, 14 (Nos. 255, 256)
Ref: LC, p. 87

BIULLETEN' OB"EDINENNAGO KOMITETA ROSSIISKOI EMIGRATSII
Paris, 1914

1914:   Aug. 15 (No. 1)

BIULLETEN' PRODOVOL'STVENNOGO OTDELA MOSKOVSKOGO SOVETA
RABOCHIKH I KRASNOARMEISKIKH DEPUTATOV
Moscow, 1918, daily

1918:   Oct. 20-26, Nov. 3-21, 24-30 (Nos. 220-225, 232-245, 248-253)
Ref: LC, p. 87

BIULLETEN' TSENTRAL'NAGO PRODOVOL'STVENNAGO BIURO VSEROSSII-
SKAGO ZHELEZNODOROZHNAGO SOIUZA
Moscow, 1918, semiweekly

1918:   Oct. 23, Nov. 13, 16, 23 (Nos. 18, 24, 25, 27)
Ref: LC, p. 87

BIULLETENI MUZEIA SODEISTVIIA TRUDU, SOSTOIASHCHEGO PRI MOS-
KOVSKOM OTDELENII RUSSKOGO TEKHNICHESKOGO OBSHCHESTVA
Moscow, 1905

1905:   Nos. 1-2 (Microfilm)

BODRAIA MYSL'
Krest'ianskaia i rabochaia gazeta.
St. Petersburg, 1913, semiweekly

1913-1914: Dec. 22 - Jan. 17 (Nos. 2, 4-7, 9-11)
Ref: Beliaeva 423; Columbia 31

BODROST'
> Paris, 1934-1940, weekly

1936-1939: Nos. 70-255
1940:   Feb. 15 (No. 259)
> Ref: Columbia 32

BOEVAIA PRAVDA
> [The Daily Red Army Newspaper. Published by the Political
Section of the 7th Army and the Administration for Political Education
of the Petrograd Military District.]
> Petrograd, 1919, daily

1919:   Sept. 7, 20, Oct. 5, Nov. 22 (Nos. 1, 12, 25, 68)
1920:   Mar. 12, Apr. 15, 16-22, 27 (Nos. 57, 80-86, 90)
> Ref: LC, p. 46

BOL'SHEVISTSKII PUT'
> Organ Viazemskogo raikoma VKP(b), raiispolkoma i raiprof-
soveta. [Organ of the Viazma district committee of the Communist
Party and the district executive committee and the district professional
Soviet.]
> Viazma, 1931

1931:   Apr. 20 (No. 87)

BOL'SHEVISTSKOE ZNAMIA
> [Organ of the Odessa Provincial and City Committees of the
Communist Party (of Bolsheviks) of the Ukrainian SSR and of the
Provincial and City Soviets of Toilers' Deputies.]
> Odessa, 1940, daily

1945:   July 17, Sept. 30-Nov. 2 (Nos. 140, 194-217)
> Ref: LC, p. 136

BOR'BA
> [Published by the District Committee of the Russian Communist
Party (of Bolsheviks) and the District Executive Committee.]
> Balashov, 1921

1921:   Nov. 7 (No. 117)
1922:   Mar. 12 (No. 28)
> Ref: LC, p. 9

BOR'BA
>Moscow, 1905, daily

1905: 1-9 (microfilm)
>Ref: Beliaeva 446

BOR'BA
>Izdanie TS. K. S. -D. Latinskogo Kraia.
>Riga

1906: Nos. 1-7, 9, 10
1907: Nos. 12, 13, 15, 16, 17
1908: No. 18
1909: No. 18 [all nos. on microfilm]

BOR'BA
>Organ Peterburgskogo Professional'nogo Soiuza Torgovo-Promy-
shlennykh Sluzhashchikh.
>Petrograd

1917: Nos. 1-5 (microfilm)
>Ref: LC, p. 46

BOR'BA
>Organ stalingradskogo okrkoma VKP(b), Okrispolkoma, Gorsoveta
i Okrprofbiuro. [Organ of the Stalingrad District Committee of the Communist Party, the District Executive Committee, the City Soviet and
the District Professional Bureau.]
>Stalingrad, 1917, daily

1928: Dec. 29 (No. 303)
1929: Jan. 30 (No. 22)

BOR'BA
>Organ TSentral'nago Komiteta sotsial-demokraticheskoi partii
Gruzii. [Organ of the Central Committee of Social Democratic Georgia.]
>Tiflis, daily

1921: Jan. 1 - Feb. 16 (No. 1-7, 9-29, 31-36)
>Ref: LC, p. 169

BOR'BA

Organ TSaritsinskogo Gub. komiteta RKP(b) i Gub. ispolnit. kom. sovetov rabochikh, krest'ian. i krasnoarm. deputatov. [Organ of the Tsaritsyn Province Committee of the Russian Communist Party and the Province Executive Committee of the Soviets of Workers, Peasants and Red Army Deputies.]
Tsaritsyn, 1917

1921:　Oct. 30 (No. 542)

BRITANSKII SOIUZNIK

Izdanie ministerstva informatsii Velikobritanii. [Published by the Minister of Information of Great Britain.]
Moscow, weekly

1945:　July 1-22, Aug. 5-26, Sept. 2, 30, Oct. 7-Nov. 25, Dec. 9
(Nos. 26-29, 31-34, 36, 39, 40-47, 49)

BUNTOVSHCHIK

[Organ for Propoganda of the Ideas of Anarchism.]
Tomsk, 1918

1918:　Apr. 7 (No. 1)

Ref: LC, p. 171

BUREVIESTNIK

[Organ of the Federation of Anarchist Groups.]
Petrograd, 1917, daily

1917:　Nov. 28, Dec. 3, 19 (Nos. 13, 18, 31)
1918:　Jan. 27, Feb. 17, Apr. 9-11 (Nos. 19, 25, 58-60)
Ref: LC, p. 46

BURIAT-MONGOL'SKAIA PRAVDA

[Organ of the Buriat-Mongolian Provincial Committee of the All-Union Communist Party (of Bolsheviks) and of the Supreme Soviet of the Buriat-Mongolian A. S. S. R.]
Ulan-Ude, 1924, daily

1933:　June 14 (No. 135)
Ref: LC, p. 174

C

CHERNAIA METALLURGIIA
> Organ Narodnogo Komissariata Chernoi Metallurgii S. S. S. R.
> [Organ of the People's Commissariat of Black Metallurgy of the U. S. S. R.]
> Title varies: <u>Torgovyi Biulleten'</u>, <u>Torgovaia Gazeta</u>, <u>Torgovo-promyshlennaia Gazeta</u>, <u>Za Industrializatsiiu</u>, <u>Industriia</u>
> Moscow, 1922, three times a week

1922: Jan. 31, Feb. 9, Mar. 30, May 6, 9 (Nos. 5, 8, 31, 47, 49)
1925: Apr. 17, 18, Aug. 5 (Nos. 88, 89, 177)
1926: Jan.-Dec. (Nos. 1, 3-122, 131-137, 139-258, 260-301)
1927: Jan.-Dec. (Nos. 4, 146-149, 151-170, 172-297)
1928: Jan.-Dec. (Nos. 1-21, 23-85, 87-285, 288-302)
1929: Jan.-Dec. (Nos. 22, 23, 25, 26, 27, 29-35, 37-110)
1933-1940: all issues

CHERNOE ZNAMIA
> Ezhenedel'nyi organ Vladivostokskogo soiuza revol. anarkhistov-kommunistov. [Organ of the Vladivostok Association of Revolutionary Anarchists and Communists.]
> Vladivostok, 1918, weekly

1918: March 12 (No. 5)
> Ref: LC, p. 179

CHERNOMORSKII MAIAK
> Novorossiisk, daily

1920: Jan. 21, 22 (No. 416, 417)
> Ref: Columbia 40; LC, p. 135

CHERNOMORSKIIA GUBERNSKIIA VEDOMOSTI
Novorossiisk

1919:   July 9 (No. 11)

CHERTOVA PERECHNITSA
Organ iziashchnoi grusti i vnezapnago uzhasa. Vykhodit pri
blizhaishem uchastii Ark. Averchenko, Ark. Bukhova, I. M.
Vasilevskago i dr.
Petrograd, daily

1917:   May 26 (No. 4)
Ref: Columbia 41; LC, p. 47

CHESTNYI SLON
Ezhenedel'naia literaturno-satiricheskaia gazeta. L'honnête
eléphant.
Paris, weekly

1945:   Mar. 3 - Dec. 8 (Nos. 1-30)
Ref: Columbia 42

CHURAEVKA
Literaturnaia gazeta Kruzhka iskusstv, nauki i literatury.
Churaevka KH. S. M. L. v Kharbine.
Kharbin

1932:   Dec. 27 (No. 7 [1])

D

DALEKAIA OKRAINA
　　　　Vladivostok, 1907, daily

　　1918:　July (Nos. 3591, 3594, 3595)
　　　　　　　　　　　　Ref: Beliaeva 2063; Columbia 46;
　　　　　　　　　　　　　　LC, p. 179

DAL'NEVOSTOCHNAIA TRIBUNA
　　　　Vladivostok, 1921, daily

　　1921:　Apr. 2 (No. 52)
　　　　　　　　　　Ref: LC, p. 180

DAL'NEVOSTOCHNAIA ZHIZN'
　　　　Ezhednevnaia nezavisimaia obshchestvenno-politicheskaia
　　gazeta.
　　　　Vladivostok, June 15, 1921, daily

　　1921:　June 15 - July 16 (Nos. 1-26)
　　　　　　　　　　Ref: LC, p. 180

DAL'NEVOSTOCHNOE OBOZRENIE
　　　　The Far-Eastern review.
　　　　Vladivostok, 1919, daily

　　1919:　Sept. 25, 30, Oct. 23, Nov. 5 - Dec. 25 (Nos. 161, 164, 184,
　　　　　　185, 187-190, 192-193, 196, 199-220, 222-228)
　　1920:　Mar. -? (Nos. 283, 295-298, 332-335, 346, 358-359, 365, 386-
　　　　　　394, 396-340, 406, 409-419, 421-424, 430-441, 458, 459, 461-
　　　　　　467, 469)
　　Note:　Number and/or date of issue often not the same on different
　　　　　　pages of same issue, e. g. , assigning of date or number to
　　　　　　some issues is arbitrary.
　　　　　　　　　　Ref: Columbia 47; LC, p. 180

DAL'NEVOSTOCHNYE IZVESTIIA
Ofitsial'nyi organ rabochego i krest'ianskogo pravitel'stva po delam Dal'nego Vostoka. [Organ of the Workers' and Peasants' Government for Far Eastern Affairs.]
Khabarovsk, 1918, daily

1918:   Apr. 10 (No. 50), May 9 (No. 69)

Ref: LC, p. 26

DAL'NEVOSTOCHNYI KAZAK
Odnodnevnaia gazeta. Izdanie Soiuza kazakov na Dal'nem Vostoke.
Kharbin, 1936

1936:   March 17-30

DAUGAVPIL'SKII GOLOS see NASH DAUGAVPIL'SKII GOLOS

DELO ROSSII
Gazeta politicheskaia, ekonomicheskaia i finansovaia, izdatel'-stvo Iokogamskogo otdela vostochnago natsional'no-gosudarstvennago ob''edineniia.
Tokyo, 1920, semiweekly
1920:   March 20-26, Apr. 5-May 18, July 10-16 (Nos. 1-2, 4-9, 16-17)

DELO ZHIZNI
Ezhednevnaia politicheskaia i literaturnaia gazeta.
Moscow, 1907, daily

1907:   Nos. 8-16 (Microfilm)

DEN'

Organ sotsialisticheskoi mysli. [Organ of socialist thought.]
Subsequently published as: Novyi den', Nov. 20, 1917; Noch', Nov. 22, 1917; Polnoch', Nov. 24, 1917; V temnuiu noch', Nov. 25, 1917; Vol'naia glukhaia noch', Nov. 26, 1917; Griadushchii den', Nov. 28, 1917; Den', Dec. 1, 1917-Jan. 3, 1918; Novyi den', Feb. 14-22, 1918; Den', Mar. 27-29, 1918; and Novyi den', Apr. 13-May 17, 1918.
Petrograd, 1912, daily

1913:   Nos. 256(344) + suppl. "Literatura i iskusstvo," Nos. 334, 354, Dec. 9, 13
1914:   Nos. 193, 194, 231, + special issue to No. 196, 202
1915:   Nos. 128, 331, 335, 336, 341, 348, 355

(Continued on next page)

DEN' (continued)

    1917:   Nos. 1, 2, 4, 7, 8, 11, 12, 13, 15-17, 19-36, 38-44, 46-49, 51, 54-58, 60, 61, 63, 65, 67, 68, 71, 72, 74, 77, 82, 85, 87-90, 92, 93-95, 101-110, 117, 121, 126-127, 132, 133, 135-139, 141-143, 147-149, 150, 151, 152, 154, 156, 157, 159, 164-166, 168, 169, 174, 177, 181, 182, 184, 187-191, 193-198, 200-209, 210-226, 228-232 (Mar.-Dec.)

    1918:   Nos. 1, 2, 4, 7 (Jan. 3, Mar. 27-29, Apr. 2)

                                                Ref: Beliaeva 2147; Columbia 49; LC, p. 47

DEN' KOMMERSANTA I ORIENTALISTA

        Odnodnevnaia akademicheskaia gazeta studentov Instituta oriental'nykh i kommercheskikh nauk v Kharbine.

        Kharbin, 1931

    1931:   Jan. (No. 8)

DEN' RUSSKAGO REBENKA

        Izdanie Kharbinskago Komiteta pomoshchi russkim bezhentsam. Ves' sbor ot prodazhi postupaet na delo obrazovaniia i vospitaniia russkikh detei.

        Kharbin, 1931, one day's paper

    1931:   Apr. 7 (Mar. 25) (8 p.)

DEN' STUDENTA

        Odnodnevnaia akademicheskaia gazeta.

        Kharbin, 1930, one day's paper

    1930:   Dec. (No. 1)

DEN' VELIKOI REVOLIUTSII

        Odnodnevnaia gazeta, izdavaemaia ob''edinennymi redaktsiiami: Pravda, Krasnaia gazeta, Makhovik v pol'zu golodaiushchikh krest'ian.

        Petrograd, 1921, one day's paper

    1921:   6 p.

                                          Ref: Columbia 53; LC, p. 47

DEN' VLADIVOSTOKA

        Ezhednevnaia vecherniaia gazeta.

        Vladivostok, daily

    1918:   Mar. 21 (8), May 17 (4), 27 (14), 28 (15), July 15 (2), Aug. 10 (July 28) (Nos. 3, 47, 54-55, 92, 115)

                                          Ref: LC, p. 180

DEREVENSKAIA BEDNOTA

Ezhednevnaia krest'ianskaia gazeta izdavaemaia voennoi organizatsiei pri TSK RS-DRP. [Published by the Military Organization of the Central Committee of the Russian Social Democratic Workers' Party and Bolsheviks of the 2nd All-Russian Congress of Peasants.]
Petrograd, 1917, daily

1917:   Oct. 27 (Nov. 9), Nov. 18 (Dec. 1), 22 (Dec. 5) - 25 (Dec. 8)
Dec. 29 (Jan. 11) (Nos. 14, 32, 35-38, 63)
Ref: LC, p. 47

DEREVENSKAIA BEDNOTA I TRUDOVOE KAZACHESTVO

Ezhednevnaia krest'ianskaia i kazach'ia gazeta, izdavaemaia voennoi organizatsiei pri TSK RS-DRP i fraktsiei bol'shevikov Vtorogo vserossiiskago krest'ianskago s"ezda. [Published by the Military Organization of the Central Committee of the Russian Social Democratic Workers' Party and Bolsheviks of the 2nd All-Russian Congress of Peasants.]
Petrograd, 1917, daily

1917:   Nov. 26 (Dec. 9) (No. 39)
Ref: LC, p. 47

DEREVENSKAIA KOMMUNA

Izdanie Inogorodnogo Otdela Kommisariata Vnutrennikh Del Severnoi Oblasti. [Published by the Branch for the area outside of Petrograd of the Union of Communes of the Northern Province.]
Petrograd, 1918, daily

1919-1920: Nos. 160, 169, 298, 308-310, 315-326, 361, 375, 381, 383, 390, 394, 395, 415, 445, 450, 453, 461, 485-493, 501, 504, 507-509, 511, 517, 519, 520, 522-524, 531, 533, 538, 540-545, 547-555, 557-574, 578-580, 583, 586, 588-591, 594, 595, 597, 599-605, 610, 611, 625-666
Ref: Columbia 54; LC, p. 48

DEREVENSKAIA PRAVDA

Izdanie Petrogradskogo Gubernskogo komiteta Rossiiskoi kommunisticheskoi partii (bol'shevikov). [Published by the Petrograd Provincial Committee of the Russian Communist Party (of Bolsheviks).]
Petrograd, 1921, daily

1921:   Nov. 7 (No. 158 [227])
Ref: LC, p. 48

DEREVENSKII KOMMUNAR

Organ Griazovetskogo uezdnogo komiteta partii kommunistov-bol'shevikov. [Organ of the Gryazovets District Committee of the Party of Communists-Bolsheviks.]

Gryazovets, 3 times a week

1919:   Nov. 7 (No. 101)
1922:   Mar. 11 (No. 20 [419])

Ref: LC, p. 20

DEVIATYI VAL

Vestnik Rossiiskago natsional-sotsialisticheskago dvizheniia. Redaktor E. G. Tiurnikova.

Berlin, 1935

1935:   Oct. (No. 1)

DEVIATYI VAL

Vestnik bor'by za natsional'nuiu Rossiiu. Redaktor E. G. Volich.

Brussels, 1935

1935:   June (no No.)

DIELO NARODA

Obshchestvennaia, politicheskaia i literaturnaia gazeta Blag. gruppy P. S. R. [Published by the Blagoveshchensk Group of the Party of Social Revolutionaries.]

Blagoveshchensk, 1921, every other day

1921:   Apr. 22-Oct. 22 (Nos. 4-9, 11-19)
1922:   May 7 (No. 78 [149])

Ref: LC, p. 12

DIELO NARODA

Organ Partii Sotsialistov-revoliutsionerov. Ezhednevnaia politicheskaia i literaturnaia gazeta. [Organ of the Party of Social Revolutionaries.]

Petrograd, 1917, daily

1917:   March 15-Dec. 30 (Nos. 1-62, 64-65, 67-85, 87-131, 133-187, 189-220, 222-244) [Nov. 23 (No. 217) has been suppressed.]

Ref: Columbia 58; LC, p. 48

DIELO NARODA
>Politicheskaia i literaturnaia ezhednevnaia gazeta.
>St. Petersburg, 1906, daily

>1906:   May 4(17), 9(22) (Nos. 2, 6)

>>Ref: Beliaeva 2130; Columbia 57

DIELO NARODOV
>Organ TSentral'nago komiteta Partii sotsialistov-revoliutsionerov.
>[Organ of the Central Committee of the Party of Social Revolutionaries.]
>Petrograd, daily

>1917:   Mar. 15-Dec. 30
>1918:   Jan. 20 (Feb. 2), No. 3

>>Ref: LC, p. 49

DNI
>Russische Tageszeitung für Politik, Wirtschaft und Literatur.
>Berlin
>See (next entry) Dni; Ezhednevnaia gazeta, Paris.

DNI
>Ezhednevnaia gazeta pod redaktsiei A. F. Kerenskogo.
>Paris, 1922, daily

>1922-1928:   Nos. 1-360, 362-365, 367-525, 527-1036, 1038-1198, 1201-1945
>With No. 1465, June 30, 1928, ceased publication as a newspaper and became a weekly journal under the same title.

DOBROVOLETS
>Gazeta voisk osvoboditel'nogo dvizheniia.
>Berlin

>1944:   Oct. 29 (No. 87 [155])

DOBROVOLETS
>Izdanie Soiuza dobrovol'tsev.
>Paris

>1937:   Feb.
>1938:   Feb.

DONSKAIA RECH'
> Obshchestvenno-politicheskaia i literaturnaia gazeta.
> Rostov-on-Don, 1919, daily

> 1919: Dec. 3 (16) No. 18 (Nos. 14-19 on microfilm)
> > Ref: LC, p. 150

DRUG NARODA
> Organ gruppy men'shevikov-oborontsev. [Organ of a Group of
Mensheviks-Anti-Defeatists.]
> Petrograd, 1917

> 1917: Nov. 4, 5 (Nos. 1, 2) [microfilm]
> > Ref: LC, p. 49

DUMY BEDNIAKA
> Organ Mstiaslavskogo uezdn. komiteta RKP (bol'shevikov).
[Organ of the Mstislavl District Committee of the Russian Communist
Party (of Bolsheviks).]
> Mstislavl, 1919, semiweekly

> 1921: Nov. 7 (No. 47[190])
> > Ref: LC, p. 133

DVADTSATYI VEK
> St. Petersburg, 1906, daily

> 1906: Mar. 25(Apr. 7)-28(Apr. 10), 30(Apr. 12)-21(Apr. 13), Apr. 4
> (17), 6(19), 8(21), 10(23), (Nos. 1-4, 6-7, suppl. to No. 9, 11,
> 13, 15)
> > Ref: Beliaeva 2094; Columbia 63

DVENADTSATOE MARTA 1917-1922 GG.
> Ob"edinennoe izdanie gazet "Vlast' truda" i "Krasnyi strelok."
> Irkutsk, 1922

DVINSKII GOLOS see **NASH DAUGAVPIL'SKII GOLOS**

E

EDINENIE

 Novotorzhskii organ Soveta soldatskikh, rabochikh, krest'ianskikh deputatov i trudovoi intelligentsii. [Novotorzhok Organ of the Soviet of Solders', Workers', and Peasants' Deputies and of the Working Intelligentsia.]

 Torzhok, 1917, four times a week

1917: June 18 (No. 27)

        Ref: LC, p. 172

EDINSTVO

 Moscow

1918: Nos. 1-3 (microfilm)

EDINSTVO

 Marksistskaia rabochaia gazeta.
 St. Petersburg, 1914, weekly

1914: June, Nos. 1-4 (microfilm)

        Ref: Beliaeva 2490

EDINSTVO

 [Published by the Russian Social Democratic Organization "Edinstvo". Ed. G. V. Plekhanov.]

 Petrograd, 1917, daily

1917: Mar. 29-Nov. 17 (Nos. 1-15, 17-40, 42-54, 56-60, 62-81, 83-189, Dec. 20-30 (Nos. 2-8)
1918: Jan. 11 (no. 14) [microfilm]

        Ref: Columbia 68; LC, p. 49

EDINSTVO

 Prague, 1931, semimonthly

1932, Dec. - Jan. 1934: Nos. 1-15 (99), 17 (101) - 21 (105), 23 (107)

EDINSTVO I NEZAVISIMOST'
Organ kazakov natsionalistov.
Paris, 1935, irregular

1935:   Feb. 19, May 25, Dec. 12 (Nos. 1-3)

EDINYI FRONT NOVOI ROSSII
Bezpartiinaia gazeta trudiashchikhsia, voennykh i uchashchikhsia.
Paris

1930-1934: Dec. 1930-Sept. 1934 (Nos. 4, 5, 8-11, 13-15)
Ref: Columbia 69

EINIKAT (EDINENIE)
Organ evreiskogo antifashistskogo komiteta v SSSR.
Moscow

1945:   No. 91

EKHO
Ezhednevnaia gazeta.
Kharbin, 1925, daily

1925:   Nov. 7 (No. 150)

EKHO
Bol'shaia obshchestvenno-politicheskaia i literaturnaia gazeta.
Petrograd, daily

1917:   Dec. 28 (No. 5)
1918:   May 22 (9) (No. 110)

EKHO
Ezhednevnaia gazeta.
St. Petersburg, 1906, daily

1906:   Nos. 1-14 (June 22-July 7) [microfilm]
Ref: Beliaeva 9472; Columbia 71

EKONOMICHESKAIA GAZETA
        Ezhenedel'nik TSentral'nogo komiteta KPSS.
        Moscow, weekly

1962:   Apr. 2 (No. 14) – to present
Missing nos:
1962:   June 2, 9

EKONOMICHESKAIA ZHIZN' see FINANSOVAIA GAZETA

EKONOMICHESKAIA ZHIZN' PENZENSKOI GUBERNII
        Ezhenedel'naia gazeta Gubernskogo ekonomicheskogo sovesh-
chaniia. Vykhodit po ponedel'nikam.
        Penz, 1921, weekly

1921:   Sept. 12, 19, 26 (Nos. 1-3)
                           Ref: LC, p. 143

EKONOMICHESKII PUT'
        Ezhednevnaia gazeta Simbirskogo gubekonom-soveshchaniia i
gub-profsoveta. [Published by the Simbirsk Provincial Economic Con-
ference and the Provincial Council of Labor Unions.]
        Simbirsk, 1921, daily

1922:   March 12, No. 59 (111)
                           Ref: LC, p. 174

EKONOMIKA I KUL'TURA
        Prilozhenie k "Izvestiiam VTSIK."
        Moscow

1922:   Mar. -June (Nos. 1-3)

ELEKTROZAVOD
        Ezhednevnaia gazeta, organ partkoma i zavkoma. [Organ of the
Party and Factory Committee.]
        Moscow, 1929, daily

1932:   March 9 (No. 57)
                           Ref: LC, p. 88

EMIGRANTSKAIA MYSL'
>Ezhenedel'naia natsional'no-obshchestvennaia gazeta.
>Shanghai, 1936, weekly

>1937:   Jan. 24, Mar. 3-24 (Nos. 4[12], 6[14]-8[16])
>>Ref: Columbia 76

ENISEISKOE SLOVO
>Krasnoiarsk, 1906, daily

>1906:   Nov. 10-26 (Nos. 1-14)

ERA
>Izdanie arteli sotrudnikov i sluzhashchikh gazety. Bol'shaia literaturnaia i obshchestvenno-politicheskaia gazeta.
>Petrograd, 1918, daily

>1918:   July 16 (3) (No. 8)
>>Ref: LC, p. 50

EZHEDNEVNAIA GAZETA GOLOS TRUDOVOGO KREST'IANSTVA see GOLOS TRUDOVOGO KREST'IANSTVA

EZHEDNEVNAIA GAZETA PARTII NARODNOI SVOBODY SVOBODNYI NAROD see SVOBODNYI NAROD

EZHEDNEVNAIA IAPONSKAIA GAZETA KHARBINSKOE VREMIA see KHARBINSKOE VREMIA

EZHEDNEVNAIA VOENNAIA GAZETA KRASNAIA ARMIIA see KRASNAIA ARMIIA

EZHENEDEL'NAIA GAZETA RABOCHIKH I KREST'IAN KASHIRSKOGO UEZDNOGO SOVETA RABOCHIKH, KREST'IANSKIKH I KRASNOARMEISKIKH DEPUTATOV I UEZDNOGO KOMITETA ROSSIISKOI KOMMUNISTICHESKOI PARTII (BOL'SH.)
>Kashira, 1921, weekly

>1921:   Nov. 7 (No. 1)
>>Ref: LC, p. 25

EZHENEDEL'NAIA GAZETA VREMIA
Vykhodit po ponedel'nikam.
Berlin, 1919, weekly

1920: Sept. 13 (No. 115)
1925: Jan. 26-June 29 (Nos. 340, 346, 348, 350, 352, 353)

F

FAKEL

Organ TSentral'nogo komiteta Rossiiskoi sots.-dem. rabochei partii (ob''edinennoi). Ezhednevnaia gazeta. [Organ of the Central Committee of the Russian Social Democratic Workers' Party (United).] Continuation of Plamia.

Petrograd, Nov. 25, 1917, daily

1917:   Nov. 25 (No. 1)

Ref: LC, p. 50

FASHIST

Organ vserossiiskago natsional-revoliutsionnago tsentra.
Subtitle varies: No. 1; Jan. 1935: Organ TS. I. K. vserossiiskoi fashistskoi (natsional-revoliutsionnoi trudovoi i raboche-krest'ianskoi) partii i organizatsii.

Moscow, 1935, annual

1935:   Jan. 1 (No. 1)
1936:   Jan. 1 (No. 2)

FASHIST

Izdanie Glavnogo shtaba russkikh fashistov.
Putnam, Conn., U.S.A., 1933, monthly

1933, July-Sept. 1934, Nov. 1935, Feb. 1936-Jan. 1937, Mar.-Sept., 1937, Nov. 1937-June 1938, Aug.-Nov. 1939 (Nos. 1-12, 22, 24-30, 32-35, 37-43, 52-54)

Ref: Columbia 79

FINANSOVAIA GAZETA

Moscow

1918:   Nov. 14, 15 (Nos. 6, 7)

FINANSOVAIA GAZETA

Moscow, 1925, daily

1926:   Jan.-Oct. 31 (Nos. (588), 3 (590)-102 (698), 104 (691)-252 (839)

FINANSOVAIA GAZETA
> Organ Narkomfina SSSR, Gosbanka SSSR, Prombanka, Sel'khoz-banka, TSekombanka, Torgbanka i TS K Soiuza finbankovskikh rabotni-kov.
> Title varies: Nov. 6, 1918-Nov. 14, 1937, Ekonomicheskaia zhizn'; Nov. 16, 1937- , Finansovaia gazeta.
> Moscow, 1918, weekly

1918, Nov. 6-1940
Missing nos. (Ekonomicheskaia zhizn'):
1919: Nos. 71, 94-95, 108-109, 111, 113-117, 119-124, 126-231, 237-238, 241, 245, 249, 259, 266, 278
1929: No. 80
1932: Nos. 28-29, 48
Missing Nos. (Finansovaia gazeta):
1939: No. 88
1940: Nos. 1-14, 17-21, 23-27

> Ref: Columbia 75, 81; LC, p. 88

FINANSOVAIA GAZETA
> Politiko-finansovaia, ekonomicheskaia, promyshlennaia i bir-zhevaia gazeta. Vechernee izdanie. Osnovana V. V. Protopopovym.
> Petrograd, 1915, daily

1917: Jan. 17 (30) (No. 401)

> Ref: Beliaeva 9020; LC, p. 50

FINANSY I NARODNOE KHOZIAISTVO
> Ezhednevnaia gazeta Komissariata finansov i Soveta narodnogo khoziaistva severnoi oblasti. [Published by the Commissariat of Finance and the National Economic Council of the Northern Province.]
> Continuation of Torgovo-promyshlennaia gazeta
> Petrograd, 1918, daily

1918: Nov. 22, 24, 26 (Nos. 49, 51-52)
> Ref: LC, p. 50

FONAR'
> Gazeta patriaticheskaia, no otniud ne kontrrevoluitsionnaia.
> [A "patriotic but not counterrevolutionary" newspaper.]
> Moscow, 1917, weekly

1917: Nov. 20 (No. 10)
> Ref: LC, p. 89

FRONT MOLODYKH

Vestnik natsional'noi revoliutsii. Izdanie ezhemesiachnoe.
Paris, monthly

1930: Nov. 23

G

GALLIPOLI
Izdanie obshchestva gallipoliitsev.
Belgrad, 1923

1923:   Feb. 15-Apr. 8 (Nos. 1-2)

GALLIPOLIETZ
Gazeta posviashchennaia russkomu voinstvu na chuzhbine. Izdanie Soiuza Gallipoliitsev vo Franstsii. Editors: V. V. Orekhov, V. V. Polianskii i Evgenii Tarusskii.
Paris, 1927, irregular

1927:   No. 1

Ref: Columbia 83

GAZETA "SERET"
[Newspaper published twice a week by Germans for the Russian Army.]
1917-1918

1917:   May-Dec. (Nos. 16, 20-32, 40, 43, 44, 60, 61, 64)
1918:   Jan.-Mar. (Nos. 72, 74-79)

GAZETA DEVIATAGO OKTIABRIA
[Published by the Executive Board of the Petrograd Committee of Educational Organizations of the Army and Navy.]
Petrograd, 1917, one day's newspaper

1917:   Oct. 9 (No. 1)

Ref: LC, p. 51

GAZETA GAZET
Ezhenedel'noe, politicheskoe, literaturnoe, birzhevoe i teatral'noe obozrenie.
Petrograd, 1917, weekly

1917:   Mar. 26 (No. 3)

Ref: LC, p. 51

GAZETA-GRIVENNIK
>Petrograd, 1917, daily

> 1917:   Nov. 28 (Dec. 11) (No. 1)
>> Ref: LC, p. 51

GAZETA-KOPEIKA
> [Published by the Joint-Stock Publishing Company "Kopeika. "]
Published briefly in 1917 as Gazeta-grivennik, Gazeta-drug, and
Gazeta dlia vsekh.
>> Petrograd, 1908, daily

> 1914:   June 22, 24 (Aug. 6) (Nos. 2160 [ekstr. prib.], 2162)
> 1917:   March 10, July 5 (18) (Nos. 3104, 3200)
>> Ref: Beliaeva 1776; Columbia 86;
>> LC, p. 51

GAZETA-KOPEIKA; GAZETA DLIA VSEKH
>> Moscow, 1916, daily

> 1917:   March 6 (No. 218)

GAZETA PECHATNIKOV
>> Moscow

> 1918-1919: Nos. 2-4, 8-11, 26-27 (microfilm)

GAZETA-PROTEST SOIUZA RUSSKIKH PISATELEI
>> Odnodnevnaia gazeta.
>> Petrograd, 1917

> 1917:   Nov. 26

GAZETA VREMENNAGO RABOCHAGO I KREST'IANSKAGO PRAVITEL'STVA
>> Petrograd, 1917, daily

> 1917:   Nov. 1 (Nov. 14), 23 (Dec. 6)-Dec. 31 (Jan. 13) (Nos. 3, 16-45)
> 1918:   Jan. 4 (Jan. 17), 9(22), 19(Feb. 1), Feb. 20, Feb. 28, Mar. 7-
>> 8, 10 (Nos. 2 (47), 5(50), 12(57), 28(73), 35(80), 41(86), 42(87),
>> 44(98)
>> Continuation of Pravitel'stvennyi vestnik
>>> Ref: Columbia 85; LC, p. 51

GEORGIEVSKII DEN'
        Kharbin, 1930

   1932:   Dec. 9

GEORGIEVSKII KAVALER
        Izdanie Dal'ne-Vostochnago soiuza voennykh v Man'chzhurskoi
imperii.
        Kharbin, 1938

   1938:   Dec. 9

GEROL'D KHARBINA
        Anglo-russkaia nezavisimaia ezhednevnaia gazeta.
        Kharbin, 1933, daily

   1933:   Jan. 1 (No. 138(435))

GOD PROLETARSKOI REVOLUTSII
        25 oktiabria 1917-25 oktiabria (7 noiabria) 1918; ob''edinennaia
redaktsiia gazet "Pravda, " "Severnaia kommuna, " "Krasnaia gazeta, "
"Vooruzhennyi narod" Kollegii Peterburgskogo biuro Rossiiskogo tele-
grafnogo agenstva i komiteta sovetskikh zhurnalistov.
        Leningrad, 1918, irregular

   1918:   Nov. 9 (No. 3)
                            Ref: LC, p. 52

GOLOS
        Ezhednevnaia politicheskaia i obshchestvennaia gazeta.
        Paris, 1914, daily

  1914, Sept. 13-Jan. 17, 1915 (Nos. 1-20, 22-108) [Nos. 1-5, Sept. 13-17,
      1914 of this newspaper were published under the title Nash golos]

GOLOS
        Politicheskaia i literaturnaia ezhednevnaia gazeta.
        St. Petersburg, 1906, daily

   1906:   June 4(17)-10(23) (Nos. 12, 14-17)
                     Ref: Beliaeva 1842

GOLOS (Sofia) see GOLOS TRUDA (Sofia)

GOLOS

Samara, 1916

1916: Oct. 27 (No. 14)

Ref: Beliaeva 1841

GOLOS

Respublikansko-demokraticheskaia, ezhenedel'naia gazeta.
Shanghai, 1931, weekly

1931, Feb. 2-Sept. 20, 1932 (Nos. 3, 4, 6-14, 16, 17, 19-24, 26, 29-34, 36-39, 42, 45)

GOLOS ANARKHISTA

Ekaterinoslav (Dnepropetrovsk), 1918, weekly

1918: March 11 (No. 1)

GOLOS ANARKHII

Organ Saratovskoi svobodnoi assotsiatsii anarkhistskikh grupp.
[Organ of the Saratov Free Association of Anarchistic Groups.]
Saratov, 1917

1917: Sept. 21 (No. 2)

Ref: LC, p. 154

GOLOS AZII

Organ iaponskoi nezavisimoi mysli.
Continued as Vozrozhdenie Azii as of Feb. 15, 1933
Tientsin, daily

1932, Apr. 9-Feb. 14, 1933 (Nos. 19-23, 25-115, 117-255)

GOLOS BUKHARESTA

Bezpartiinyi politiko-ekonomicheskii organ.
Bucharest, 1933, weekly

1933: Aug. 15-Nov. (Nos. 1-13)

GOLOS KAZAKA

Periodicheskaia gazeta.
Shanghai, 1929

1930: May (No. 2)

GOLOS NARODA
>Vykhodit 1 i 15 chisla kazhdogo mesiatsa.
>Pechory, 1927, semimonthly

>1927:   March 15 (No. 1)

GOLOS NARODA
>Organ russkoi sotsialisticheskoi mysli.
>Prague, 1920

>1920:   June 26, July 6 (Nos. 5, 8)

GOLOS PISHCHEVIKA
>Moscow

>1920:   Nos. 1-5 (microfilm)

GOLOS PRAVDY
>Organ fraktsii R. S. D. R. P. (bol'shev.) pri Kronsh. S. R. i S. D.
>Ezhednevnaia gazeta. [Organ of the Faction of the Russian Social
>Democratic Workers' Party (of Bolsheviks) of the Kronstadt Soviet of
>Workers' and Soldiers' Deputies.]
>Kronstadt, 1917, daily

>1917:   Nov. 11 (Oct. 29) (No. 98)
>   Ref: LC, p. 43

GOLOS PRIKAZCHIKA
>Ezhenedel'naia gazeta, posviashchennaia interesam prikazchikov,
>kontorshchikov i drugikh sluzhashchikh v torgovykh i promyshlennykh
>uchrezhdeniiakh.
>St. Petersburg, weekly, 1906

>1906:   Nos. 1-6, 8-11, 13 (microfilm)
>   Ref: Beliaeva 1938

GOLOS PRIMOR'IA
>Gazeta ezhednevnaia, progressivnaia, vnepartiinaia, politiko-
>ekonomicheskaia i obshchestvenno-literaturnaia.
>Vladivostok, 1917, daily

>1917:   Dec. 13, 25, 27, 29
>1918:   Mar. 29, Apr. 6-7, 10, 28, June 7-8, 10, 23, 27, 29, July 1,
>   8, 13, 15, 17, 20, 25, 26 (Nos. 98, 100, 102, 178, 185-186, 188,
>   198, 230, 231, 233, 242, 245, 247, 254, 258, 260, 261, 264,
>   268, 269
>   Ref: Columbia 93; LC, p. 181

GOLOS PROLETARIIA
        Rossiiskaia Sotsial-Demokraticheskaia Rabochaia Partiia. Organ
Vyborgskogo Raiona.
        St. Petersburg

1906:   Nos. 1-3 (microfilm)
                                 Ref: Columbia 94

GOLOS RODINY; izdanie komiteta za vozvrashchenie na rodinu (Berlin) see
ZA VOZVRASHCHENIE NA RODINU; izdanie komiteta za vozvraschenie na
rodinu

GOLOS RODINY
        Obshchestvennaia i politicheskaia gazeta.
        Hague, 1918, daily

1918, May 20, June 2-July 18, 31, 1919 (Nos. 1-214, 216-313, 315-
     329)
                                 Ref: Columbia 95

GOLOS RODINY
        Vladivostok, 1917, daily

1919:   Sept. 27, Oct. 23-25 (Nos. 18, 20, 38-40)
                                Ref: LC, p. 181

GOLOS RONDA
        Organ Rossiiskogo osvoboditel'nogo narodnogo dvizheniia
(Rossiiskoe natsional-sotsialisticheskoe dvizhenie trudiashchikhsia)
        Berlin, 1933, weekly

1933:   June 8 (No. 1)
                                Ref: Columbia 378

GOLOS ROSSII
        Organ nezavisimoi russkoi politicheskoi mysli. Vykhodit
ezhednevno, krome ponedel'nikov.
        Berlin, 1919, daily

1919:   Mar. 15(2) (No. 17)
1920:   May 20(7), 23(10) (Nos. 108, 111)
1921:   Dec. 3-31 (Nos. 830-853)
1922:   Feb. 22, 25, June 27, 30-July 18, 20-25, 27, Aug. 8, 13, 27,
        Sept. 28 (Nos. 898, 901, 1000, 1002-1008, 1010-1014, 1016,
        1026, 1031, 1043, 1070)

GOLOS ROSSII
Nezavisimaia obshchestvenno-politicheskaia informatsionnaia gazeta natsional'nogo ob''edineniia.
Munich, 1949, irregular

1949: May 8-Dec. 18 (Nos. 1-9)
1950: Jan. 8-Mar. 25 (Nos. 10-18, 20-27)
Ref: Columbia 97

GOLOS ROSSII
Ezhenedel'naia obshchestvenno-natsional'naia gazeta. Ed. N. I. Plavinskii.
Continuation of Golostruda. Suppressed by the Bulgarian govt. Continued as Nasha gazeta.
Sofia, 1936, weekly

1936: June 18 - Aug. 9, 1938 (nos. 1-111)
Ref: Columbia 98

GOLOS RUSI
Ezhednevnaia politicheskaia, ekonomicheskaia i literaturnaia gazeta.
Petrograd, 1914, daily

1914: July 21-22 (Aug. 4), 23 (Aug. 5), 27 (Aug. 9), Oct. 9 (22)
Spec. suppl. issues (ekstr. prilozh.) Nos. 194-195, 196, 200, 273
Ref: Beliaeva 1948

GOLOS RUSSKOI MOLODEZHI
Organ russkoi pravoslavnoi natsional'noi molodezhi. Izdanie Russkago trudovogo khristianskago dvizheniia.
Geneva, 1938, monthly

1939: May-July (Nos. 6-8)
Ref: Columbia 99

GOLOS SIBIRI
Krasnoyarsk, 1905, three times a week

1906: May 10, 17, 24 (Nos. 31, 34, 37)
Ref: Beliaeva 1959

GOLOS SOLDATA
>Organ Petrogradskago soveta soldatskikh i rabochikh deputatov.
[Organ of the Petrograd Soviet of Soldiers' and Workers' Deputies.]
Continued as Soldatskii golos as of Oct. 27, 1917.
Petrograd, 1917, daily

1917:   May 14, Aug. 31 (Nos. 9, 102)
>Ref: LC, p. 52

GOLOS STUDENCHESTVA
>Vnepartiinaia obshchestvenno-literaturnaia gazeta.
Moscow, 1910, weekly

1910:   Sept. 30 (No. 3)
>Ref: Beliaeva 1968

GOLOS TEKSTILEI
>Organ TSK Soiuza rabochikh khlopchatobumazhnoi promyshlen-
nosti, TSK Soiuza rabochikh l'nopen'kodzhutovoi sherstianoi, shelkovoi
i trikotazhnoi promyshlennosti.
Moscow, 1922

1931:   Oct. 25 (No. 251)

GOLOS (TELEGRAMMY GOLOSA)
>Petrograd, 1914

1914:   Aug. 26

GOLOS TRUDA
>Izdanie Aleksandrovskogo, IUr'ev-Pol'skogo, Pereslavl'-
Zalesskogo i Kirzhachskogo ispolnitel'nykh komitetov Sovetov rabo-
chikh, krest'ianskikh i krasnoarmeiskikh deputatov.
Aleksandrovsk, 1917, daily

1919:   Nov. 7 (No. 39 [239])

GOLOS TRUDA
>Organ federatsii rossiiskikh rabochikh organizatsii IUzhnoi
Ameriki.
Buenos Aires, 1917, weekly

1918-1930: Nos. 2-3, 5-6, 12, 14, 17-18, 20-27, 30, 32, 34-38, 42,
47-49, 52-58, 60-71, 74-75, 79, 82-84, 87-104, 106-217, 250-
253, 255-266, 268-271, 273-275, 278-279, 282-284, 291, 293,
295, 300
>Ref: Columbia 100

GOLOS TRUDA
      Izdanie Soiuza anarkho-sindikalistskoi propagandy. [Published
by the Union for Propaganda of Anarchism and Syndicalism.]
      Continued as   Vol'nyi golos truda.
      Petrograd, 1917, weekly

1917:   Aug. 11 (24)-Nov. 8 (21), 18 (Dec. 1) (Nos. 1-17, 19)
                         Ref: Columbia 102; LC, p. 52

GOLOS TRUDA
      Gazeta stavit svoeiu zadacheiu otstaivanie klassovykh interesov
sel'skago i promyshlennago proletariata.
      St. Petersburg, 1906, daily

1906:   Nos. 1-16 (microfilm)
                         Ref: Beliaeva 1978; Columbia 101

GOLOS TRUDA
      Samara, 1916, weekly

1916:   Nos. 1-3 (microfilm)
                         Ref: Beliaeva 1977

GOLOS TRUDA
      Ezhenedel'naia obshchestvenno-politicheskaia gazeta. Organ
Russkago obshche-trudovogo soiuza v Bolgarii. Pod redaktsiei G. F.
Voloshina i N. I. Plavinskago (Otvetstvennyi redaktor)
      With No. 431/20 this newspaper consolidated with Trud March 5,
1933. In 1936 (June?) it changed title to Golos Rossii, ed. by I. Solonevich.
At the outset there were 2 numberings in the first 20 issues, a continuation
of nos. of Trud and of Golos Truda (i.e., 431, etc.). Beginning with Nov.
1933 the second numbering was omitted.
      Sofia, weekly

1933:   March-May 1936 (Nos. 1-19). For Nos. 20 [431]-75, 77-121,
        123-165 see Trud)
                         Ref: Columbia 103

GOLOS TRUDOVOGO KREST'IANSTVA
      Organ Krest'ianskogo otdela Vserossiiskogo TSentral'nogo
ispolnitel'nogo komiteta sovetov. Ezhednevnaia gazeta. [Organ of the
Peasants' Section of the All-Russian Central Executive Committee of
Soviets.]
      Moscow, 1918, daily
(Continued on next page)

GOLOS TRUDOVOGO KREST'IANSTVA (continued)

    1918: May-Nov. (Nos. 135, 141, 167-181, 183-194, 196-227, 229-231, 234, 235, 251-256, 263-272, 274-276, 279-284)

                                                        Ref: Columbia 105; LC, p. 89

GOLOS TRUZHENIKA

            Ezhenedel'naia rabochaia gazeta industrial'nykh rabochikh mira. [Weekly of the Industrial Workers of the World.]

            Chicago, 1918, weekly

    1918-1924: Nos. 2-4, 6-185, 190-238

GOLOS UDARNIKA

            Organ ozerskogo gorkoma vsesoiuznoi kommunisticheskoi partii (bol'shevik) i raionnogo soveta deputatov trudiashchikhsia moskovskoi oblasti.

            Moscow, 1945

    1945: Sept. 8, 11 (Nos. 108 [30132], 109 [30133])

GORSKAIA PRAVDA

            Organ Gorskogo oblastn. komiteta R. K. P. (b) i Gorskogo tsentral'nogo ispolnitel'nogo komiteta sovetov rab. krest'ian. krasn. kaz., gorsk. trud. deputatov G. S. S. R. [Organ of the Gorskii Provincial Committee of the Russian Communist Party (of Bolsheviks) and of the Gorskii Central Executive Committee of Soviets of Workers', Peasants', Red Army, Cossack, and Gorskii Workers' Deputies.]

            Vladikavkaz, 1921, daily

    1922: Mar. 12 (No. 59)

                                                   Ref: LC, p. 16

GRAZHDANIN

            Gazeta politicheskaia i literaturnaia.

            St. Petersburg, 1875, daily

    1890: July 19, Sept. 25-27, 29-30, Oct. 2, 5, 9, 12, 15, 17, 20, 23, 26, Dec. 13 (Nos. 198, 266-268, 270-271, 273, 276, 280, 283, 286, 288, 291, 294, 297, 345)

                                      Ref: Beliaeva 2026; Lisovskii 1106

GRIADUSHCHAIA ROSSIIA
Organ russkoi narodnoi mysli.
Continuation of Den'
Berlin, 1921, weekly

1921: Sept. 29, Oct. 6, 13, Dec. 15 (Nos. 5, 6, 7, 16)

Ref: Columbia 109

GRIADUSHCHII DEN'
Sotsialisticheskaia gazeta.
Petrograd, 1917, only 1 number was published

1917: Nov. 28 (No. 1)

Ref: LC, p. 52

GROZNENSKII RABOCHII
Ezhednevnaia massovaia rabochaia gazeta. Organ Che-
chorgbiuro VKP, Orgbiuro Sovprofa i Chechenskogo obl. ispolnitel'nogo komiteta i gorodskogo soveta r., k., k. d.
Grozny, 1928, daily

1928: Dec. 29 (No. 304 [2089])

GRUZIIA
Ezhednevnaia politicheskaia i literaturnaia gazeta.
Tiflis, daily

1920: Nov. 6 (No. 161)
1921: Jan. 1-Feb. 17 (Nos. 1-26, 29-36)

Ref: LC, p. 169

GUDOK
Gazeta TS. K. Soiuza zh.-d. i vodnogo transporta. [Organ of
the Ministry of Communications of the USSR and of the Central Committee of the Labor Union of Railroad and Waterways Workers.]
Moscow, 1920, daily

1920, May 11-Feb. 3, 1922: Nos. 1-200, 203-229, 231-238, 240-287,
290-410, 412-467, 469, 471-474, 482-484, 492-499, 501, 503-
504, 518-519
1929: Aug. 2 (No. 175/2761)

Ref: Columbia 113; LC, p. 89

GUDOK

Organ Narodnogo komissariata putei soobshcheniia.
Moscow, 1921, semiweekly

1945: Sept. 19-Nov. 21 (Nos. 113, 115-116, 118, 122, 139)
1948: Jan. 30, Feb. 1, 4, 6, 15, Mar. 10, Apr. 16, Oct. 9, 12
(Nos. 13-16, 20, 30, 46, 121, 122)

Ref: Columbia 113; LC, p. 89

GUN-BAO

Kharbin, 1926, daily

1928: Nos. 333, 336, 338-339, 344, 347-351, 353, 437, 464, 482, 489,
494, 516, 524, 528-531, 534-535, 542, 564-565, 567-568, 594,
596-597, 602-611
1929: Nos. 620, 622, 624, 625d-627, 631, 639d, 646-647, 650-657,
659, 662, 668-670, 673-682, 684, 686, 689-695, 697-706, 708-
711, 713-719, 722-727, 729-731, 733-740, 742-753, 755-756,
758, 762, 763, 765, 766d, 770-771, 773-777, 778d, 779-781-
782d-785d, 786, 787d, 791, 792d, 793-794, 796-798, 800, 802,
805d, 806-810, 813d, 814d-815d, 816-819d, 821-823, 824d, 826,
828-829, 832, 833, 834d-836d, 837-839, 842, 845d, 846-847,
848d, 849-850, 852-853, 854d, 857-858, 859d, 860-864, 913
1930-1932: Nos. 1281, 1345-1370, 1374-1375, 1377-1386, 1388-1391, 1393-
1414, 1416-1426, 1428-1453, 1455-1474, 1476-1494, 1496-1500,
1502, 1504-1506, 1508-1511, 1513-1517, 1519-1520, 1522-1530,
1532-1541, 1543-1553, 1556-15 , 1561-1562, 1564-1573, 1575-
1576, 1579-1586, 1588-1600, 1602-1608, 1610-1617, 1619-1622,
1625, 1628-1629, 1632-1635, 1638-1640, 1642, 1644-1654, 1656-
1658, 1660-1667, 1669-1674, 1676-1678, 1680-1682, 1685-1691,
1693-1695, 1697-1698, 1700-1703, 1705 (1931-1932)
1933: No. 1863

I

IALTA

Gazeta obshchestvennoi i kurortnoi zhizni IUzhnago berega Kryma. Izdanie ezhenedel'noe s ezhednevnymi pribavleniiami.

Yalta, 1893, weekly

1894:   Jan. 11 (No. 2)
1896:   Sept. 26 (No. 38)

_____Ezhednevnoe pribavlenie k gazete "IAlta."

1894:   Jan. 20, Apr. 24, Aug. 10-20, Sept. 10, Oct. 1-15, 18-28 (Nos. 13, 75, 124, 132, 147, 163-174, 176-182, 229-230)
1895:   Jan. 3-4, Nov. 23, Dec. 9 (Nos. 209, 220)
1896:   Jan. 6, Mar. 3, May 24, June 2, July 2, 17, Sept. 28 (Nos. 3, 40, 91, 98, 118, 128, 175)

Ref: Lisovskii 2291

IMPERSKAIA ROSSIIA

Organ Rossiiskago sotsial-natsionalisticheskago imperskago dvizheniia.

Paris, irregular

1937:   Jan.-June, Nov. (Nos. 1-4)
1938:   Apr., Sept. (Nos. 5, 7)

Ref: Columbia 116

IMPERSKII KLICH

Organ Rossiiskago Imperskago Soiuza.
Paris, 1932, monthly

1932, June 25-July 1936 (Nos. 1-28)

Ref: Columbia 117

INDUSTRIIA see CHERNAIA METALLURGIIA

INFORMATSIONNYI BIULLETEN'

Izdanie Soiuza russkikh invalidov v Bolgarii.
Sofia, 1933 (?)

1933:   Jan.-Aug. (Nos. 8-11)

INFORMATSIONNYI LISTOK SHTABA 1-GO ARMEISKAGO KORPUSA RUSSKOI
ARMII
>
> Bulgaria, 1922

1922: May 21, 28 (Nos. 38, 40)

INVALID
>
> Odnodnevnyi vypusk. Otvetstvennyi redaktor prof. N. Esperov.
> Kharbin, 1936

1936: Nov. 15

IRBITSKII IARMAROCHNYI LISTOK
>
> Vykhodit ezhednevno v period iarmarki s 25-go ian. po 1-e marta.
> Irbit, 1863, appears daily each year from Jan. 25 to March 1.

1901: Jan.-Feb. (Nos. 7, 19, 20)
>
> Ref: Lisovskii 766; Beliaeva 3623

ISKRA
>
> Moscow

1918: Nos. 2-3

ISKRA
>
> Tsentral'nyi organ Rossiiskoi sotsial-demokraticheskoi rabochei
> partii. [Central organ of the Russian Socialist Workers' Party.]
> Geneva, 1900

1900, Dec.-Oct. 8, 1905: Nos. 1-112.

ISKRA
>
> Organ men'shevikov-internationalistov. Rossiiskaia sotsial-
> demokraticheskaia rabochaia partiia.
> Petrograd, 1917, weekly

1917: 2-122 (microfilm)
>
> Ref: LC, p. 52

ISKUSSTVO KOMMUNY
>
> Izdanie Otdela Izobrazitel'nykh Iskusstv Narodnogo komissariata
> Narodnogo Prosveshcheniia. [Published by the Department of Graphic
> Arts of the People's Commissariat of Public Instruction.]

1918, Dec. 7-Apr. 13, 1919 (Nos. 1-19)
>
> Ref: LC, p. 53

ITOGI SEMI DNEI
New York, weekly

1940: June 17, 25 (Nos. 1, 2)

Ref: Columbia 120

IUG ROSSII
Bezpartiinaia obshchestvenno-politicheskaia i literaturnaia gazeta.
Sevastopol, 1919, daily

1920: June 25, Oct. 9 (22) - 10 (23), 17 (30), 23 (Nov. 5) (Nos. 72 [245],
153 [348] - 154 [349], 160 [355], 165 [360])

Ref: Columbia 123; LC, p. 156

IUZHNAIA GAZETA
Kiev, 1910, daily

1917: Oct. 21-22, Nov. 9, 15 (Nos. 2437, 2438, 2450, 2456)

Ref: LC, p. 30

IUZHNOE SLOVO
Pri blizhaishem uchastii akademikov I. A. Bunina i N. P. Konda-
kova.

Odessa, 1919

1919: Nov. 26 (Dec. 9), Dec. 11 (24) (Nos. 84, 96)

Ref: Columbia 126; LC, p. 137

IUZHNYE VEDOMOSTI
Gazeta politicheskaia, obshchestvennaia i ekonomicheskaia.
Simferopol, 1906, daily

1906: No. 25
1913: No. 244
1920: Nos. 65, 66, 126, 127, 129, 153, 162, 166, 181, 182, 183, 212-
214

IUZHNYI KRAI
Kharkov, 1880, daily

1919: (microfilm)

Ref: LC, p. 27

IZO

Vestnik otdela izobrazitel'nykh iskusstv N. K. P.
Moscow, 1921 (?)

1921: Mar. 10 (No. 1)

IZVESTIIA BRIANSKOGO GUBERNSK. ISPOLNITEL'NOGO KOMITETA SOVETOV
RABOCHIKH, KREST'IANSKIKH I KRASNOARMEISKIKH DEPUTATOV I GUB-
KOMA K. K. P. (b.)
Briansk, 1921

1921: Nov. 7, No. 233 (793)
Ref: LC, p. 12

IZVESTIIA DANILOVSKOGO UEZDNOGO ISPOLNITEL'NOGO KOMITETA
SOVETOV KREST'IANSKIKH RABOCHIKH I KRASNOARMEISKIKH DEPUTATOV
Danilov, 1919, twice a week

1921: Nov. 5 (No. 68)
Ref: LC, p. 16

IZVESTIIA ELATOMSKOGO UEZDNOGO KOMITETA ROSSIISKOI KOMMUNISTI-
CHESKOI PARTII. (BOL'SHEVIKOV)
Sasovo, 1920

1921: Nov. 7 (No. 33 [82])
Ref: LC, p. 155

IZVESTIIA ISPOLNITL'NOGO KOMITETA SARATOVSKOGO GUBERNSKOGO
SOVETA KREST'IANSKIKH DEPUTATOV
Saratov, 1917

1917: Nov. 4 (No. 1)
Ref: LC, p. 154

IZVESTIIA ISPOLNITEL'NOGO KOMITETA SOVETA RABOCHIKH, KREST'-
IANSKIKH I MATROSSKIKH DEPUTATOV GORODA SEVASTOPOLIA
Title varies: May 1919, Izvestiia Sevastopol'skogo revoliutsion-
nogo komiteta
Sevastopol, 1919, daily

1919: May 3-9, 11-15, 21, 24, 27-28, 31, June 11-12, 15, 18-21 (Nos.
6-11, 13-16, 21, 24, 26-27, 29, 37-38, 41, 43-46 (microfilm)
Ref: LC, p. 156

IZVESTIIA KALIAZINSKOGO UISPOLKOMA, UEZDNOGO KOMITETA R. K. P.
(BOL'SHEVIKOV) I UEZDNOGO KOMITETA ROSTA
Kaliazin, 1919, weekly

1921: Nov. 6 (No. 44 [117])

Ref: LC, p. 23

IZVESTIIA KERCHENSKOGO OKRUZHNOGO ISPOLKOMA I OKRKOMA R. K. P.
Kerch, 1921

1922: March 12 (No. 174)

Ref: LC, p. 26

IZVESTIIA KOMISSARIATA GORODSKIKH KHOZIAISTV SOIUZA KOMMUN
SEVERNOI OBLASTI
Continuation of Izvestiia Petrogradskago gorodskogo obshchest-
vennago upravleniia.
Petrograd, 1918, semiweekly

1918: Sept. 25-Dec. 21, Nos. 1, 3-6, 8, 10, 12, 13-14, 16, 19, 23-25
Ref: LC, p. 53

IZVESTIIA KREST'IANSKIKH DEPUTATOV; EZHEDNEVNAIA NARODNAIA
GAZETA
St. Petersburg, 1906, daily

1906: May 30 (10)

Ref: Beliaeva 3366; Columbia 128

IZVESTIIA KRONSHTADTSKOGO SOVETA RABOCHIKH, MATROSSKIKH I
KRASNOARMEISKIKH DEPUTATOV
Kronshtadt, 1919

1919: June 6 (May 24) (No. 123)

Ref: LC, p. 43

IZVESTIIA MOSKOVSKOGO SOVETA RABOCHIKH DEPUTATOV
Moscow, 1917, daily

1917: June 17 (30) (No. 88)

Ref: Columbia 129

IZVESTIIA MOSKOVSKOI PECHATI
Moscow, 1917

1917:   Mar. 1

IZVESTIIA PETROGRADSKAGO GORODSKOGO OBSHCHESTVENNAGO
UPRAVLENIIA
Izdanie Petrogradskoi gorodskoi dumy.
Continued as Izvestiia Komissariata gorodskikh khoziaistv
Soiuza kommun severnoi oblasti.
Petrograd, 1918, semiweekly

1918:   Apr. 17(4), 20(7), May 15(2), June 8(May 26) - July 6, 13 -
Sept. 11, 18-21 (Nos. 25, 26, 32, 39-47, 49-66, 68, 69
Ref: LC, p. 53

IZVESTIIA PETROGRADSKOGO SOVETA RABOCHIKH I KRASNOAR-
MEISKIKH DEPUTATOV
Title varies:
a) Izvestiia petrogradskogo soveta rabochikh i soldatskikh
deputatov, nos. 1-25; Mar. 16, 1918, Apr. 17, 1918.
b) Izvestiia petrogradskogo soveta rabochikh i krasnoarmeiskikh deputatov, no. 26-61; Apr. 18, 1918–June 1, 1918.
c) Severnaia kommuna; izvestiia tsentral'nogo ispolnitel'-
nogo komiteta sovetov krest'ianskikh, rabochikh i krasnoarmeiskikh
deputatov severnoi oblasti i petrogradskogo soveta rabochikh i
krasnoarmeiskikh deputatov, nos. 1-193; June 2, 1918 - Dec. 31,
1918 and nos. 1(194) - 103(296); Jan. - May 11, 1919.
d) (again) Izvestiia petrogradskogo soveta rabochikh i
krasnoarmeiskikh deputatov, nos. 104(296) - ; May 12, 1919 - .
Petrograd, 1918, daily

1918:   Mar. 16 - June 1 (Nos. 1-61). [As Severnaia Kommuna]
June 2 - Dec. 31 (Nos. 1-4, 7, 11-13, 48, 58, 64-66, 68-
69, 71-73, 77-78, 80-81, 83, 85-152, 154, 156-160, 162-
165, 167, 169-193)
1919:   [As Severnaia Kommuna] Jan. - May 11 (nos. 1(194) -
103 [296], [again as Izvestiia ...] May 12 - Dec. 31 (nos.
104 [297] - 135, 138-144, 146-149, 151, 153-157, 163, 167,
170-171, 179-180, 184, 186, 192, 198-200, 202-203, 206,
209-211, 216-222, 224-226, 231, 235-243, 245, 247-268,
273-293, 295-297, 299 [494])
1920:   Jan. - Dec. (nos. 1-44, 46-168)
1921:   Jan. 4 - Apr. 16 (nos. 1-7, 9, 14-17, 26-31, 34-35, 37-55,
57-68, 70, 72, 75-77, 79-82)

IZVESTIIA PETROGRADSKOGO SOVETA RABOCHIKH I SOLDATSKIKH DEPU-
TATOV see IZVESTIIA PETROGRADSKOGO SOVETA RABOCHIKH I KRASNO-
ARMEISKIKH DEPUTATOV

IZVESTIIA PETROKOMMUNY
Organ Petrogradskoi potrebitel'skoi kommuny. [Organ of the
Petrograd Consumers' Cooperative.]
Title varies: issue of Nov. 7, 1920 under the title, Izvestiia
Petrogubkommuny.
Petrograd, irreg.

1919: Nov. 7
1920: Nov. 7

Ref: LC, p. 54

IZVESTIIA REVEL'SKAGO SOVETA RABOCHIKH I VOINSKIKH DEPUTATOV
Revel, 1917, daily

1917: March 17 (30), 23 (Apr. 5), 29 (Apr. 11), 30 (Apr. 12), Apr.
8 (21)-11 (24), 13 (26)-16 (29), 25 (May 8), 26 (May 9), 29 (May
12)-May 3 (16), 7 (20), 11 (24)-17 (30), 21 (June 3), 28 (June 10),
June 1 (14)-3 (16), 6 (19), 8 (21), 9 (22), 11 (24), 15 (28)-17 (30).
(Nos. 6, 11, 15, 16, 21-23, 25-28, 34, 35, 38-41, 45, 48-52,
56, 60, 63-65, 67, 69, 70, 72, 75-77)

IZVESTIIA REVOLIUTSIONNOI NEDELI; IZDANIE KOMITETA PETROGRAD-
SKIKH ZHURNALISTOV
Petrograd, 1917, daily

1917: Feb. 27 - Mar. 5 (nos. 1-10)

Ref: LC, p. 54

IZVESTIIA ROSTOVO-NAZHICHEVANSKOGO S. R. n S. D.
Rostov-on-Don

1917: No. 16 (microfilm)

IZVESTIIA SARATOVSKOGO SOVETA RABOCHIKH I KR.-ARM. DEPUTATOV, GUBISPOLKOMA, GUBKOMA VKP I GUBPROFSOVETA

        Saratov, 1917, daily

1918: Jan.-June 22 (nos. 1-2, 4-7, 21-22, 32-34, 36, 38-50, 52-68, 70-82, 84, 86, 88-103, 105-122)

1928: Feb. 29, Apr. 11, 13, 18, 20-24, 26-28, May 5-13, 16, 17, June 2, 6, 10 (nos. 51, 86, 88, 91, 93-96, 98-100, 103-110, 112, 113, 127, 129, 133)

                                      Ref: LC, p. 154

IZVESTIIA SOVETA RABOCHIKH DEPUTATOV

        S predisloviem i primechaniiami Dm. Sverchkova i s prilozheniem fotograficheskikh snimkov "Izvestii". Leningrad Gosudarstvennoe izdatel'stvo, 1925.

        At head of title: Otdel Leningradskogo gubernskogo komiteta RKP(b) po izucheniiu istorii Oktiabr'skoi revoliutsii i RKP(b) Leningradskii istpart...

        Reprint.

1905: Oct. 17-Dec. 14 (nos. 1-10 [nos. 2-8 on microfilm])

IZVESTIIA SOVETA RABOCHIKH I KREST'IANSKIKH DEPUTATOV GORODA ROSTOVA, IAROSLAVSKOI GUB.

        Rostov, 1918, 3 times a week

1919: Nov. 7 (no. 125 [209])

                                Ref: LC, p. 149

IZVESTIIA SOVETOV DEPUTATOV TRUDIASHCHIKHSIA SSSR

        Title varies:

        a) Izvestiia Petrogradskago sovieta rabochikh deputatov, nos. 1-4; Feb. 28-Mar. 3, 1917.

        b) Izvestiia Petrogradskago sovieta rabochikh i soldatskikh deputatov, no. 5-131; Mar. 5-July 30, 1917.

        c) Izvestiia tsentral'nago ispolnitel'nago komiteta i Petrogradskago sovieta rabochikh i soldatskikh deputatov, no. 132-183; Aug. 1-Sept. 28, 1917.

        d) Izvestiia tsentral'nago ispolnitel'nago komiteta sovietov rabochikh i soldatskikh deputatov, nos. 184-207; Sept. 29-Oct. 26, 1917

        e) Izvestiia tsentral'nago ispolnitel'nago komiteta i Petrogradskago sovieta rabochikh i soldatskikh deputatov, nos. 208-260; Oct. 27-Dec. 24, 1917.

        f) Izvestiia tsentral'nago ispolnitel'nago komiteta sovietov krest'ianskikh, rabochikh i soldatskikh deputatov i petrogradskago sovieta rabochikh i soldatskikh deputatov, nos. 261-264; Dec. 28-Dec. 31 and nos. 1-39, 1918.

g) <u>Izvestiia vserossiiskago tsentral'nago ispolnitel'nago komiteta</u>
<u>sovietov krest'ianskikh, rabochikh, soldatskikh i kazach'ikh deputatov i</u>
<u>petrogradskago sovieta rabochikh i soldatskikh deputatov</u>, nos. 40-45;
1918.

h) <u>Izvestiia Vserossiiskogo tsentral'nogo komiteta sovetov</u>
<u>krest'ianskikh, rabochikh, soldatskikh i kazach'ikh deputatov</u>, no. 46;
1918.

i) Same title as above plus <u>i moskovskogo soveta rabochikh i</u>
<u>krasnoarmeiskikh deputatov</u>, no. 127; 1918-no. 155; 1923.

j) <u>Izvestiia tsentral'nogo ispolnitel'nogo komiteta SSSR i</u>
<u>vserossiiskogo tsentral'nogo ispolnitel'nogo komiteta sovetov rabochikh,</u>
<u>krest'ianskikh i krasnoarmeiskikh deputatov</u>, no. 156; 1923 - no. 20;
1938.

k) <u>Izvestiia sovetov deputatov trudiashchikhsia SSSR</u>, no. 21;
1938- .

Moscow, 1917, daily

1917 - June 1946
1946, Aug. - to present
<u>Missing nos.</u>:
1924:   Aug. 7
1926:   Sept. 2
1938:   July 24-25
1946:   all of July, Aug. 21-31, Sept. 21
1948:   all of Mar., Apr., and May
1956:   Aug. 17
1957:   Jan. 27, Oct. 17
1958:   June 11

<u>IZVESTIIA SOVETOV DEPUTATOV TRUDIASHCHIKHSIA SSSR</u>
Moscow, 1917, daily

1917:   Mar. 1 - Dec. 24 (nos. 1-260)
<u>Missing nos.</u>:
Nos. 89, 194, 204, 206, 211, 214, 220, 224, 231, 236, (pp. 1-9 of) 237,
245, 247

<u>IZVESTIIA TSENTRAL'NAGO ISPOLNITEL'NAGO KOMITETA I PETROGRAD-</u>
<u>SKAGO SOVIETA RABOCHIKH I SOLDATSKIKH DEPUTATOV.</u> Petrograd,
see <u>IZVESTIIA SOVETOV DEPUTATOV TRUDIASHCHIKHSIA SSSR.</u> Moscow.

<u>IZVESTIIA TSENTRAL'NAGO ISPOLNITEL'NAGO KOMITETA SOVETOV</u>
<u>KREST'IANSKIKH, RABOCHIKH I SOLDATSKIKH DEPUTATOV I PETRO-</u>
<u>GRADSKAGO SOVETA RABOCHIKH I SOLDATSKIKH DEPUTATOV.</u>
Petrograd, see <u>IZVESTIIA SOVETOV DEPUTATOV TRUDIASHCHIKHSIA</u>
<u>SSSR.</u> Moscow.

IZVESTIIA TSENTRAL'NAGO ISPOLNITEL'NAGO KOMITETA SOVETOV
RABOCHIKH I SOLDATSKIKH DEPUTATOV. Petrograd, see IZVESTIIA
SOVETOV DEPUTATOV TRUDIASHCHIKHSIA SSSR. Moscow.

IZVESTIIA TSENTRAL'NOGO ISPOLNITEL'NOGO KOMITETA SSR I VSEROS-
SIISKOGO TSENTRAL'NOGO ISPOLNITEL'NOGO KOMITETA SOVETOV
RABOCHIKH, KREST'IANSKIKH I KRASNOARMEISKIKH DEPUTATOV.
Moscow, see IZVESTIIA SOVETOV DEPUTATOV TRUDIASHCHIKHSIA SSSR.
Moscow.

IZVESTIIA TVERSKOGO SOVETA RABOCHIKH, KREST'IANSKIKH I KRASNO-
ARMEISKIKH DEPUTATOV
   Organ Soveta professional'nykh soiuzov i fabrichno-zavodskikh
komitetov. [Organ of the Soviet of Labor Unions and of Factory and
Plant Committees.]
   Tver, 1918, daily

1918: June 4(22) (No. 66)
         Ref: LC, p. 23

IZVESTIIA ULAN-BATOR-KHOTO
   Title varies: Nos. 1-133 Urginskaia gazeta; No. 134 Urginskie
Izvestiia; No. 135 Izvestiia Ulan-Bator-Khoto.
   Ulan Bator Khoto, 1924

1924: Nos. 73-76, 81-82, 88, 107, 111-113, 123-139
1925: Nos. 150-160, 176, 178-180, 183-193, 220-223, 228-232, 238-
    241
1926: Nos. 247, 260, 262-263, 267, 285, 294, 303-305, 315, 320,
    338-339, 341
1927: Nos. 345-352, 357, 360-374, 376-377, 379-386, 389-394, 397-
    400, 417-418, 420-423, 426-438
1928: Nos. 450-451, 463-468, 471-473, 485-486, 488-494, 503, 512-
    517, 521-523

IZVESTIIA VITEBSKOGO GUBISPOLKOMA I GUBKOMA R.K.P. (BOL'SHEVI-
KOV)

Vitebsk, 1918, daily

1919: Nov. 7 (No. 252)
1921: Nov. 7 (No. 254)
1922: March 12 (No. 59)

Ref: LC, p. 179

IZVESTIIA VLADIVOSTOTSKAGO SOVETA RABOCHIKH I SOLDATSKIKH
DEPUTATOV

Vladivostok, 1917, daily

1917: Dec. 14(27), 16(29) (Nos. 194, 196)

IZVESTIIA VSEBASHKIRSKOGO TSENTRAL'NOGO ISPOLNITEL'NOGO KOMI-
TETA SOVETOV RABOCHIKH, KREST'IANSKIKH, KRASNOARMEISKIKH
DEPUTATOV I BASHKIRSKOGO OBLASTNOGO KOMITETA RKP (b)

Sterlitamak, 1920, 3 times a week

1921: Nov. 6 (No. 36)

Ref: LC, p. 163

IZVESTIIA VSEROSSIISKAGO SOVETA KREST'IANSKIKH DEPUTATOV

Petrograd, 1917, daily

1917: July 6 (No. 50)
1918: May 13, 16, June 11 (Nos. 5, 7, 29)

Ref: LC, p. 55

IZVESTIIA VSEROSSIISKAGO TSENTRAL'NAGO ISPOLNITEL'NAGO
KOMITETA SOVETOV KREST'IANSKIKH, RABOCHIKH, SOLDATSKIKH
I KAZACH'IKH DEPUTATOV I PETROGRADSKAGO SOVETA RABOCHIKH
I SOLDATSKIKH DEPUTATOV. Petrograd, see IZVESTIIA SOVETOV
DEPUTATOV TRUDIASHCHIKHSIA SSSR. Moscow.

IZVESTIIA VSEROSSIISKOGO TSENTRAL'NOGO KOMITETA SOVETOV
KREST'IANSKIKH, RABOCHIKH, SOLDATSKIKH I KAZACH'IKH DEPU-
TATOV. Moscow, see IZVESTIIA SOVETOV DEPUTATOV TRUDIASH-
CHIKHSIA SSSR. Moscow.

IZVESTIIA VSEROSSIISKOGO TSENTRAL'NOGO KOMITETA SOVETOV KREST'-
IANSKIKH, RABOCHIKH, SOLDATSKIKH I KAZACH'IKH DEPUTATOV I
MOSKOVSKOGO SOVETA RABOCHIKH I KRASNOARMEISKIKH DEPUTATOV.
Moscow, see IZVESTIIA SOVETOV DEPUTATOV TRUDIASHCHIKHSIA SSR,
Moscow.

IZVESTIIA VSETATARSKOGO TSENTRAL'NOGO ISPOLNITEL'NOGO KOMITETA
SOVETOV OBLASTNOGO KOMITETA R.K.P. I KAZANSKOGO SOVETA
> Kazan, daily

> 1922:   Mar. 12 (No. 59 [653])
>> Ref: LC, p. 25

IZVESTIIA VYSHNEVOLOTSKOGO UEZDNOGO SOVDEPA
> Vyshnii Volochek, 1919

> 1919:   Nov. 7 (No. 126 [209])
>> Ref: LC, p. 186

IZVESTIIA ZAGRANICHNAGO SEKRETARIATA ORGANIZATSIONNAGO
KOMITETA ROSSIISKOI SOTSIAL DEMOKRATICHESKOI RABOCHEI PARTII
> Zurich

> 1915:   Feb. 22, June 14
> 1916:   Feb. 5
> 1917:   Jan.

IZVESTIIA ZAGRANICHNOGO SEKRETARIATA ORG. KOMITETA
> Paris, 1915-1917

> 1915-17:   Nos. 1-8 (microfilm)

IZVIESTIIA PETROGRADSKAGO SOVIETA RABOCHIKH DEPUTATOV.
Petrograd, see IZVESTIIA SOVETOV DEPUTATOV TRUDIASHCHIKHSIA SSSR.
Moscow.

IZVIESTIIA PETROGRADSKAGO SOVIETA RABOCHIKH I SOLDATSKIKH
DEPUTATOV. Petrograd, see IZVESTIIA SOVETOV DEPUTATOV
TRUDIASHCHIKHSIA SSSR. Moscow.

K

K OB"EDINENIIU
>Informatsionnyi biulleten' Ob"edineniia natsional'no-progressivn. i demokratich. russkoi emigratsii v Korol. S. KH. C.
>Belgrade, 1926 (?)

>1926: May (No. 1)

KAMCHATSKAIA PRAVDA
>Organ kamchatskogo obkoma, petropavlovskogo gorodskogo komiteta vsesoiuznoi kommunisticheskoi partii (bol'shevikov) i oblastnogo soveta deputatov trudiashchikhsia. [Organ of the Kamchatka Provincial Committee of the Petropavlovsk City Committee of the All-Union Communist Party (of Bolsheviks) and of the Provincial Soviet of Toilers' Deputies.]
>Petropavlovsk on the Kamchatka, 1923, daily

>1945: Mar. 27 (No. 60)

>>>Ref: LC, p. 144

KAMMUNAR (Kharkov) see KOMMUNIST (Kharkov)

KANADSKII GUDOK
>Organ russkikh rabochikh Kanady.
>Toronto, Ontario, 1931

>1931: Nos. 4-8, 10-13
>1932: Nos. 1-2, 4-5, 7-15, 17-42
>1933: all except No. 97
>1934: all except Nos. 122-130, 132-146, 149-153, 158-159, 165, 167-170, 172-201, 208-210, 218, 220, 221
>1935: Nos. 223-225, 227-230, 239-242, 245-257, 263-280

KARPATORUSSKII GOLOS; NEZAVISIMAIA EZHEDNEVNAIA GAZETA
>Uzhgorod, 1932, daily

>1932: June 5, 11, 14, 16, 28, Aug. 17, Oct. 14, 16 (Nos. 18, 21, 23, 25, 34, 71, 116, 117)

>>>Ref: Columbia 135

KARPATORUSSKOE SLOVO
New York, 1935-38, semimonthly

1935, June-Nov. 1938 (Nos. 1-49, 51-57, 59-78) [No. 40 has never
appeared--an error in numbering]

KAZACH'E SLOVO
Vykhodit po voskreseniiam.
Paris, 1923, weekly

1923:   Dec. 9 (No. 3)

KAZACHII NABAT
Ezhemesiachnik, nezavisimaia gazeta istoricheskoi kazach'ei
mysli.
Title varies: Nov. 1933 - Jan. 1934, Nos. 11-12 Kazachii nabat;
Apr. 20, 1934 - Feb. 8, 1935, Nos. 1(13) - 8(20) Nabat kazachestva;
March 1953 - No. 1(21) Kazachii nabat.
Prague, 1933, irregular

1933:   Nov. (No. 11)
1934:   Jan.-Nov. (Nos. 12-19)
1935:   Feb.-Mar. (No. 20-21)
1937:   Mar.-June (No. 22-24)
1940:   Jan. (Nos. 30-31)

KAZACHII PUT'
Paris, 1934

1934:   Oct. 18
1935, June 28, Sept. 15-Oct. 11, 1936 (Nos. 1, 3, 4-6)

KAZAKHSTANSKAIA PRAVDA
Organ tsentral'nogo komiteta i Alma-Atinskogo obkoma KP(b)
Kazakhstan. [Organ of the Central Committee and the Alma-Ata
Provincial Committee of the Communist Party of Kazakhstan.]
Alma-Ata, 1922, daily

1945:   Mar. 16, June 1, 5, Aug. 3-5, 10-12, 15-29, Sept. 5-7,
        11-21, Oct. 6, 12-13, 16, 19-23, 27-28, Nov. 3-7, 10-11, 23-
        27, 30, Dec. 1, 7, 9-14, 18, 21 (52, 109, 112, 160-2, 164-7,
        169-79, 183-4, 187-94, 205, 209-10, 212, 214-7, 220-1, 225-
        32, 238-41, 243-4, 248, 250-3, 256, 258
                            Ref: Columbia 144; LC, p. 2

KAZARMA

Organ Voennoi organizatsii pri Ob"edinennom komitete. (Rossii-skaia sotsial-demokraticheskaia rabochaia partiia)
Leningrad (?)

1906, Feb.-March 1907: Nos. 1-13

KHARBIN TORGOVYI
Kharbin

1933: Jan. 1 (No. 89)

KHARBINSKII VESTNIK
Ezhednevnaia gazeta.
Kharbin, 1903, daily

1904: Apr. 7 (No. 166)

Ref: Beliaeva 9061

KHARBINSKOE VREMIA
Ezhednevnaia gazeta. Zaregistrirovano v iaponskom General'nom konsul'stve v Kharbine. Organ nezavisimoi mysli.
Kharbin, 1931(?), daily

1932: Nos. 34, 42-45, 47-51, 53, 55, 57-64, 66-76, 100-101, 104-106, 108-116, 119-122, 124-133, 135-143, 154-159, 181-330, 332, 334-352, 357-358

1933: Nos. 1-14, 16-53, 55-60, 62-81, 83-88, 90-100, 102-209, 211-218, 220-231, 232-237, 239-249, 251, 253-258, 342, 348, 353

1934: Nos. 4, 6-9, 11-12, 16, 20, 24-25, 62, 64, 75, 111-113, 116, 123-126, 128-146, 148-158, 160-162, 164-174, 176-183, 185-189, 194-200, 220-221, 228-231, 233, 240-241, 245-252, 257-260, 263-266, 311, 314-317, 349-354, (356-360?)

1935: Nos. 337, 338, 342-348

1936: Nos. 61-62, 72, 76, 78-79, 81, 94-96, 99-101, 166-169, 272-275, 280, 283-286, 293-297, 299, 303, 305, 328

1937: Nos. 65-67, 72-75, 86-88, 92-94, 97

Ref: Columbia 149

KHLEB I VOLIA
Ezhenedel'nyi organ Federatsii soiuzov russkikh rabochikh Soed. Shtatov i Kanady.
New York, 1919, weekly

1919: Feb. 26, July 31, Nov. 6 (Nos. 1, 23, 37)

KIEVLIANIN

Literaturnaia i politicheskaia gazeta IUgo-Zapadnago kraia.
Kiev, 1864, daily

1917: Jan. 21, Apr. 1, July 13, Aug. 5, 9, 10, Sept. 3, 8, 23, Oct. 6,
12, 17, 21, 27, Dec. 8 (Nos. 21, 87, 166, 186, 189, 190, 207,
211, 222, 233, 238, 242, 246, 251, 269)
1919: Aug. 21, 22, 25, 27, Sept. 1, 3, 5 (Nos. 1, 2, 5-6, 10, 11, 13)

Ref: Lisovskii 808; Beliaeva 3843;
Columbia 152; LC, p. 30

KIEVSKAIA MYSL'

Kiev, 1916, daily

1916: Nov. 1 - Dec. 30 (Nos. 304-306, 308, 310-312, 314-333, 335,
337-342, 344-358, 360-362)
1917: Oct. 21-22 (Nos. 254-255)

Ref: Columbia 153; LC, p. 30

KIEVSKYI KOMMUNIST

Kiev

1919: March 13-15, 18 (Nos. 38[46] - 40[48], 42[50]) (microfilm)

KINO

Organ Glavnogo upravleniia kino-fotopromyshlennosti pri SNK
SSSR i TsK kino-fotorabotnikov. [Organ of the Committee on Cinema-
tography of the Council of People's Commissars of the U.S.S.R.]
Moscow, 1924, 5 times a month (every 6 days)

1935-1936
Missing nos. :
1935: Nos. 1-5, 24
1936: Nos. 30(742) - 31(743), 36(746) - 52(764), 57(769)

Ref: Columbia 156; LC, p. 94

KIZIL UZBEKISTON

Uzbekiston kommunist (bol'shevik) lar partirasi Markazii
komiteti, Toshkent oblast, shakhar komitetlari va Uzbekiston S.S.R.
obii sovetining organi.
Tashkent

1947: Apr. 16-18 (Nos. 77-78 [6752-6753])
1949: July 23 (No. 144 [7334])

KLICH

Organ TSentral'nogo komiteta Rossiiskoi sots.-dem. rabochei
partii (ob"edinennoi). Ezhednevnaia gazeta. [Organ of the Central
Committee of the Russian Social Democratic Workers' Party (United).]
Continuation of Zaria. Continued as Plamia as of Nov. 24, 1917.
Petrograd, 1917

1917:   Nov. 23 (No. 1) the only No. published
Ref: LC, p. 56

KLICH NA POMOSHCH'

Odnodnevnaia gazeta Gubkomissii pomoshchi golodnomu
rebenku.
[Published by the Provincial Commission for Relief to Starving
Children.]
Samara (Kuibyshev), 1921, one day's newspaper
Ref: LC, p. 44

KOLKHOZNIK TATARII

Oblastnaia gazeta, izdanie Tatobkoma VKP(b). Vykhodit v
kazhduiu piatidnevku.
Kazan , 1930 (?), every five days

1930:   July 19 (No. 50)

KOLOKOL

Odnodnevnaia gazeta pamiati A. I. Gertsena. Izdanie Muzeia
revoliutsii.
Petrograd, 1920, one day's newspaper

1920:   Jan. 21

Ref: Columbia 162; LC, p. 56

KOMMERCHESKAIA ROSSIIA

Gazeta nauchnaia, obshchestvennaia politiko-ekonomicheskaia,
morskaia, torgovo-promyshlennaia i finansovaia.
Odessa, Khersonsk. gub., 1905, daily

1905:   Nos. 113, 237, 240, 241, 244, 262, 270 (microfilm)
Ref: Columbia 164; Beliaeva 4047

KOMMUNA
>Anarkhicheskaia gazeta.
>Paris, 1905 (?)

>1905: Dec. (No. 1)

KOMMUNA
>Ezhenedel'nyi organ Federatsii internatsional'nykh grupp RKP.
>[Organ of the Federation of International Groups of the Russian Commu-
>nist Party.]
>>Petrograd, 1918, weekly

>>1919: Jan. 30, Feb. 10 (Nos. 13, 15)
>>>Ref: LC, p. 56

KOMMUNA
>Ezhednevnaia gazeta. Organ Samar. gub. komiteta R. K. P. i
>Gub. ispolnitel'nogo komiteta sovetov. [Organ of the Samara Provin-
>cial Committee of the Russian Communist Party and of the Provincial
>Executive Committee of Soviets.]
>>Samara, 1919, daily

>>1921: Sept. 27-28, Oct. 12, 13 (Nos. 833, 834, 846, 847)
>>1922: Mar. 12 (No. 974)
>>>Ref: LC, p. 44

KOMMUNA
>Ezhednevnaia gazeta Voronezhskogo obkoma VKP(b), Oblispolkoma,
>Oblprofsoveta i Gorkoma VKP(b).
>>Voronezh, daily

>>1936: Feb. 23-Aug. 6 (Nos. 44, 46, 47, 57-59, 61-62, 65-67,
>>>69-71, 77, 79, 81, 85, 88, 91, 92, 94, 99, 102, 104, 106,
>>>108, 109, 111-113, 115, 118, 121, 124, 125, 127, 128,
>>>130, 132, 133, 138, 139, 141, 142, 144, 180)

KOMMUNAR
>Ezhednevnaia rabochaia gazeta. Izdanie TSentral'nogo komiteta
>Rossiiskoi kommunisticheskoi partii (b). [Published by the Central
>Committee of the Russian Communist Party (of Bolsheviks).]
>>Moscow, 1918, daily

>>1918: Oct. 20-26, Nov. 3-21, 24-30 (Nos. 11-16, 23-36, 39-44)
>>1919: Mar. 16, Apr. 1, 3 (Nos. 58[128], 70[140], 72[142])
>>>Ref: Columbia 165; LC, p. 95

KOMMUNAR
>Organ Tul. gubispolkoma soveta rab. , kr. i kr. -arm. deputatov i Tul'skogo gubkoma RKP(b). [Organ of the Tula Provincial Committee of Soviets and of the Tula Provincial Committee of the Russian Communist Party (of Bolsheviks).]
>>Tula, 1918, daily

>1922: Mar. 12 (No. 59[1103])
>>>>Ref: LC, p. 172

KOMMUNIST
>Organ TSentral'n. i Bakinsk. komit. Azerbaidzh. kommun. p. (bol'shevikov) Aztsika i Baksoveta. [Organ of the Central Committee and the Baku Committee of the Communist Party (of Bolsheviks), of the Revolutionary Committee of the Azerbaidzhan SSR and of the Baku Soviet of Workers', Peasants', and Red Army Deputies.]
>>Baku, 1920, daily

>1921: Nov. 7 (No. 255[456])
>>>>Ref: LC, p. 8

KOMMUNIST
>Organ TSentral'nogo komiteta i Erevanskogo komiteta Kommunisticheskoi partii (b) Armenii. [Organ of the Central Committee and of the Yerevan Committee of the Communist Party of Armenia.]
>>Yerevan, 1934, daily

>1945: July 1 (No. 131)
>>>>Ref: Columbia 166; LC, p. 187

KOMMUNIST
>Organ TSentral'nogo i Kievskogo gorodskogo komitetov Kommunisticheskoi partii (bol'shevikov) Ukrainy. [Organ of the Central Committee and the Kiev Committee of the Ukrainian Communist Party (of Bolsheviks).]
>>Absorbed by Radians'ka Ukraina as of Feb. 2, 1943.
>>Kiev, 1919, daily

>1919: Mar. 20-22, Apr. 2, 17-26, 29-30 (Nos. 15[43]-17[45], 26[54], 38[66]-43[71], 45[73]-46[74]
>>>>Ref: LC, p. 31

KOMMUNIST

Organ tsentr. kom. KP(b)U. [Organ of the Central Committee of the Communist Party (of Bolsheviks) of the Ukraine.]

Continued as <u>Kammunar</u> as of Mar. 16, 1919, later resuming original title.

Kharkov, 1919, daily

1921: Nov. 30, Dec. 4, 18, 21 (Nos. 270[565], 274[566], 286[581], 288[583])

Ref: LC, p. 28

KOMMUNIST

Ezhednevnaia gazeta Donskogo komiteta KP i Donispolkoma. [Published by the Don Committee of the Communist Party and the Don Executive Committee.]

Rostov, 1921, daily

1922: Mar. 12 (No. 35[192])

Ref: LC, p. 150

KOMMUNIST

Izdanie Serpukh. uezdkoma RKP(b) i Sov. r. k. i kr. dep. [Published by the Serpukhov District Committee of the Russian Communist Party (of Bolsheviks) and the Soviet of Workers', Peasants' and Soldiers' Deputies.]

Serpukhov, 1919, daily

1921: Nov. 6 (No. 252)

Ref: LC, p. 155

KOMMUNIST

Organ Varnavinskogo uezd. ispolnitel'nogo komiteta sovetov i Uezd. komiteta RKP (bol'shevikov). [Organ of the Varnavino District Executive Committee of Soviets and the District Committee of the Russian Communist Party (of Bolsheviks).]

Varnavino, 1920

1921: Nov. 7 (No. 22)

Ref: LC, p. 176

KOMMUNIST TADZHIKISTANA
Organ TSentral'nogo komiteta Stalinabadskogo obkoma i gorkoma
KP(b) Tadzhikistana i Verkhovnogo soveta Tadzhikskoi SSR. [Organ of
the Central Committee and the Stalinabad City and Provincial Committees of the Communist Party of Tadzhikistan and of the Supreme Soviet
of the Tadzhik S. S. R.]
Stalinabad, 1929, daily

1945: Aug. 1-5, Aug. 9-Sept. 8, Sept. 11, Sept. 14-Oct. 21,
Oct. 24-Dec. 5, Dec. 18-26, 29-30 (Nos. 146-149,
151-172, 174, 176-203, 205-234, 243-249, 251-252)
Ref: Columbia 168; LC, p. 162

KOMMUNISTICHESKII INTERNATSIONAL
Izvestiia Kiril. uezd. isp. k-ta soveta krest'iansk., rab. i
kr.-arm. dep. Piatidnevnaia raboche-krest'ianskaia gazeta. [Pub-
lished by the Kirillov District Executive Committee of the Soviet of
Toilers' Deputies.]
Kirillov, 1917, irregular

1919: Nov. 7 (No. 70[226])
Ref: LC, p. 37

KOMMUNISTICHESKII PUT'
Gazeta Stavropol'skogo uezdkoma RKP i Uispolkoma. [Published
by the Stavropol District Committee of the Russian Communist Party
and the District Executive Committee.]
Stavropol-Samarskii, 1921, semiweekly

1921: Nov. 7 (No. 59)
Ref: LC, p. 163

KOMMUNISTICHESKII TRUD
Organ Moskovskogo komiteta RKP i Moskovskogo soveta R. i K.D.
[Organ of the Moscow Committee of the Russian Communist Party and
of the Moscow Soviet of Workers' and Peasants' Deputies.]
As of Feb. 7, 1922, continued as Rabochaia Moskva.
Moscow, daily

1920: Nov. 13, 14 (Nos. 196, 197)
1921: July 22, Aug. 2-Dec. 31 (Nos. 392, 401, 422-517, 519-524,
526-529)
1922: Nos. 1(530)-25, 27
Ref: LC, p. 95

KOMSOMOL'SKAIA PRAVDA
Organ TSentral'nogo i Moskovskogo komiteta VLKSM. [Organ of the Central Committee of the All-Union Lenin Communist Youth League.]
Moscow, May 24, 1925, daily

1929-1941
1943-1947
1948: Jan.-Dec. (Nos. 1, 32, 34, 38, 72, 104-114, 116-119, 121-127, 125-307, 308-310)
1949-1953
Missing nos.:
1930: Nos. 207, 245, 327
1932: No. 295
1933: No. 228
1938: No. 143
1939: Nos. 5, 199
1940: Nos. 1-97, 99-108, 111, 117-119, 122-124, 132, 261-267, 269, 272-279, 281, 284-286, 289-291, 294-296, 301
1941: Nos. 150, 164-165, 234, 236, 238, 259
1943: Nos. 63, 199
1944: Nos. 3, 13, 19, 265
1945: Nos. 24, 67, 146
1948: Nos. 2-31, 33, 35-37, 39-71, 73-103, 115, 120, 128-134
1953: No. 104
Ref: Columbia 169; LC, p. 95

KOOPERATIVNOE DELO
Ezhednevnaia obshchestvenno-ekonomicheskaia, kooperativnaia i torgovaia gazeta. Organ TSentrosoiuza. [Organ of the Central Union of Cooperatives.]
Moscow, Feb. 1, 1922, daily

1922: Feb. 18 (No. 16)
Ref: LC, p. 96

KOOPERATIVNYE BIULLETENI PRIKAMSKIKH SOIUZOV
Izdanie Prikamskogo soiuza potrebitel'nykh obshchestv i Prikamskogo kreditno-kooperativnogo soiuza. [Published by the Unions of Consumers' and Credit Cooperatives of the Kama area.]
Sarapul, 1919, irregular

1919: Aug. 15 (No. 1)
Ref: LC, p. 153

KOOPERATSIIA
> Izdanie O-va p-lei "Kooperatsiia". [Published by the Consumers' Association "Kooperatsiia v Moskve".]
> Moscow, 1918

1919: July 31 (No. 54)

> Ref: LC, p. 97

KOSTROMSKAIA ZHIZN'
> Vecherniia ekstrennyia telegrammy.
> Kostroma

1914: Aug. 27 (No. 47)

KOSTROMSKOI LISTOK
> Gazeta literaturnaia, politicheskaia i obshchestvennaia.
> Kostroma, 1898, three times a week

1898: Nos. 1, 3

> Ref: Lisovskii 2732; Beliaeva 4125

KRASNAIA ARMIIA
> Gazeta Politicheskogo upravleniia Ukrainskogo voennogo okruga.
> Kharkov, three times a week

1928: May 24 (No. 290)

KRASNAIA ARMIIA
> Ezhednevnaia voennaia gazeta.
> [Published by the Military Department of the Publishing House of the All-Russian Central Executive Committee of the Soviet of Workers', Red Army, Peasants', and Cossacks' Deputies.]
> Moscow, Sept. 1918, daily

1918: Oct. 20-26, Nov. 3-6, 10-13, 16-17 (Nos. 102-107, 114-116, 118-120, 123-124)

> Ref: LC, p. 97

KRASNAIA ARMIIA
> Voennaia gazeta Petrogradskoi trudovoi kommuny. [Military newspaper of the Petrograd Labor Commune.]
> Continuation of Rabochaia i krest'ianskaia armiia i flot.
> Petrograd, 1918, daily

1918: May 1-July 31 (Nos. 1-75)

> Ref: Columbia 173; LC, p. 56

KRASNAIA BASHKIRIIA

Organ Bashkirskogo oblastnogo komiteta VKP (b), TS IK
sovetov Bashkirii i Bashprofsoveta. [Organ of the Bashkir Provincial
Committee and the Ufa City Committee of the All-Union Communist
Party (of Bolsheviks), of the Supreme Soviet of the Bashkir A. S. S. R.
and of the Ufa City Soviet of Toilers' Deputies.]
Ufa, 1920, daily

1928:   Apr. 27, May 27 (Nos. 98, 122)

KRASNAIA GAZETA

Izd. Petrogradskogo sov. rab. i sold. deputatov. Izd.
Leningradskogo soveta R. i K.D. [Published by the Petrograd Soviet
of Workers' and Soldiers' Deputies.]
Leningrad, Jan. 25, 1918, daily

1918-1921
1922:   Mar. 12 (No. 58)
1927:   Aug. 11 (No. 214)
1934:   Aug. 3-Dec. 30 (Nos. 177-300)
1935:   May 21 (No. 115)
Missing nos. :
1918:   Nos. 40, 42, 45, 48, 50, 51, 53, 55, 56-61, 64, 69, 70, 72,
        75, 84, 98, 101, 107, 109, 111, 116-120, 123, 125-131,
        133-135, 137-139, 157-159, 165, 167, 171, 173, 177, 186-189,
        191, 193, 195, 202, 205-207, 209, 211-213, 219, 222, 229,
        231, 233, 238, 243, 254, 257-259, 261, 263-274, 277
1919:   Nos. 1-52, 54-56, 60-69, 71, 75-82, 84-86, 88-89, 96-99,
        101, 102, 104-106, 108-111, 113, 114, 116-117, 119-126, 128,
        130-133, 135, 136, 138, 140-142, 144, 147-150, 157-167,
        170-174, 176-183, 186, 187, 189-191, 194-195, 197, 199, 200,
        203, 204-205, 211, 213, 219-221, 223, 225, 227, 232, 243,
        244, 247, 248, 251-253, 255, 264-266, 268, 271-275, 285,
        290, 293
1920:   Nos. 4, 6, 21-31, 33-36, 38, 40, 41, 46, 49-52, 57, 60-64,
        68, 81, 89-93, 97, 115, 119, 121, 122, 124, 127-130, 133-135,
        137-168, 185, 192, 264, 266, 270-end of year
1921:   Nos. 1-23, 25-167, 169, 170-191, 193-274
1934:   Nos. 186, 187, 210-214, 216-222, 239, 241, 253, 262, 289,
        297

Ref: Columbia 175; LC, p. 57

KRASNAIA PRAVDA
Organ of the Orlov Provincial Committee of the Russian Communist Party (of Bolsheviks) and of the Provincial Executive Committee of Soviets of Workers', Peasants' and Red Army Deputies.
Orel, daily

1921: Nov. 7 (No. 148 [153])

Ref: LC, p. 142

KRASNAIA STEP'
Organ kalm. obkoma VKP(b), oblispolkoma i oblprofsoveta.
Astrakhan, 1922, semiweekly

1928: Jan. 31, Feb. 13, Mar. 8-15, Apr. 2-May 10, 17, 21, 24, June 4, 7 (Nos. 9,12, 19-21, 26-37, 39, 40, 42, 43)

KRASNAIA TATARIIA
Ezhednevnaia gazeta Tatarskogo oblastnogo komiteta Vsesoiuznoi kommunisticheskoi partii (bol'shevikov), Tsentral'nogo ispolnitel'nogo komiteta Soveta . . . Soveta professional'nykh soiuzov Tatarskoi Sotsialisticheskoi Sovetskoi Respubliki i Kazanskogo gorodskogo soveta.
Kazan, 1917, daily

1927: Aug. 18 (No. 187)
1928: Apr. 29, May 29 (Nos. 99, 122)

KRASNAIA VOLNA
Organ Ostashkovskogo uispolkoma i ukoma R. K. P. [Organ of the Ostashkov District Committee of the Russian Communist Party.]
Ostashkov, 1918, semiweekly

1921: Nov. 7 (No. 35)

Ref: LC, p. 143

KRASNAIA ZVEZDA
TSentral'nyi organ narodnogo komissariata oborony Soiuza.
[Central Organ of the Ministry of Defense of the USSR.]
Moscow, 1924, daily

1925: Oct. 17, 27, 28 (Nos. 238, 246-247)
1928: Nov. 7 (No. 254)
1930: July 12 (No. 160)
1932 - 1940
1941: Jan. 1 - Oct. 16 (Microfilm)
1942: Jan. 1 - Feb. 27 (Microfilm); May 24-28 (Nos. 120-123)

(Continued on next page)

KRASNAIA ZVEZDA (continued)

 1932-1940
 1941: Jan. 1-Oct. 16 (Microfilm)
 1942: Jan. 1-Feb. 27 (M); May 24-28 (Nos. 120-123)
 1943: Jan. 1-31, Feb. 4-21, 24-Mar. 10, 14, 20-24, 31-Apr. 7, 20-
   Aug. 24, 25-Dec. 31 (Nos. 1-25, 28-43, 45-57, 61, 66-69,
   75-90, 92-199, 200-309) (M); Apr. 3 (No. 78)
 1944: July 3-Aug. 30 (Nos. 94-206)
 1945: Apr. 27-Dec. 30 (Nos. 99-306)
 1947: Jan. 1-Dec. 31 (Nos. 1-307) (Microfilm)
 1948: Aug. 1-Dec. 31 (Nos. 181-310) (Microfilm)
 1949: Jan. 1-Apr. 29, May 1-4, 6-9, 12-13, 18, 21-29, June 1, 3-12,
   15-18, 21, 23-25, 28-30, July 2-6, 8-13, 15-Aug. 6, 9-27, 30-
   Oct. 19, 21-Dec. 31 (Nos. 1-100, 102-103, 105-106, 110-111,
   115, 118-125, 127, 129-137, 139-142, 144, 146-148, 150-152,
   154-157, 159-163, 165-184, 186-202, 204-247, 249-309) (M)
 1950: Nov. 29, Dec. 8 (Nos. 282, 289) (Microfilm)
 1951: Apr. 24-29, May 24-27, June 15, Dec. 25, 30 (Nos. 95-100,
   119-122, 138, 300, 305) (Microfilm)
 1952: Feb. 15, 26-27, 29, Mar. 2-7, 12, 13, 15, 16, 19-21, 23, 26,
   28, Apr. 1, 4-6, 9-16, 18-22, 27-29, May 1, 2, 5, 11, 14-18
   (Nos. 39-48, 49, 51, 53-57, 61, 62, 64, 65, 67-69, 71, 73-75,
   78, 81-86, 89-91, 93-96, 101, 102, 104, 105, 108, 111, 113-
   117) (Microfilm)
 1958: Jan. -cont.
Missing nos. :
 1932: No. 272
 1938: No. 18
 1940: Nos. 1-15, 16-51, 53, 61, 63, 71, 94, 97, 100-105, 108-113,
   116, 118, 121, 300
 1942: No. 122
 1944: Nos. 110-130, 132-137, 142-170, 173, 177-189, 192-205
 1945: Nos. 110-152, 186-191, 195, 198, 242, 247, 253, 295, 298
             Ref: Columbia 176; LC, p. 97

KRASNAIA ZVEZDA

   Ezhednevnaia gazeta politicheskogo upravleniia Sredne-Aziatskogo
voennogo okruga.
   Tashkent

 1928: Nov. 7 (No. 254)

KRASNAIA ZVEZDA see also KRASNOARMEISKII SPRAVDCHNIK

KRASNOARMEETS

Krasnoarmeiskaia gazeta Politupravleniia PRIVO. Vykhodit tri raza v nedeliu.

Samara, three times a week

1928: Jan. 24-28, Feb. 11, 14, April 3-28, May 3-17, 22-24, 29-
June 14, Oct. 19-24, Nov. 2, 13-14, 20-24, Dec. 11, 26 (Nos.
703-705, 711-712, 731-741, 743-749, 751-752, 754-760, 825-
828, 833, 837, 838, 841-844, 855, 864
1929: Jan. 22 (No. 877)

KRASNOARMEISKAIA PRAVDA

Organ Politupravleniia Revvoensoveta Zapfronta. [Organ of the Political Administration of the Revolutionary Military Counsel of the Western Front.]

Smolensk, 1921, daily

1921: Nov. 7 (No. 117)
1922: March 12 (No. 41)

Ref: LC, p. 161

KRASNOARMEISKII SPRAVOCHNIK

Prilozhenie k gazete "Krasnaia zvezda."
Moscow, semiweekly

1925: Oct. 14 (No. 77 [137])

KRASNOE PRIAZOV'E

Ezhenedel'naia krest'ianskaia gazeta--organ Azovskogo raikoma VKP(b) i Ispolkoma sovetov.

Azov-Don, 1921, weekly

1928: Apr. 8 (No. 15 [382])

KRASNOE PRIKAM'E

Organ Okruzhkoma VKP(b), Okrispolkoma i Okrprofbiuro.
Sarapul, 1920, daily

1928: Apr. 6, 28, May 1 (Nos. 82, 100, 102)

KRASNOE ZNAMIA
>Organ Kubokrushkoma VKP(b) Kubanskogo Okrispolkoma, Okruzhnogo sofprofa i krasnodarskogo gorodskogo soveta. [Organ of the Kuban District Committee of the All-Union Communist Party (of Bolsheviks), of the Kuban District Executive Committee, of the District Soviet of Labor Unions and of the Krasnodar City Soviet.]
>Krasnodar, 1920, daily

1921:   Dec. 4 (No. 488)
1922:   Mar. 12 (No. 58)
1928:   Mar. 21, Apr. 10, 14, 20-22, May 8, 11, 12 (No. 68, 85, 89, 92-94, 104, 107, 108)
>Ref: LC, p. 40

KRASNOE ZNAMIA
>Organ Tikhvinskogo ukoma RKP(b), izdanie Rosta. [Organ of the Tikhvin District Committee of the Russian Communist Party (of Bolsheviks).
>Tikhvin, 1918, semiweekly

1921:   Nov. 7 (No. 66 [405])
>Ref: LC, p. 171

KRASNOE ZNAMIA
>Organ Dal'nevostochnogo biuro i Vladiv. kom. RSDRP (bol'shevikov).
>Vladivostok, 1917, daily

1918:   Apr. 5 (Mar. 23), 9 (Mar. 27), 19 (6), 20 (7), 23 (10), 27 (14)
>Nos. 158 (62), 161 (65), 170 (74), 171 (75), 173 (77), 219 (122)
>Ref: Columbia 177; LC, p. 181

KRASNOIARETS
>Krasnoyarsk, 1906

1906:   Oct. 21-29 (Nos. 1-2)
>Ref: Beliaeva 4142

KRASNOIARSKII RABOCHII
>Ezhednevnyi organ Krasnoiarskogo okruzhnogo komiteta VKP(b), Okruzhnogo ispolnitel'nogo komiteta i Okrprofsoveta. [Organ of the Krasnoyarsk Regional and City Committees of the All-Union Communist Party (of Bolsheviks) and of the Regional Soviet of Toilers' Deputies.]
>Krasnoyarsk, 1905, daily

(Continued on next page)

KRASNOIARSKII RABOCHII (continued)

1905:   Nos. 2, 3, 5 (microfilm)
1921:   Nov. 7 (No. 248)
1922:   March 12 (No. 58)
1928:   March 24, 31, Apr. 3, 5, 15, 19, 22-25, May 1, 4, 10, 12-15, 17-18 (Nos. 71[2921], 77[2927], 79, 81, 90[2940], 92[2942], 95-97, 101, 102[2952], 107, 109-111)

Ref: Beliaeva 4149, LC, p. 41

KRASNYI BALTIISKII FLOT
Organ politicheskogo otdela Revoliutsionnogo voennogo soveta Baltiiskogo flota. [Organ of the Political Section of the Revolutionary Military Soviet of the Baltic Fleet.]
Petrograd, 1919, daily

1919:   July 10, Aug. 20, 27, Sept. 3, 10, 13, 24, Oct. 1, 7, Dec. 11 (Nos. 29, 41, 43, 45, 47-48, 51, 53, 55, 80)
1920:   Jan. 6, 10, Feb. 28, Sept. 14, 23-Oct. 21, 26-28, Nov. 2 (Nos. 3[91], 4[92], 24[112], 92[180], 96[184]-108[196], 110 [198], 111[199], 113[201]-114[202])

Ref: LC, p. 57

KRASNYI FLOT
Organ komissariata voennomorskogo flota. [Organ of the Ministry of the Armed Forces of the USSR.]
Moscow, 1938, six times a week

1941:   Jan. 1-Aug. 29 (Nos. 1, 31-130, 133-137, 142-144, 146-161, 163-169, 172, 175-176, 179-181, 185-187, 189, 194-195, 197, 199-203)
1945:   July 1-24, Sept. 30 - Oct. 5, 16 (Nos. 153-159, 161-172, 231-235, 244)

Ref: Columbia 178; LC, p. 98

KRASNYI GORNIAK
Ezhednevnaia rabochaia gazeta. Organ Krivorogskogo okrparkoma, Okrispolkoma i Okrprofsoveta.
Krivoi Rog, 1924, daily

1928:   May 8-10, June 2-6, 8, 9 (Nos. 105[716]-107[718], 127[738]-129[740], 131[742], 132[743]

KRASNYI MIR

Organ Kostromskogo gubernskogo ispoln. k-ta sovetov i gub. k-ta RKP (bol'shevikov). [Organ of the Kostroma Provincial Executive Committee of Soviets and of the Provincial Committee of the Russian Communist Party (of Bolsheviks).]
Kostroma

1919: Nov. 7 (No. 111 [incomplete])
1921: Nov. 6 (No. 250)
1922: Mar. 12 (No. 57)

Ref: LC, p. 39

KRASNYI NABAT

Vtoraia oktiabr'skaia godovshchina. IUbileinyi nomer gazety "Krasnyi nabat."
Moscow, 1919

1919: Nov. 7 (Oct. 25)

KRASNYI OKTIABR'

Odnodnevnyi nomer; organ Ispolnitel'nogo komiteta Kineshem. soveta rabochikh, krest'ian i krasnoarmeiskikh deputatov i uezdnogo kom. RKP (bol'shevikov). [Organ of the Executive Committee of the Kineshma Soviet and of the District Committee of the Russian Communist Party.]
Kineshma, 1919, one day's newspaper

Ref: LC, p. 37

KRASNYI OKTIABR'

Odnodnevnaia gazeta. Izdanie Shenkurskogo otd. Vserossiiskogo kommunisticheskogo soiuza zhurnalistov. [Published by the Shenkursk Group of the All-Russian Communist Association of Journalists.]
Shenkursk, 1919, one day's newspaper

1919: Nov. 7 [Oct. 25]

Ref: LC, p. 160

KRASNYI PAKHAR'

Organ Ardatovskogo uezdn. komiteta RKP i uezdnogo ispolnitel'n. komiteta. [Organ of the Ardatov District Committee of the Russian Communist Party and of the District Executive Committee.]
Ardatov, 1921

1921: Nov. 7, (No. 45)

Ref: LC, p. 5

KRASNYI PAKHAR'

Organ Starorusskogo soveta rabochikh, krest'ianskikh i krasno-armeiskikh deputatov i uezdnogo komiteta RKP. [Organ of the Staraia Russa Soviet of Workers', Peasants' and Soldiers' Deputies and of the District Committee of the Russian Communist Party.]
Staraia Russa, 1919, semiweekly

1919:   Nov. 7 (No. 21)

Ref: LC, p. 162

KRASNYI PUT'

Ezhednevnaia gazeta Usmanskogo ukomparta i Ispolkoma. [Published by the Usman District Party Committee and the Executive Committee.]
Usman, 1917, daily

1921:   Nov. 7 (No. 198 [931])

Ref: LC, p. 175

KRASNYI SEVER

Organ Vologodskogo gubern. komiteta VKP(b), Gub. ispolnitel'nogo komiteta s. r. kr. i kr. dep. i gub. soveta professional'nykh soiuzov.
Vologda, 1919, daily

1926:   Oct. 24 (No. 244 [2231])

KRASNYI SPORT

[Organ of the All-Union Committee for Physical Culture and Sport of the Council of People's Commissars of the U. S. S. R. and of the All-Union Central Council of Labor Unions.]
Continued as Sovetskii Sport.
Moscow, 1933, irreg. 3 times a week, weekly

1945:   June 19, Aug. 7-Nov. 27 (Nos. 25, 32, 35, 36, 38-41, 46, 48)

Ref: LC, p. 99

KRASNYI TRUBACH

Organ Politotdela i gruppy Zapfronta. [Unit organ of the Political Section and of the Western Front.]
Gomel, daily

1920:   July 10-11 (Nos. 30-31)

Ref: LC, p. 18

KRASNYI UGLEKOP

Organ Cheremkhovskogo raionnogo komiteta RKP, Soiuza gornora-
bochikh i Iruglia. [Organ of the Cheremkhovo District Committee of the
Russian Communist Party, of the Miners' Union and of the Irkutsk Coal
Administration.]
Cheremkhovo, 1921, semiweekly

1922:   March 11 (No. 15)
Ref: LC, p. 14

KRASNYI VES'EGONSK

Organ uezdno-gorodskogo komiteta Ves'egonskoi organizatsii
Rossiiskoi kommunisticheskoi partii. [Organ of the District and City
Committees of the Vesyegonsk Organization of the Russian Communist
Party.]
Vesyegonsk, weekly

1921:   Nov. 5, Dec. 3 (Nos. 90, 92-93)
Ref: LC, p. 177

KRASNYI VOIN

Organ Politupravleniia Otd. Kavkazskoi armii. [Organ of the
Political Administration of the Caucasian Army.]
Tiflis, 1918

1921:   Nov. 7 (No. 249)
Ref: LC, p. 169

KREST'IANIN I RABOCHII

Ob''edinennyi organ ispolnitel'nogo biuro Primorskogo oblast-
nogo soveta krest'ianskikh deputatov i Vladivostokskogo soveta rabochikh
i soldatskikh deputatov. [United Organ of the Executive Bureau of the
Maritime Province Soviet of Peasants' Deputies and of the Vladivostok
Soviet of Workers' and Soldiers' Deputies.]
Vladivostok, 1918, daily

1918:   Apr. 9 (March 27)-10 (March 28), 18(5), 20(7), 23(10), June 9
(May 27), 21 (8), 27 (14) (Nos. 39, 40, 47, 49, 51, 85, 94, 98)
Ref: LC, p. 181

KREST'IANSKAIA GAZETA DLIA NACHINAIUSHCHIKH CHITAT'

Moscow

1931:   Oct. 19 - Dec. 31 (Nos. 55-65)
1932:   Jan. 6-29, Feb. 12, 28, March 17 (Nos. 1-4, 6, 8, 10)

KREST'IANSKAIA PRAVDA
Izdanie Luzhskogo okruzhnogo komiteta Vsesoiuznoi kommunisticheskoi partii (bol'shevikov) i Okruzhnogo ispolnitel'nogo komiteta Sovetov
rabochikh, krest'ianskikh i krasnoarmeiskikh deputatov.
Luga, 1918, three times a week

1928: Nov. 10, 24, Dec. 29 (Nos. 127, 133, 146)

KREST'IANSKAIA PRAVDA
Gazeta Gubernskoi komissii pomoshchi golodaushchim. [Pub-
lished by the Provincial Committee for Hunger Relief.]
Samara, semiweekly

1921: Nov. 7 (No. 2)

Ref: LC, p. 44

KREST'IANSKAIA PRAVDA
Izdanie Stalingradskogo gubkoma VKP(b) i Gubispolkoma sovetov.
Stalingrad, 1922

1927: May 4 (No. 35)
1928: June 20 (No. 48)

KREST'IANSKAIA RUS'
Ezhenedel'naia gazeta dlia krest'ian i rabochikh.
Nos. 1 to 13 were published as a supplement to the newspaper
Svoboda; starting with No. 14 it was published separately.
Warsaw, 1921, weekly

1921, May 25-March 3, 1922 (Nos. 1-20, 33)

KREST'IANSKAIA UKRAINA
Organ Vseukrainskago Ob''edinennago Krest'ianskago Soveta.
Vienna, semimonthly

1925: Jan. 20 (No. 3)

KREST'IANSKAIA ZHIZN'
Organ Kuznetskogo ukoma VKP (b) i Usipolkoma (Sar. g.)
Kuznetsk, semimonthly

1928: May 9, June 10 (Nos. 33 [284], 42 [293])

KREST'IANSKAIA ZHIZN'
> Krest'ianskaia gazeta Vologodskogo gubkoma VKP(b)
> Vologda, weekly

   1928:   March 28-Apr. 25, May 16-30, Nov. 14-23 (Nos. 12-16, 18-20, 43-44)

KREST'IANSKII DEPUTAT
> St. Petersburg, 1906, daily

   1906:   June 21, July 6 (Nos. 2, 10)
> > Ref: Beliaeva 4183; Columbia 184

KREST'IANSKOE SLOVO
> Organ Leidenpol'skogo okruzhkoma VKP(b), Okrispolkoma, Okrprofbiuro i Okrpotrebsoiuza.
> Lodeinoe Pole, 1918

   1928:   Apr. 28 (No. 33 [506])

KRYMSKII KOLKHOZNIK
> Organ OK VKP(b) Krymtsika i Soiuza kolkhozsoiuzov.
> Simferopol, semiweekly

   1930:   June 7 (No. 3)

KRYMSKII VESTNIK
> Sevastopol, 1888, daily

   1920:   Sept. 6(19), 8(21), 17(30), Oct. 16(29) - 18(31), 23 (Nov. 5)
> (Nos. 198-199, 205, 229-231, 235)
> > Ref: Lisovskii 1940; Beliaeva 4217;
> > Columbia 186; LC, p. 157

KUBANSKII PUT'
> Ezhednevnaia politicheskaia, ekonomicheskaia i literaturnaia gazeta.
> Ekaterinodar, 1919, daily

   1920:   Feb. 1 (No. 24 [84])
> > Ref: LC, p. 40

KUL'TARMEETS

Izdanie "Krest'ianskoi gazety dlia nachinaiushchikh chitat'."
Moscow, weekly

1931:   Oct. 19, Nov. 13, Dec. 23, 31 (Nos. 55, 58, 64-65)
1932:   Jan. 20 (No. 3)

Ref: LC, p. 100

KUL'TURA I ZHIZN'

Gazeta otdela propagandy i agitatsii TSentral'nogo Komiteta
VKP(b). [Published by the Department for Propaganda and Agitation of
the Central Committee of the All-Union Communist Party (of Bolsheviks).]
Moscow, June 28, 1946, three times a month

1950:   Aug. 20, 31, Sept. 10, 30, Oct. 11, 21, 31 (Nos. 23[151] - 25[153],
27[155] - 30[158]
1951:   Jan. 11, Feb. 28 (Nos. 1[165], 6[170])

Ref: Columbia 187; LC, p. 100

KUR'ER

Kostroma

1914:   Aug. 28, (No. 26)

Ref: Beliaeva 4293

KUR'ER

Ezhednevnaia gazeta (politiki, literatury i obshchestvennoi
zhizni).
Moscow, 1898, daily

1899:   Nov. 3 (No. 304)

Ref: Lisovskii 2651; Beliaeva 4294

KUR'ER

Gazeta stavit svoeiu zadacheiu otstaivanie klassovykh interesov
promyshlennogo i sel'skogo proletariata.
St. Petersburg, 1906, daily

1906:   Nos. 1-17, 20-23 (microfilm)

Ref: Columbia 188; Beliaeva 4296

KUSTARNYI KRAI LENINSKOGO UKOMA VKP(b), UISPOLKOMA I UPROFBIURO

Leninsk, Mosk. Gub., semiweekly

1928:   Feb. 19 (No. 14 [158])

KUZBASS
Organ Kol'chuginskogo raikoma RKP, Raikoma gornorabochikh, Rudoispolkoma i Rudoupravleniia. Ezhednevnaia gazeta. [Organ of the Kol'chugino District Committee of the Russian Communist Party of the Miners' District Committee and of the Administration of Mining.]
Kolchugino, daily

1922:   March 12 (No. 49)

Ref: LC, p. 39

KUZBASS
Organ Kuznetsk. OK VKP(b), OIK i Okrprofbiuro. Ezhednevnaia gazeta.
Shcheglovsk, daily, 1922

1928:   Nov. 25 (no. 274 [1745])

KZYL TATARSTAN. OZBL TATARSTAN
Kazan, daily

1928:   May 17, July 4, 19 (Nos. 111[2780], 152[2821], 165 [2834])

L

LEDIANOI POKHOD
Vladivostok

1921:   Feb. 6

LEMKO

Organ lemkovskogo soiuza v S. SH. i Kanade.
Cleveland, 1928

July 21, 1932 - Nov. 16, 1933 (Nos. 27-32, 35-38, 42, 44)

LEMKOVSHCHINA

Russian paper, official organ of the lemkos' committee of the
United States of America.
New York, 1922, semimonthly

1925:   Jan. 1, Apr. 1-May 15, Aug. 16, Dec. 1 (Nos. 1, 4-6, 13, 15)
1926:   May 1-15 (Nos. 9-10)

LENINGRADSKAIA PRAVDA
[Organ of the Leningrad Provincial Committee and of the City
Committee of the Communist Party of the Soviet Union and of the
Provincial and City Soviets of Toilers' Deputies.]
Title varies: from 1918 to Jan. 30, 1924 Petrogradskaia pravda;
Organ of the Provincial Bureau of the Central Committee of the Russian
Communist Party, of the Petrograd Provincial Committee of the Russian
Communist Party, of the Petrograd Provincial Labor Union Council and
of the Provincial Assembly.
Leningrad, 1918, daily

1918-1925
Missing nos. :
1918:   Nos. 63(288)-79(305), 81(307)-118(344), 120-175, 177-221, 223-
232, 234-236, 238, 246, 247, 250-277, 279(506) – to the end of
the year
1919:   Nos. 1-4, 6-13, 15, 17-19, 21, 23-30, 34, 37-39, 41, 46, 52,
69, 72, 78, 80, 83, 136, 151, 162, 171, 231, 242, 265
1921:   Nos. 24, 139

(Continued on next page)

LENINGRADSKAIA PRAVDA (continued)

1922: Nos. 11, 18, 39, 74-169, 176, 179, 190, 198, 200, 201, 206, 212, 216, 220, 237, 240, 242, 244-246, 278, 285

1923: Nos. 31, 59, 73-76, 78-94, 102, 114, 115, 118-144, 155, 167, 168, 194, 198-200, 214, 259

1924: Nos. 1, 2, 5

1925: Nos. 217, 221, 265, 269, 290, 293

Ref: Columbia 345, 193; LC, pp. 66, 58

LETUCHII LISTOK MEN'SHEVIKOV-INTERNATSIONALISTOV
Petrograd

1917: No. 1 (microfilm)

LISTOK OB''IAVLENII
Vladivostok, daily

1919: Dec. 4 (No. 25) (microfilm)

LISTOK PETERBURGSKAGO KOMITETA EVREISKOI SOTS. -DEM. RAB.
PARTII (PAEOLEITSION)
Petrograd, 1917, weekly

1917: Mar. 11 (No. 1)

Ref: LC, p. 58

LISTOK PRAVDY see PRAVDA

LISTOK REMESLENNYKH RABOCHIKH
St. Petersburg, 1908

1908: (microfilm)

LITERATURA I ISKUSSTVO
Organ pravleniia soiuza sovetskikh pisatelei SSSR komiteta po delam iskusstv pri SNK SSSR i komiteta po delam kinematografii pri SNK SSSR. [Organ of the Board of the Union of Soviet Writers of the USSR, of the Committee for Arts of the Council of People's Commissars of the USSR, and of the Committee for Cinematography of the Council of People's Commissars of the USSR.]
See Literaturnaia gazeta; organ soiuza sovetskikh pisatelei.
Moscow.

Ref: Columbia 198; LC, p. 101

LITERATURNAIA GAZETA

Organ Pravleniia Soiuza sovetskikh pisatelei. [Organ of the Board of the Union of Soviet Writers of the USSR.]

From Jan. 6, 1942 to Nov. 1944, published jointly with Sovetskoe iskusstvo under the title Literatura i iskusstvo. Resumed publication under original title as of Nov. 7, 1944.

Moscow, 1929, every three days

1932:   Oct. 26, 29 (Nos. 48, 49)
1935:   Jan. 30 - Dec. (No. 6-72)
1936:   Jan. -July (Nos. 1-46)
1937:   Jan. -Dec. (Nos. 1-71)
1938:   Jan. -Dec. (Nos. 1-72)
1939:   Jan. -Dec. 26 (Nos. 1-71)
1940:   Jan. 5, 15, Feb. 7 (Nos. 1, 3, 7)
1942:   Feb. -Aug. (Nos. 8, 10, 19, 26, 28, 34-35)
1944:   Aug. 12 (No. 33)
1945:   May 1-5, July 14-28, Sept. 1-Dec. 22 (Nos. 18-19, 30-32, 37-52)
1946:   Dec. 28 (No. 52)
1947:   May 9 (No. 19)
1948:   Jan. -Dec. (Nos. 1-104)
1949:   Jan. -Dec. (Nos. 1-104)
Jan. 1950 - to present
Missing nos. :
1935:   Nos. 23, 29, 42, 47, 61, 69
1936:   Nos. 34-35
1937:   Nos. 16, 64
1938:   No. 63
1939:   Nos. 12-13, 15, 31, 37, 51, 61
1950:   Nos. 24, 26, 29, 32, 49, 50-51
1960:   Mar. 5, July 12

Ref: Columbia 200; LC, p. 102

LITERATURNYI LENINGRAD

Organ Leningradskogo orgkomiteta Soiuza sovetskikh pisatelei pod redaktsiei B. Asaf'eva, P. Bauze, I. Brodskogo (i dr.). [Organ of the Leningrad Section of the Union of Soviet Authors.]

Leningrad, weekly

1934:   Apr. 8-Dec. 26 (Nos. 16, 20-21, 25-30, 32-46, 49-64)

Ref: LC, p. 58

LIUBOV' (Mesiachnik)
          Mayfield, Pa., 1915, monthly

1932:   Dec. 5 (No. 12)

LOKOMOTIV
          Professional'nyi organ, posviashchennyi interesam zhelez-
nodorozhnikov.
          St. Petersburg, semimonthly

1907:   Nos. 3-4 (microfilm)
                        Ref: Beliaeva 4506

LONDONSKII SPRAVOCHNYI LISTOK
          Vykhodit dva raza v mesiats. Redaktor-izdatel' P. M. Loviagin.
          London, 1930, semimonthly

1930:   Dec. 20-1934, July (Nos. 1-63, 65)

LUCH
          Organ legitimno-monarkhicheskoi mysli.
          Belgrade, 1931, semimonthly

Nov. 17, 1932-July 1933 (Nos. 43-57)

LUCH
          Murom, 1918

1921:   Nov. 7 (No. 84[270])

LUCH
          Organ TSentral'nogo Komiteta rossiiskoi sotsial-demokraticheskoi
rabochei partii [ob''edinennoi]. Ezhednevnaia gazeta. [Organ of the
Central Committee of the Russian Social Democratic Workers' Party
(United).]
          Continuation of Rabochaia gazeta, continued as Zaria and Novyi
Luch.
          Petrograd, 1917, daily

1917:   Nov. 19 (No. 1)
                        Ref: Columbia 201: LC, p. 59

LUCH

Rabochaia Gazeta.
St. Petersburg, 1912, daily

1912-1914 (microfilm)

Ref: Beliaeva 4528; Columbia 201

L'VOVSKII VESTNIK

Izdavaemaia pri Upravlenii voennago General-gubernatorstva
Galitsii.
Lvov, 1915, daily

1915:   May 28-29 (Nos. 87-88)

Ref: Beliaeva 4538

L'VOVSKOE VOENNOE SLOVO

Izdavaemoe Shtabom-Glavnokomanduiushchago armiiami Iugo-
Zapadnago fronta. Voennaia, politicheskaia, obshchestvennaia i litera-
turnaia gazeta.
Lvov, 1914

1914:   Sept. 26-Oct. 17, 19-Nov. 19, 22-Dec. 29, 31
1915:   Jan. 7, 11, 12, 16-23, 25, 26, 31-Feb. 2, 5-10, 12-20, 22-
        Apr. 1, 14-23, 30, May 5
        (Nos. 1-18, 20-43, 46-81, 83-90, 94, 95, 99-105, 107-108,
        113-115, 118-122, 124-131, 133-140, 150, 151, 158, 164, 168)
        Ref: Beliaeva 4539

M

MAIAK

        Gazeta P. K. Priiuta-uchilishcha b. "Russkii dom" v Kharbine.
Odnodnevnaia gazeta.
        Kharbin, 1930, one day's newspaper

    1930:   June

MAIAK KOMMUNY

        Ezhednevnaia rabochaia gazeta Sevastopol'skogo ispokoma i
okruzhkoma RKP. [Published by the Sevastopol Executive Committee
and the District Committee of the Russian Communist Party.]
        Sevastopol, daily

    1922:   Dec. 21 (No. 273 [584])
    1923:   Jan. 4 (No. 2 [594])
                       Ref: LC, p. 157

MAKHOVIK

        Organ Petrogradskogo gubernskogo soveta professional'nykh
soiuzov. [Organ of the Petrograd Government Council of Labor Unions.]
        Petrograd, 1921, daily

    1921:   Nov. 16 (No. 226)
                       Ref: Columbia 203; LC, p. 59

MALEN'KAIA GAZETA

        [Published by the Non-Party Socialists.]
        Continued as Narodnaia gazeta as of July 13, 1917.
        Petrograd, 1914, daily

    1917:   Mar. 5-8(21), 10(23), Mar. 31 (Apr. 18), July 5 (18), (Nos. 57
           [865]-59 [867], 68 [876?], 74 [873], 154 [913]
                   Ref: Beliaeva 4559; Columbia 204;
                       LC, p. 59

MASHINOSTROENIE
Organ Narodnogo komissariata mashinostroeniia i Narodnogo komissariata oboronnoi promyshlennosti. [Organ of the People's Commissariats for Heavy, Medium and General Machine Building.]
Moscow, 1937, irregular

1937:   Sept. 27 (No. 8)

Ref: LC, p. 103

MECH'
Warsaw, Nos. 1-20 were published as a weekly journal, beginning with No. 21 it became a weekly newspaper.

1934-1939: Oct. 7, 1934-Aug. 1939 (Nos. 21-32, 34-269)

Ref: Columbia 205

MEDITSINSKII RABOTNIK
Organ Narodnogo komissariata zdravookhraneniia SSSR. [Organ of the Ministry of Health of the USSR and of the Ministry of Health of the RSFSR.]
Moscow, 1938, weekly, semiweekly

1945:   Feb. 15, 21-Mar. 21, May 5, June 28-July 19, Aug. 2, 16, 20, Sept. 13-20, Oct. 4-11, Nov. 1, 29 (Nos. 8, 10-15, 28, 36-39, 42, 44, 46, 48-49, 52-53, 56, 60

Ref: Columbia 206; LC, p. 103

MINSKAIA GAZETA
Minsk, 1912, daily

1918:   Dec. 1-2 (Nos. 2029-2030)

Ref: Beliaeva 4696; LC, p. 83

MINSKII GOLOS
Minsk, 1909, daily

1918:   Dec. 1-4 (Nos. 2908-2910)

Ref: Beliaeva 4707; LC, p. 84

MIR
Vykhodit ezhednevno krome posleprazdnichnykh dnei.
Moscow, 1918, daily

1918:   Aug. 5, 25, 30 (Nos. 11, 19, 22)

Ref: LC, p. 104

MIR NARODOV

Organ Mezhdunarodnago otdela Vserossiiskago TS IK soveta rabochikh, soldatskikh i krest'ianskikh deputatov. Izdaetsia dlia bezplatnago rasprostraneniia sredi nemetskikh brat'iev soldat. Vykhodit ezhednevno pod redaktsiei Karla Radeka.

Petrograd, 1918, daily

1918: Jan. 26(Feb, 8) - 27(Feb.9), 30(Feb. 12) - Feb.15(2), 17(4) Nos. 27-28, 30-33, 35

MLADOROSSKAIA ISKRA

Soiuz molodezhi vo Frantsii.
Paris, 1931, semimonthly

1931, Aug. 1-Feb. 1935 (Nos. 1-43)

Ref: Columbia 210

MLADOROSSKII BIULLETEN' see NA RASSVETE

MLADOROSSKOE SLOVO

Saõ Paulo, 1934, weekly

1934: Dec. 8, 15 (Nos. 15, 16)
1935: Nov. 23, Dec. 7 (Nos. 65, 67)

MOLODAIA MYSL'

Organ russkoi molodezhi.
Paris, bimonthly

1935: Apr. 28-July (Nos. 1-3)

MOLODAIA ROSSIIA

Ezhenedel'naia obshchestvennaia, politicheskaia i literaturnaia gazeta.

St. Petersburg, 1906, weekly

1906: No. 1 (microfilm)

Ref: Beliaeva 4817

MOLODOE SLOVO

Obshchestvenno-politicheskaia gazeta, organ Soiuza mladorossov v Bolgarii.

Sofia, 1932

1931, Oct. -Nov. 1933 (Nos. 12-18, 20)
1936: Oct. -Nov. (Nos. 28-29)

MOLODOI RABOCHII

Ezhednevnaia gazeta rabochei molodezhi, organ Sibkraikoma, Novosibirskogo okruzhkoma VLK SM i Kraisofprofa. [Organ of the Siberian Regional Committee of the Novosibirsk District of the All-Union Lenin Communist Youth League and of the Regional Labor Union.]
Novosibirsk, daily

1930: March 4, 15, 16, 18, 22, 25, 26 (Nos. 52[400], 61[469]-62[470], 63[471], 66[478], 68[480], 69[481])
Ref: LC, p. 136

MOLVA

Bol'shaia literaturnaia i obshchestvenno-politicheskaia gazeta. Petrograd, 1918, daily

1918: June 10 (28), 12 (30) (Nos. 4, 6)
Ref: Columbia 215; LC, p. 60

MOLVA

St. Petersburg, 1905, daily
1905: Dec. 25 (Jan 7, 1906) (No. 17)
Ref: Beliaeva 4806; Columbia 216

MOLVA

Ezhenedel'naia gazeta.
Warsaw, 1932, daily

1933: Apr. 1-Dec. 28 (Nos. 70-84, 87, 89-95, 97-99, 101-104, 106-110, 112-113, 115, 117, 119, 121, 123, 125-126, 128, 130, 132, 134, 136-137, 139, 141, 143, 145, 147, 149, 151, 153, 156, 159-162, 164-166, 168, 170-171, 173, 175, 177, 179, 182, 187-188, 190, 192, 195, 197-198, 201, 203, 205, 209-210, 212, 214, 216, 218, 220, 222, 226, 228, 232, 235-236, 242, 246, 250, 255, 257, 259, 261, 263, 265, 268, 270-271, 274, 277, 279, 281-282, 284, 286, 288, 290, 292, 294-295)
1934: Jan. (Nos. 2, 5, 7, 10-11, 13, 15, 17, 19, 21, 23, 25)
Ref: Columbia 217

MORIAK

Obshcherossiiskii organ morskikh i rechnykh sudovykh komand.
Sub-title varies: Nos. 1-11, Organ chernomorskikh sudovykh komand.
Vienna

1912: Feb. 20, May 5, 25 - June 25, Aug. 25 - Sept. 12, 1913 (Nos. 2, 6, 8-9, 11-14)
Ref: Columbia 218

MORSKOI FLOT
        Organ Ministerstva morskogo flota i TsK profsoiuza rabochikh
morskogo transporta. [Organ of the Ministry of the Ocean Fleet and of
the Central Committee of the Labor Union of Maritime Transport
Workers.]
        Absorbed by Rechnoi transport as of Mar. 17, 1953.
        Moscow, 1943, semiweekly

1949:   Mar. 4 - Dec. 30 (Nos. 35-104)
1950:   Jan. 4 - 11 (Nos. 1-3)
                      Ref: LC, p. 104

MORSKOI LISTOK

1909:   No. 1
1915:   Nos. 1-2 (microfilm)

MOSKOVSKAIA GAZETA
        Ezhednevnyi sotsial-demokraticheskii organ.
        Moscow, 1905, daily

1905:   No. 9 (microfilm)
                      Ref: Beliaeva 4865

MOSKOVSKII BOL'SHEVIK
        Organ MK i MGK VKP(b) Moskovskogo oblastnogo i gorodskogo
sovetov deputatov trudiashchikhsia. [Organ of the Moscow Committee
and of the Moscow City Committee of the All-Union Communist Party
(of Bolsheviks) and of the Moscow Provincial and City Soviets of
Toilers' Deputies.]
        Continuation of Rabochaia Moskva
        Moscow, 1939, daily

1939:   Dec. 2 (No. 223)
1945:   July 1-20, 22, 27-28, Sept. 6-Dec. 29 (Nos. 153-169, 171, 175-
        176, 210-213, 216-219, 221-273, 275-284, 286-305)
               Ref: Columbia 221; LC, p. 105

MOSKOVSKII GOLOS
        Politicheskaia obshchestvennaia tserkovnaia i literaturnaia
ezhenedel'naia gazeta.
        Moscow, 1906, weekly

1906:   Dec. 21 (No. 38)
                      Ref: Beliaeva 4882

MOSKOVSKII LISTOK
>Moscow, 1881, daily

1917:   Mar. 4 (No. 50)

>Ref: Lisovskii 1492; Beliaeva 4890

MOSKOVSKIIA VEDOMOSTI
>Moscow, 1756, daily

1894:   Sept. 17 (No. 255)
1895:   Feb. 1-8 (Nos. 32-39)
1900:   Sept. 30 (Oct. 13), Nov. 17(30), 18 (Dec. 1), 20 (Dec. 3) - 25 (Dec. 8), (Nos. 270, 318, 319, 321-326)
1901:   Feb. 21 (Mar. 6), 21 (Mar. 7), 24 (Mar. 9), Mar. 31 (Apr. 13) - Apr. 11 (24), 29 (May 12) - May 9 (22), (Nos. 51, 52, 54, 89-98, 116-126)
1902:   Mar. 2 (15), 6 (19), 27 (Apr. 9) (Nos. 60, 64, 85)
1903:   Jan. 1 (14) - Sept. 30 (Oct. 13) (Nos. 1-267)
1904:   Jan. 1 (14) - June 30 (July 13) (Nos. 1-38, 40-48, 50-71, 73-115, 120-131, 133-178)
1906:   Sept. 23 (Oct. 6) (No. 232)
1917:   June 22 (July 5) (No. 132)

>Ref: Beliaeva 4874; Columbia 223;
>LC, p. 106; Lisovskii 6

MUKDEN
>Ezhednevnaia vecherniaia gazeta. Pod red. C. I. Klerzhe.
>Mukden, 1930, daily (originally published as a weekly
paper)

1931:   July 16 - Dec. 31 (Nos. 21-29, 31, 33, 34, 40-41, 43-93)
1932:   Jan. - Sept. 20 (Nos. 94-129, 132-162, 184-297)

MYSL'
>Politicheskaia, obshchestvennaia i literaturnaia gazeta.
>Paris, 1914, daily

Nov. 15, 1914 - March 14, 1915 (Nos. 1-48, 50-62, 64-101)
>Ref: Columbia 226

MYSL' TRUDA
>Krest'ianskaia i rabochaia gazeta.
>St. Petersburg, 1914, three times a week

1914:   Apr. 20 - May 23 (Nos. 1-11)

>Ref: Beliaeva 4946; Columbia 229

N

NA BOR'BU
      Izdanie Shenkurskogo ispolkoma i komiteta R. K. P.
(bol'shevikov). [Published by the Shenkursk Executive Committee
and the Committee of the Russian Communist Party (of Bolsheviks)].
      Shenkursk, 1919, 3 times a week

1919:   Nov. 7 (82)
                            Ref: LC, p. 160

NA DNEPROSTROE
      Prilozhenie k gazete "Ukrainskii ekonomist" (organ EKOSO
U. S. S. R. n. p., 192 ?)
      6 p.

NA GRANITSE
      Pogranichnaia, weekly

1937, Mar. 7–June 9, 1940 (Nos. 101–103, 105–110, 112–184, 186–220,
     222–226, 228–235, 238–247, 249–259, 261)

NA RASSVETE
      Title varies: Nos. 1–7, Mladorosskii biulleten'; May 2, 1937,
No. 8 - Na rassvete.
      San Francisco, 1936, monthly, irregular

1936, Feb. 11–Feb. 1938 (Nos. 2, 6–10, 12–14, 16–17)

NA SMENU
      Organ Dal'nevostochnogo biuro Vsesibirskogo ob''edineniia s. -r.
molodezhi.
      Vladivostok, 1921

1921:   Feb. (No. 2)

NA STRAZHE
>Organ TSentral'nogo i Moskovskogo sovetov Osoviakhima.
Vykhodit po chetnym chislam.   (Organ of the Central and Moscow
Councils of the Society for the Promotion of Defense and Aero-
Chemical Development.)
>Moscow, every other day.

1934:   Mar. 28 (No. 4)

Ref: LC, p. 106

NA STRAZHE
>Organ voennoi ligi. [Organ of the Military League.]
Petrograd, Aug. 4, 1917, weekly

1917:   Aug. 28 (Sept. 10) (Nos. 2-3)

Ref: LC, p. 60

NA STRAZHE RODINY
>Odnodnevnaia gazeta R. O. V. S. [Russkii obshche-voinskii soiuz.]
Kharbin

1932:   June
1934:   Apr. 8

NABAT
>Vestnik russkoi natsional'no-patrioticheskoi pravoslavno-
khristianskoi mysli.
>Subtitle through Dec. 1952: - Vestnik natsional'no-patrioticheskoi pravoi demokraticheskoi mysli rossiiskoi emigratsii.
>Published by Bratstvo Sv. Georgiia.
Munich, 1950, monthly

1950:   July 20 - Nov. 26 (1-10)
1951:   Jan. 21 - July 8, Aug. 19, Oct. 14, 23 (Nos. 11-20, 23, 26, 29)
1952:   Jan, Mar 2 - Dec. (Nos. 30-31, 33-39)
1953:   Jan. - Dec. (Nos. 40-43)
1954:   Jan. - Sept. (Nos. 44-50)

Ref: Columbia 232

NABAT
>Russkaia ezhenedel'naia gazeta; vykhodit po voskresen'iam.
[Organ of the Confederation of Anarchistic Organizations "Nabat".]
Odessa, weekly

1919:   Jan. 20 (No. 15)

Ref: LC, p. 138

NABAT

Gazeta podlinno-russkaia, periodicheskaia. Organ 150-millionnogo russkogo krest'ianstva.

Paris, irregular

1930-1933: May-Feb. (Nos. 1-13)

Ref: Columbia 234

NABAT

Ezhednevnaia gazeta Serpukhovskogo uezdkoma R. K. P. (b) Uispolkoma i Serpukhovskogo otdela Vseros. profsoiuza tekstil'shchikov. [Organ of the Serpukhov District Committee of the All-Union Communist Party (of Bol'sheviks), the District Executive Committee, the UPB and the Serpukhov District Organs.]

Serpukhov, 1919, daily

1922: March 12 (No. 4)
1929: June 14, 21 (Nos. 134 (2176), 140 (2182)

Ref: LC. p. 155

NABAT

Organ Konfederatsii anarkhistskikh organizatsii Ukrainy "Nabat".

Ukraine, n. p. 1919

1919: May 5, 12, 26, June 2, 9, July 7, 21 (Nos. 14-18, 22, 25)

NABAT KAZACHESTVA, Prague see KAZACHII NABAT, Prague

NABAT REVOLIUTSII

Organ Vserossiiskogo TSentral'nogo ispolnitel'nogo komiteta Sov. rab. i sold. dep. (pervogo sozyva), staviashchii svoei zadachei ob"edinenie vsekhdemokraticheskikh sil strany dlia vozstanovleniia grazhdanskikh svobod, bor'be za skoreishii pochetnyi mir i zashchity Vsenarodnogo uchreditel'nogo sobraniia. Izdaetsia pri blizhaishem uchastii chlenov TS IK I. G. TSeretelli, V. M. Chernova, F. I. Dana i dr. [Organ of the All-Russian Central Executive Committee of Soviets of Workers' and Soldiers' Deputies (of the First Assembly).]

Subsequently published as Za svobodu, Za svobodu naroda, Za svabodu i pravo, and Za pravo naroda.

Petrograd, 1917

1917: Dec. 6 (No. 1)

Ref: LC, p. 60

NACHALO
Ezhednevnaia obshchestvennaia i politicheskaia gazeta. Le debut; quotidien Russe de Paris.
Paris, 1916, daily

1916:   Oct. 18-19, Oct. 22-Nov. 15, Nov. 17-22, Nov. 24-Dec. 14, Dec. 20, Dec. 31 (Nos. 16-18, 20-39, 41-45, 47-64, 69, 78)
1917:   Jan. 7, 11, 18, Mar. 9-22 (Nos. 83, 86, 92, 134-145)
Ref: Columbia 236

NACHALO
Sotsialdemokraticheskaia gazeta.
St. Petersburg, 1905, daily

1905:   Nov. 13 (26) - 30 (Dec. 13), Nos. 1-14
Ref: Beliaeva 5136

NACHALO
Petrograd, daily

1918:   No. 2 (microfilm)

Ref: LC, p. 60
Columbia 237

NAKANUNE
Ezhednevnaia gazeta.
Berlin, 1922, daily

1922-24
Missing Nos. :
1922:   Nos. 2-11, 13-17, 21, 27, 29, 40, 48, 56, 62, 73-74, 81, 88, 101-103, 111, 114, 120-121, 123, 127-131, 133, 139, 142, 147-148, 163-164, 173-174, 180, 186, 196, 206-207, 209-210, 213, 218
1923:   No. 322
1924:   Nos. 6(523), 9(527), 64(581)

Supplements:

_____ Inostrannaia zhizn'; Nos. 1-8, suppl. to Nos. 20-116 (Jan. 25- May 23, 1924

_____ Nakanune; literaturnoe prilozhenie pod redaktsiei gr. A. N. Tolstogo. Apr. 30, 1922-Apr. 20, 1924; Nos. 1-34, 38, 45, 47, 51, 54, 55-57, 90

(Continued on next page)

NAKANUNE (continued)

_____ Nakanune; Ekonomicheskoe obozrenie. Pod redaktsiei prof. G. G.
Shvittau.
      Berlin, weekly
1922: Oct. 5 - Dec. 14 (Nos. 17-21, 23-27)
1923: Jan. 25 (No. 32)
                        Ref: Columbia 238

NAKANUNE

      Ezhenedel'nik politiki, literatury i obshchestvennoi zhizni.
Moscow, weekly

1918: Apr., (Nos. 1, 2, 4)

NAROD see VECHERNIAIA GAZETA NAROD

NAROD
      Ezhednevnaia politicheskaia i literaturnaia gazeta.
St. Petersburg, 1896, daily

1896: Dec. 4(16), No. 4
                   Ref: Lisovskii 2507

NARODNAIA ARMIIA
      Organ Soveta Soiuza ofitserov - respublikantsev narodnoi
armii. [Organ of the League of Republican Officers of the
National Army.]
      Petrograd, 1917, irreg.

1917: March 22 (No. 6)
               LC, p. 61

NARODNAIA DUMA
      Ezhednevnaia gazeta.
St. Petersburg, 1906, daily

1907: Mar. 21 (Apr. 3), Mar. 24 (Apr. 6)
               Ref: Beliaeva 5027
                  Columbia 241

NARODNAIA DUMA
      St. Petersburg, 1906, daily

1907: No. 1-21 (microfilm)
            Ref: Columbia 241, Beliaeva 5027

NARODNAIA GAZETA
       Ezhenedel'naia sotsialisticheskaia gazeta.
       New York, 1918, weekly

   1918, March 21-Aug. 14, 1919, (Nos. 1-39, 41-52,
      53-74)

NARODNAIA GAZETA
       St. Petersburg, 1907, daily

   1907:   Nos. 1-4 (microfilm)
                     Ref: Columbia 242, Beliaeva 5025

NARODNAIA GAZETA
       Gazeta vnepartiinykh sotsialistov. [Organ of the non-party
socialists.]
       Continuation of Malen'kaia gazeta. Continued as Narodnaia molva
as of 1917.
       Petrograd, 1917, daily

   1917:   July 13 (26), No. 1
                     Ref: LC, p. 61

NARODNAIA GAZETA
       Organ russkoi narodnoi partii na Slovakii.
       Presov, 1924, semimonthly

   1932:   Nos. 16-24
   1934:   Nos. 1-2, 17-18, 35-36
   1935:   Nos. 9-10, 13-14

NARODNAIA GAZETA
       Rostov na Donu, daily

   1919:   Aug. 13 (No. 110)
                     Ref: LC, p. 150

NARODNAIA VOLIA
       Gazeta ezhednevnaia.
       Vladivostok, daily

   1921:   July 31-Aug. 5, 7, 9 (Nos. 1-5, 7-8)

NARODNOE DELO
Organ Komiteta gruppy sotsialistov-revoliutsionerov severo-zapadnoi oblasti Rossii.
Revel

1920: Nos. 56-58, 69-70, 76, 80-81, 84-85, 87-89, 91-93, 95-102, 105-108, 110-112
1921: Nos. 1-7, 9-30, 32-38, 40-55, 57
1921: Special unnumbered issue dated Feb. 28
On March 13, 1921, the newspaper was suppressed; beginning with March 15, continued as Za narodnoe dielo.

NARODNOE KHOZIAISTVO
Ezhednevnaia gazeta. V gazete prinimaiut uchastie postoiannye sotrudniki priostanovlennoi do sudebnogo prigovora gazety "Nasha zhizn' ".
St. Petersburg, 1905, daily

1906: Jan. 5(18) (No. 18)
Ref: Beliaeva 5079

NARODNOE SLOVO
Ezhednevnaia politicheskaia i literaturnaia gazeta. Organ Trudovoi Narodno-Sotsialisticheskoi Partii. Petrograd.
Petrograd, 1917, daily

1917: Nos. 20-29; 31-37; 59-60; 62; 75-83; 86-98; 94-117; 119-123; 125-129
June 27 - Nov. 9 [old style]. (Issues in original and on microfilm)
1918: No. 19 (184)

NASH DAUGAVPIL'SKII GOLOS
Bezpartiinyi i nezavisimyi organ progressivnoi latgal'skoi obshchestvennosti.
Daugavpils, Latviia, 1925, twice a week

1932: Nos. 97-100, 103-105
1033 - 1938

Title varies: To Aug. 4, 1933, Dvinskii golos
Aug. 4, 1922 - Aug. 24, 1934, Nash Dvinskii golos
Aug. 24, 1934, Nash Daugavpil'skii golos

Missing Nos. :
1933: 35, 59
1933: 11, 35
1935: 44, 45
1938: Nos. 34(494), 82(542)-83(543), 99 - to end of the year.

NASH DVINSKII GOLOS see NASH DAUGAVPIL'SKII GOLOS

NASH GOLOS , Paris, see GOLOS; EZHEDNEVNAIA POLITICHESKAIA I
OBSHCHESTVENNAIA GAZETA, Paris.

NASH GOLOS

Izd. Sots.-Dem. rab. partii, ob''edinennoi.
St. Petersburg, 1905, daily

1905:   Dec. 18(31) (No. 1)
Continuation of Sievernyi golos.
Ref: Beliaeva 5144
Columbia 249

NASH GOLOS

Samara, 1915, daily

1915:   No. 12
1916:   Apr. 24 - May 1 (Nos. 13, 14, 17, 18, 20-29)
Ref: Beliaeva 5142

NASH KONVEIER

Organ iach. VKP(b) i fabkoma f-ki Moskvashvei No. 5 im.
Profinterna. [Organ of the Party Cell of the All-Union Communist
Party (of Bolsheviks) and of the Factory No. 5 "Profintern".]
Moscow

1932:   Jan. 8, Feb. 4 (Nos. 31[46], 2[48])
Ref: LC, p. 106

NASH KRAI

Gazeta severo-zapadnoi Novgorodchiny. Izd. Tikhvinskogo
soveta krest'ianskikh, rabochikh i krasnoarmeiskikh deputatov.
[Published by the Tikhvin Soviet of Peasants' and Workers' Deputies.]
Tikhvin, 1918, twice a week

1919: Nov. 7 (No. 88[152])

Ref. LC, p. 171

NASH PUT'

Ezhednevnaia politicheskaia, literaturnaia i ekonomicheskaia
gazeta.
Ekaterinoslav, 1907, daily
1907:   Nos. 3, 7, 8, 9, 13 (microfilm)
Ref: Beliaeva 5175

NASH PUT'
>
> Ezhednevnyi organ russkoi natsional'noi mysli za rubezhom.
Glavnyi redaktor K. V. Rodzaevskii.
>> Kharbin, 1933, daily

1934: Apr. 26, Nov. 20-28, Nos. 101, 301-304
1935: Nov. 5 - 16, Nos. 282(710), 283, 287, 288, 290, 291, 293
1936: Jan. 17 - Sept. 13, Nos. 12, 14, 20, 107(870 incomp.),
128(891), 142(905), 182(945), 190(953), 211(947), 225(988),
239(1040)
1937: Jan. 6 - July 17, Nos. 6-14, 62-65, 87-95, 178-179, 182,186
>> Ref: Columbia 252

NASH PUT'
>
> Organ slavianskogo edineniia.
> Omsk, 1919

1919: Oct. 20 (Oct. 7) (No. 6)

NASH PUT'
>
> Ezhemesiachnaia gazeta russkikh rabochikh.
> French title: Notre chemin.
> Paris, 1933, monthly

1933: June - Oct. (Nos. 2-6)

NASH PUT'
>
> Tiantsin, 1926, daily

1927: July 19-24, 28; Aug. 2, 4-5, 9-10, 12-18, 20-21, 30; Sept. 3, 6,
9, 13-18; Oct. 9, 12-13 (Nos. 162-167, 170, 173, 177, 180-181,
183-184, 186-187, 190-191, 198-202, 204, 207, 210-215, 233,
235-236)
Defective Nos.:
1927: Nos. 173, 183, 186, 187, 190, 202, 207, 211, 212, 213, 214,
236

NASH VEK
>
> Ezhenedel'naia gazeta.
> Berlin, 1931, weekly

1931: Nov. 29-Jan. 1, 17-Apr. 10, May 1-June 5, Oct., Nov. 13
1932-Apr. 1933: (Nos. 4-8, 10-22, 25-30, 47, 50-72)

NASH VEK

Petrograd, Nov. 1917, daily

1917, Nov. 30 (Dec. 13)-Aug. 3, 1918 (Nos. 1-2, 5-20, 22-134 (158)
Continuation of Vek and Novaia riech
Ref: LC, p. 61

NASHA ARMIIA

Gazeta voennaia, obshchestvennaia i literaturnaia.
Omsk, Sept. 24, 1919, daily

1919:   Sept. 24-Oct. 3, 6-17, 20-24 (Nos. 1-8, 11-19, 21-25)
Ref: LC, p. 139

NASHA DOLIA

Moscow, 1906, weekly

1906 - 1907: Nos. 1-3 (microfilm)
Ref: Beliaeva 5191

NASHA GAZETA

Kharbin

1933:   Jan. 1, Feb. 12, 19, 50 (Nos. 1, 36, 43, 50)

NASHA GAZETA

Omsk, daily

1919:   Sept. 12 (No. 23)
Ref: LC, p. 139

NASHA GAZETA

Organ russkoi molodezhi Zarubezh'ia. [Editor: A. A. Illukevich]
Riga, 1930, monthly

1931:.   May 20 (No. 8/9)

NASHA GAZETA

Saratov, 1915, weekly

1915:   No. 1-3, 5-6, 8-9, (microfilm)
Ref: Beliaeva 5188

NASHA GAZETA
   Ezhenedel'naia obshchestvenno-natsional'naia gazeta.
  Redaktor Bs. Levashev.
   Sofia

  1938, Oct. 19-Jan. 18, 1940 (Nos. 1-65)
   Continuation of <u>Golos Rossii</u>.
           Ref: Columbia 258

NASHA GAZETA
   Ezhednevnaia Pekin-Tian'tszin-Mukdenskaia gazeta.
   Tientsin, 1928, daily

  1934: Sept. 14 (No. 2016)

NASHA PRAVDA
   Organ Uispolkoma i Ukoma RKP(b). [Organ of the District
  Executive Committee of the Russian Communist Party (of Bolsheviks).]
   Kozlov, 1919

  1922: March 11 (No. 30 [491])
          Ref: LC, p. 83

NASHA PRAVDA
   Organ TSentr. i Erivansk. kom. KPA i POBR. [Organ of the
  Central Committee and the Yerevan Committee of the Communist
  Party of Armenia and of the POBR.]
   Yerevan, 3 times a week

  1922: March 12 (No. 30)
         Ref: LC, p. 187

NASHA RECH'
   Ezhednevnaia, vnepartiinaia, obshchestvenno-literaturnaia i
  ekonomicheskaia gazeta.
   Bukharest, 1922, daily

  1926: Nov. 29-Dec. 31 (Nos. 303, 310, 312-316, 318-330, 332-334)
         Ref: Columbia 260

NASHA RECH'
   Bezpartiinaia, demokraticheskaia, progressivnaia gazeta.
   Chicago, 1941, twice a week

  1941: March 12 - June 21 (Nos. 1-10, 12-25)
   Continuation of <u>Vse novosti</u>, which was suppressed with No. 40,
   Feb. 20, 1941.

NASHA RECH'

Continuation of Rech'. Continued as Svobodnaia Rech' as of Nov. 19, 1917.

Petrograd, Nov. 16, 1917, daily

1917:　Nov. 16 (No. 1-2)

Ref: Columbia 261

NASHA RECH'

Vladivostok, 1922, daily

1922:　Apr. 26-May 13, 19-25, June 19, 21-30, July 2-5, 9-17, (Nos. 1-17, 19-27, 44, 46-55, 57-60, 64-72) (Most numbers are in poor condition)

Ref: LC, p. 182

NASHA VERNOST'

Petrograd

1917:　Nos. 2, 21, 25

NASHA VOL'NOST'

Ezhednevnaia politicheskaia, obshchestvenno-literaturnaia i kazach'ia gazeta.
Continuation of Vol'nost'.
Petrograd, 1917, daily

1917:　Nov. 26 (Dec. 9), No. 2

Ref: LC, p. 62

NASHA ZARIA

Organ demokraticheskoi gosudarstvennoi mysli.
Omsk, Dec. 31, 1918, daily

1919:　Feb. 23-Aug. 27 (Nos. 41, 116-120, 122-135, 139-149, 151-154, 156-164, 169, 172-179, 181-186)

Ref: Columbia 264
LC, p. 139

NASHA ZARIA

Tientsin, 1928

1934:　Sept. 14 (No. 2016)
1941:　Mar. 18 (No. 4088)

NASHA ZHIZN'
        Ezhednevnaia obshchestvenno-politicheskaia, literaturnaia i
ekonomicheskaia gazeta bez predvaritel'noi tsenzury. Redaktor
izdatel' prof. L. V. Khodskii.
        St. Petersburg, 1905, daily

1905:   Jan. 16(29), 19(Feb. 1) - Feb. 5(18), June 17(30) - 21 (July 4),
        29 (July 12) - 30 (July 13), July 5 (18) - 8 (21), Nos. 61, 64-81,
        124-128, 135-137, 144, 146, 148, 150.
                            Ref: Beliaeva 5198, 1904
                                  Columbia 266

NASHA ZHIZN'
        Natsional'nyi nezavisimyi demokraticheskii organ evreiskoi
mysli.
        Shanghai, 1941, weekly

1945:   Nov. 23 (No. 14(209)

NASHA ZHIZN'
        Sofia, irregular

1933:   Jan. 22 - Sept. (Nos. 53-74)
                        Ref: Columbia 267

NASHE DELO
        Irkutsk

1919:   Nos. 2, 195, 240, 243, 255-264, 267-273, 275-278, 283-296
        (Aug. - Dec.) (microfilm)

NASHE DELO
        Ezhenedel'naia gazeta
        Moscow, 1906, weekly

1906:   Nos. 1-10 (microfilm)
                        Ref: Beliaeva 5238

NASHE DELO
        Ezhenedel'naia gazeta pod redaktsiei G. A. Aleksinskogo.
    Organ politicheskii, obshchestvennyi, literaturnyi i khudozhestvennyi.
        Paris, weekly

1939, Nov.--Jan. 13, 1940: Nos. 1-2, 4-8
                        Ref: Columbia 268

NASHE EDINSTVO

Petrograd, 1917, daily (Pod red. G. V. Plekhanova)

1917: Nos. 2, 9-13 (microfilm)
1918: No. 14 (microfilm)

Ref: LC, p. 62

NASHE EKHO

Ezhednevnaia politicheskaia i literaturnaia gazeta.
St. Petersburg, 1907, daily

1907: March 25, 31 - Apr. 3, 10 (Nos. 1, 6-8, 14)

Ref: Beliaeva 5253

NASHE SLOVO

[Continuation of Novoe Slovo.]
Moscow, 1918, daily

1918: Apr. 13(March 31), May(Apr. 20), 12(Apr. 29), 15(2), 17(4),
22(9), 25(12), 26(13), June 12(May 30) (Nos. 1, 4, 16, 21, 23,
25, 29, 32-33, 43)

Ref: LC, p. 106

NASHE SLOVO

Obshchestvennaia i politicheskaia gazeta.
Paris, 1914, daily

1915: Jan. - Dec. (1-108, 110-115, 117-158, 162-164, 167-169, 171-178,
181-196, 198-199, 201-203, 206, 208-219, 221, 223-240, 243-257,
259-279)
1916: Jan. - Dec. (Nos. 1-204, 207-213)
Beginning with Jan. 1, 1916, merged with Golos and since that
date carries double numbering.

Ref: Columbia 272

NASHE VREMIA

Vestnik svobodnoi mysli rossiiskoi emigratsii.
Munich, 1946, weekly, fortnightly, irreg.

1948: May - July, (Nos. 5, 6, 8-11)
1949: Feb., Dec. (Nos. 12-13)
1950: May (No. 14)
Subtitle varies: up to Dec. 1949. "Organ nezavisimoi
obshchestvennoi politicheskoi mysli narodov poraboshchennykh
bol'shevizmom."

Ref: Columbia 273

NASHI DNI
Politicheskaia, obshchestvennaia i literaturnaia gazeta.
Petrograd, Jan. 29, 1918, weekly

1918:   March 18(5), Apr. 1 (March 19) (Nos. 7, 9)
Ref: Columbia 277; LC, p. 62

NASHI VEDOMOSTI
Vecherniaia gazeta. Izdanie sotrudnikov "Birzhevykh
Vedomostei".
Petrograd, 1918, daily

1918:   Jan. 12 - Jan. 26 (Nos. 3-9, 12)
Continuation of Vedomosti which, in turn, is one of the news-
papers continuing Birzhevyia vedomosti.
Continued as Novyia Vedomosti.
Ref: LC, p. 62

NASHI VESTI
Izdanie upravleniia soiuza b. chinov Russkogo Korpusa.
Russian bulletin "Our News".
New York, bi-monthly

1952, Feb. 1 - Dec. 15, 1955 (No. 1/2138 - No. 92/2230)

NATSIONAL-REVOLIUTSIONER
Izdanie TSentral'nogo Komiteta Natsional-Revoliutsionnogo
Soiuza.
Paris, 1927, fortnightly

1927:   Nos. 1-4, 8
Ref: Columbia 279

NATSIONAL'NYE SOIUZY RUSSKOI MOLODEZHI ZA RUBEZHOM
Obshchaia informatsiia organizatsionnogo biuro po
ob"edineniiu i sozyvu s"ezda russkoi natsional'noi molodezhi.
Paris

1930:   April 15 - May 15 (Nos. 2-3)

NEDELIA
Gazeta dlia russkikh voennoplennykh v Avstrii.
Vienna, weekly

1916:   Nos. 1, 2, 9-10

NEUMOLCHNOE SLOVO

Ezhednevnaia politicheskaia i literaturnaia gazeta; organ Tsentral'nogo komiteta trudovoi narodno-sotsialisticheskoi partii. [Organ of the Central Committee of the People's Socialist Workers' Party.]

Petrograd, daily
Est. Oct. 29, 1917

1917: Nov. 29(Dec. 12) - 30(Dec. 13), Nos. 1-2
Ref: LC, p. 63

NEVSKAIA GAZETA

St. Petersburg, 1906, daily
1906: Nos. 1-10 (microfilm)
Ref: Columbia 285
Beliaeva 5272

NEVSKAIA ZVEZDA

St. Petersburg, 1912, 3 times per week

1912: Mar. 10(Feb. 26) - July 7(June 24) Nos. 1-14
Ref: Beliaeva 5273

NEVSKII GOLOS

Politicheskaia gazeta.
St. Petersburg, 1912, twice a week

1912: Nos. 1-9 (May-August) (microfilm)
Ref: Columbia 286
Beliaeva 5275

NEZAVISIMYI GORETS

Organ revoliutsionno-demokraticheskoi i sotsialisticheskoi mysli. Vykhodit raz v nedeliu po ponedel'nikam.
Tiflis, 1921, weekly

1921: Jan. 24-Feb. 14 (Nos. 1-4)
Ref: LC, p. 169

NIKOLAEVSKII VESTNIK

(Vykhodit ezhednevno). Izdanie voennykh vlastei g. Nikolaeva. [Also has a German title "Anzeiger fuer Nikolajew".]

1918: Apr. 12, 30 - May 14 (Nos. 8, 23-26)

NIVA

Petrograd, weekly

1917:   Nov. 11 (No. 45) (microfilm)

NIZHEGORODSKAIA KOMMUNA
Organ Nizhegorodskogo gubernskogo komiteta Rossiiskoi kommunisticheskoi partii Gubernskogo i gorodskogo sovetov rabochikh, krasnoarmeiskikh i krest'ianskikh deputatov. [Organ of the Nizhnii Novgorod Provincial Committee of the Russian Communist Party and of the Provincial and City Soviets.]
Nizhnii Novgorod, 1921, daily

1921:   Nov. 6 (No. 253)
Ref: LC, p. 20

NOCH'
Sotsialisticheskaia gazeta.
Petrograd, 1917, daily

1917:   Nov. 22-23 (Nos. 1-2)
Continuation of Den'. Continued as Polnoch'.
Ref: LC, p. 63

NOVAIA DEREVNIA
Ezhednevnaia gazeta Gomel'skogo komiteta Rossiiskoi kommunisticheskoi partii (bol'shevikov). [Published by the Gomel Provincial Committee of the Russian Communist Party (of Bolsheviks).]
Gomel, daily

1922:   March 12 (No. 226)
Ref: LC, p. 19

NOVAIA DEREVNIA
Ezhenedel'naia krest'ianskaia gazeta. Organ Semipalatins-kogo gubkoma VKP(b) i Gubispolkoma.
Semipalatinsk, 1925, weekly

1928:   Mar. 9, Apr. 20, May 1, 11, 18, June 1, 8 (Nos. 10(111), 16(117), 17(118), 19(120), 20(121), 22(123), 23(124)

NOVAIA GAZETA
Petrograd, May 29, 1918, twice daily

1918: May 29 (No. 1)

Ref: LC, p. 63

NOVAIA MYSL'
Nikolaev, 1943, semi-weekly

1944: Feb. 20 (No. 17)

NOVAIA PETROGRADSKAIA GAZETA
Politicheskaia i literaturnaia.
Continuation of Petrogradskaia Zhizn'.
Petrograd, Dec. 3, 1917, daily

1918: Feb. 14, Mar. 1, 25, June 14 (1), Aug. 4 (Nos. 23, 36, 121, 164)

Ref: LC, p. 63

NOVAIA RABOCHAIA GAZETA
St. Petersburg, 1913, daily

1913: Nos. 1-45 (Aug. - Sept.) (microfilm)

Ref: Columbia 292; Beliaeva 5384

NOVAIA RECH'
Continuation of Svobodnaia rech' and Vek; continued by Nash Vek as of Nov. 30 (Dec. 13), 1917.
Petrograd, 1917, daily

1917: Nov. 28 (Nos. 1-2)

Ref: Columbia 293; LC, p. 63

NOVAIA ROSSIIA
Kharkov

1919: Nos. 134-140; 142-143 (Oct.-Nov.) (Microfilm)

NOVAIA ROSSIIA
        Ezhednevnaia demokraticheskaia gazeta.
        Revel, Mar. 12, 1919, daily

   1919:   Mar. 12, 14-20, 27, Apr. 8, 11-12, 16, 20, 24-26, July 11,
        15-29, 31, Aug. 2-4, 23, Sept. 4-5, 8-11, 16, 22, Oct. 8, 10,
        13-15 (Nos. 1, 3-8, 13, 23, 26-27, 30, 32, 34-36, 82, 85-97,
        99, 101-102, 119, 129-130, 132-135, 139, 144, 158, 160, 162-164)
                         Ref: LC, p. 164

NOVAIA ROSSIIA
        Sofia

   1922, Nov. 22 - May 11, 1923 (Nos. 7, 9-10, 12, 15-18, 22, 24, 26
        29-37, 39-40, 42, 44-46, 49-54, 57-60, 62, 68-73, 76-77)

NOVAIA RUS'
        Gazeta vnepartiinykh sotsialistov. [Newspaper of Non-Party
Socialists.]
        Petrograd, Est. Aug. 27, 1917, daily

   1917:   Aug. 27(9), Sept. 23(Oct. 6) - 30(Oct. 13), Oct. 8(21), 11(24)
        (Nos. 1, 12-18, 24, 26)
                     Ref: Columbia 295
                         LC, p. 63

NOVAIA RUSSKAIA ZHIZN'
        Organ russkoi osvoboditel'noi natsional'no-gosudarstvennoi
mysli.
        Continuation of Russkaia zhizn'.
        Helsingfors, 1919, daily

   1919:   Dec. 19 (No. 13)
   1920:   Jan. 20-Dec. 31 (Nos. 14, 16, 145, 189, 192-201, 203-219,
        221-227, 229, 231, 236, 238-239, 241, 244, 246-248, 251-254,
        258, 259, 261, 263, 264, 266, 268)
   1921:   Nos. 1, 3-12, 14-15, 17-32, 34-35, 37-130, 132-187, 192-201,
        204-205, 208-213, 215, 218-223, 228-253, 258-277, 280-287,
        290-302
   1922:   Jan.-May 2 (Nos. 1-7, 10-65, 68-86, 88-109, 114-24)

NOVAIA TEKHNIKA
        Prilozhenie k "Torgovo-promyshlennoi gazete".
        Moscow, twice a month, irreg.

   1929:   Aug. - Dec. 29 (Nos. 16-24)

NOVAIA ZARIA
San Francisco, Calif., daily

1929: Mar. 28(No. 83)
1931: Aug. 1 - Dec. 2 (Nos. 669-754)
1932: Jan. 30, May 13, June 8 - Dec. 31 (Nos. 792, 894, 881-900, 902-922, 924-989, 1020, 1022-24)
Jan. 5, 1933 - Dec. 1938 (Nos. 1026-28, 1030-37, 1039-1049, 1052, 1054-2526)
1939: Jan. - Dec. (Nos. 2527-2637, 2639-2777)
Jan. 1940 - Dec. 1945 (Nos. 2778-4170, 4172-4284)
Ref: Columbia 297

NOVAIA ZHIZN'
Obshchestvenno-literaturnaia sotsial-demokraticheskaia gazeta.
Petrograd, est. 1917, daily

1917: Nos. 1-102, 104-110, 113-114, 116-139(134), 141(136)-143(137), 145(139)-169(163), 171(165)-186(180), 188 (182)-187(181), 189(183), 191(185)-200(194), 202(196), 206(200)-211(205), 213(207)-214(208), May 1(Apr. 18) - Dec. 31, 1917(Jan. 13, 1918)
1918: Nos. 2(216)-7(221), 9(223)-15(229), 17(231)-30(244), 32(246)-54(269), 56(271), 68(283)-69(284), 71(286)-72(287), 74(289), 76(291), 77(292), 79(294)-84(299), 86(301)-139(354), Jan. 4(17)-July 16
Jan. 3 (16) never published
No. 36 (250), Mar. 8 (Feb. 23) also numbered 37 (251) on last page
Ref: Columbia 298; LC, p. 64

NOVAIA ZHIZN'
Shanghai, daily

1945: Nov. 18-24, 27-30, Dec. 6, 10, 16, 20, 22, 23 (Nos. 1657-1663, 1666-1669, 1675, 1678, 1685, 1689, 1691, 1692)
1946: Jan. 4-5, 7-8, 14-17, 19, 22-27, 28-30, Feb. 7-9, 12-16, 18-22, 25, 27, Mar. 2, 4-9, 11-16, 18-23, 25-27, 29-30, Apr. 5-6, 8-13, 23-26, May 3, 7-8, 14. (Nos. 1703-1704, 1706-1707, 1713-1716, 1718, 1721-1725, 1727-1728, 1736-1738, 1741-1745, 1747-1751, 1754, 1756, 1759, 1761-1766, 1768-1773, 1775-1780, 1782-1784, 1786-1787, 1793-1794, 1796-1801, 1811-1814, 1820, 1824-1825, 1831)

NOVAIA ZHIZN'
>> Vechernii vypusk.
>> Shanghai, daily

1945: Nov. 17, 19-23, 26-29, Dec. 5, 15, 19, 21-22 (Nos. 1656, 1658-1662, 1665-1668, 1674, 1684, 1688, 1690-1691)
1946: Jan. 3, 4, 14-16, 22-25, 28-29, Feb. 8, May 13 (Nos. 1702-1703, 1713-1717, 1721-1724, 1727-1728, 1737, 1830)

NOVOE NARODNOE SLOVO
>> Ezhednevnaia politicheskaia i literaturnaia gazeta. Organ TSK
Trudovoi Narodno-Sotsialist. Partii.
>> Petrograd, 1917, daily

1917: Nos. 3, 4, 5, 7, 8, 9 (Dec. 3 - Dec. 10 [old style]) (Microfilm)

NOVOE RUSSKOE SLOVO
>> New York, 1911, daily

1927: July 8 (No. 5276)
1932: Nov. - Dec. (Nos. 7219-7258, 7260-7267, 7269-7277, 7279)
1933 - 1945
1946: Nos. 12300-12552, 12554, 12556, 12558, 12560-12604, 12606-12665
1947: Nos. 12666-12905, 12907-13033
1948: Jan. - Dec. (Nos. 13034-13398
1949: Jan. 1 - Dec. 31 (Nos. 13399-13763
1950: Jan. 1 - Dec. (Nos. 13764-14128
1951: Jan. - Dec. (Nos. 14130-14172, 14375-14477)
1965: Jan. - to present
Missing Numbers:
1933: Nos. 7325, 7493, 7500, 7513-7514, 7519-7520, 7522-7527, 7531, 7534, 7536, 7546-7548, 7554, 7566, 7574, 7576, 7597, 7602, 7612, 7631
1934: Nos. 7663, 7667-7668, 7670-7696, 7701-7751, 7757-7774, 7790-7794, 7816-7817, 7824-7850, 7852-7930, 7932-7934, 7937-7943, 7945, 7993, 7996
1935: 8010, 8013-8116, 8031-8034, 8036-8037, 8040-8046, 8048-8049, 8059-8060, 8062, 8064-8073, 8085, 8095-8099, 8102-8106, 8109-9110, 8123, 8134-8138, 8159, 8174, 8211, 8214, 8343, 8345, 8349-8361, 8364
1936: 8465, 8473-8479, 8529, 8542, 8545, 8570, 8592, 8667
1937: 8745, 8765, 8837, 8856, 9092-9098
1938: 9407-9413, 9427-9433, 9441
1939: 9511-9517, 9552-9559, 9616, 9679-9685, 9700-9706, 9708, 9721-9727, 9735 (Oct. 1) to the end of the year

(Continued on next page)

NOVOE RUSSKOE SLOVO (continued)

    1940: Nos. 10059, 10069
    1941: No. 10410
    1042: No. 10876
    1945: Nos. 11928, 12151, 12259, 12280-12281
    1946 - 1964

Ref: Columbia 300

NOVOE SLOVO
         Berlin, 1933, irregular

May 1933 - Oct. 1939 (Nos. 1-267)
1940: July - Dec. (Nos. 31-51)
1941: Jan. - Sept. (Nos. 1-13, 14-16, 20, 22, 27, 30, 31, 36-38)
1942: Feb. - Dec. (Nos. 14, 16, 29, 34, 35, 38-40, 42-49, 51, 55, 57, 59, 60, 73, 77, 91)
1943: Jan. - Dec. (2-20, 22-27, 28, 30-32, 34, 39, 41-44, 46-48, 50-54, 56, 61, 62, 67, 72-74, 78, 81, 83-88, 91-93, 95, 97-98, 100-104)
1944: Jan. - July (4, 6-15, 17-19, 21, 23, 28, 29, 31-36, 38-41, 43-48, 50-57, 59)

Ref: Columbia 301

NOVOE SLOVO (NUEVA PALABRA)
         Ezhenedel'naia gazeta.
         Buenos Aires, 1950, weekly

1950, Feb. 2-Nov. 1960 (Nos. 1-341, 347-348)

Ref: Columbia 302

NOVOE SLOVO
         Moscow, 1918, daily

1918: Jan. 17, 28, Feb. 14(1), 19(6), Mar. 9(Feb. 24), 19(6), 22(9), 28(15), 31(18), Apr. 2(Mar. 20) (Nos. 2, 12, 15, 17-18, 25, 32, 35, 40, 43, 44)
      With April 13, 1918, continued as Nashe Slovo.

Ref: LC, p. 107

NOVOE VREMIA
         Petrograd, 1868, daily

1876, Apr. 1-Oct. 26, 1917 (many issues on microfilm)
(Continued on next page)

<u>NOVOE VREMIA</u> (continued)

Missing numbers:

1876:   June 1, 28, 30, Nov. 1-30

1877:   Jan. 1 - Aug. 31, Oct. 1 - Dec. 31

1878:   Feb. 1 - Mar. 31, May 1 - July 13, Aug. 1 - Dec. 31

1879-80: July 1 - Sept. 30, Nov. 1 - June 30, Aug. 1 - Dec. 31

1882:   Jan. 1 - Apr. 30, June 1 - Dec. 31

1883-84: Jan. 1 - Feb. 28, June 1 - Oct. 31, Dec. 1 - July 31

1884:   Sept. 1 - 30, Nov. 1 - 30

1885:   Mar. 1 - Apr. 30

1886:   Mar. 1 - 31

1887:   Jan. 1 - 31, June 1 - 30, Sept. 1 - Nov. 30

1888:   Jan. 1 - 31, Mar. 6, Apr. 1 - 30, July 1 - Oct. 31

1889:   Jan. 1 - Feb. 28, May 1 - July 31, Oct. 1 - Nov. 30

1890:   Feb. 2 - 3, 6 - 7, 9 - 11, 13 - 14, 16, Mar. 2, 23 - 25,
        Apr. 1 - 12, 14 - 16, 24 - 25, 27 , 29 - 30, May 1 - 31,
        Aug. 1 - 31, Nov. 1 - Dec. 31

1891:   Feb. 28(p. 1-2), Mar. 1 - 31, Apr. 21, June 6, July 7,
        Aug. 1 - Oct. 31, Dec. 23 - 30

1892:   Nov. 1 - 28

1893:   Dec. 1 (p. 1-2), 5, Mar. 1 - Apr. 30, Sept. 16

1896-97: Apr. 1 - 30, Dec. 1 - Feb. 28, June 1 - July 31, Oct. 1 - 31,
        Dec. 1 - 31

1900:   Jan. 4 (p. 1-4), 11 (p.1-4), 31, May 1 (p.1-2), Dec. 1, 6, 7, 14,

1901:   July 19 - 31, Dec. 1 (p. 1-2)

1902:   Feb. 28 (p. 3-4)

1903:   May 30, 31, Sept. 1 - Nov. 30

1904:   Feb. 1 - 28, Mar. 1, June 16, July 11, Aug. 10, Sept. 8,
        Oct. 1 - 2, Oct. 30 - 31, Dec. 18

1905:   Feb. 2 - 4, Mar. 1 - Apr. 3, June 1 (p. 1-2), 6, July 19 - 31,
        Nov. 20, 30, Dec. 13, 26 (p. 1-2), Dec. 27 (p.1-2)

1906:   May 4

1907:   May 1 - 31

1908:   Mar. 1 - May 31, Aug. 1 - Sept. 30

1909:   Jan. 1 - May 31, June 1 (p. 1-2), Sept. 1 - Mar. 31

1910:   May 1 - Dec. 31

1911:   Feb. 1 - May 31, June 1 - 30, Aug. 1 - Sept. 30, Nov. 1, Dec. 31

1912:   Feb. 1 - May 31, July 1 - Aug. 31

1913:   Jan. 1 (p. 1-4), Mar. 30-31, Apr. 11 - June 30, July 21 - 31,
        Oct. 1 - 20

1913:   Oct. 21 (p. 1-4)

1914:   Feb. 1 - Apr. 30, Sept. 6, 8, 24, 29 - 31

1915:   Mar. 23, Apr. 4, 8, 21, Aug. 1 - 19, 31, Nov. 23, Dec. 10,
        14 - 21

1916:   Jan. 1 - 19, Jan. 21 - Feb. 6, 8 - 22, Mar. 6 - 31, July 12 - 13,
        20

Ref: Lisovskii 964, Columbia 305
                                    LC, p. 64, Beliaeva 5419

NOVOLADOZHSKAIA KOMMUNA

Organ Novoladozhskogo uezdnogo komiteta Rossiiskoi
kommunisticheskoi partii (bol'shevikov), uezdispolkoma sovetov
rabochikh, krest'ianskikh i krasnoarmeiskikh deputatov. [Organ of
the Novaia Ladoga District Committee of the Russian Communist
Party (of Bolsheviks) and of the District Executive Committee of
Toilers' Deputies.]

Novaia Ladoga, 3 times a week

1919:   Nov. 7 (No. 30 (74))

Ref: LC, p. 134

NOVOROSSIISKII TELEGRAF

Gazeta politicheskaia, ekonomicheskaia i literaturnaia.
Odessa, 1869, daily

1894:   Aug. 22(Sept. 3), Oct. 4(16), 12(24) - 13(25), 24-25(Nov. 5-6)
(Nos. 6209, 6247, 6255-6256, 6266-6267) (mutilated)

Ref: Lisovskii 1001

NOVOSTI

Ezhenedel'naia gazeta.
Munich, 1947, weekly

1947:   May - Dec. (Nos. 1-18, 21-24, 27, 31, 32)
1948:   Jan. - Apr. (Nos. 33-45, 47, 49)

Ref: Columbia 307

NOVOSTI

Ezhednevnaia obshchestvennaia, politicheskaia i literaturnaia
gazeta.

Paris, 1914, daily

1914:   Aug. 24-28, Sept. 6-Dec. 12 (Nos. 1-4, 13-110)
1915:   Mar. 5, Apr. - Apr. 20, Aor. 22 - May 30 (Nos. 180, 201-216,
218-248)

Ref: Columbia 308

NOVOSTI DNIA

Kiev, 1917, daily

1918:   Sept. 8-Nov. 17
Missing numbers:
(Nos. 5, 12-21, 52, 53, 61)

Ref: LC, p. 32

NOVOSTI DNIA
        Bezpartiinaia politicheskaia, obshchestvennaia i literaturnaia
gazeta.
        Kiev, 1917

1918:   Nov. 20(7), No. 59
                    Ref: LC, p. 32

NOVOSTI DNIA
        Ezhednevnaia politicheskaia, obshchestvennaia i literaturnaia
gazeta.
        Moscow, 1883, daily

1896:   May 17 (No. 4647)
              Ref: Lisovskii 1638, Beliaeva 5464

NOVOSTI I BIRZHEVAIA GAZETA
        St. Petersburg, 1880, daily

1890:   March 22(Apr. 3), 27(Apr. 8), (Nos. 80, 85)
1894:   Dec. 30 - 31 (Jan. 11-12, 1895), (Nos. 358 - 359)
1895:   Jan. 31(Feb. 12), Apr. 1. (13), May 9(21), 11(23) - 15(27),
        23(June 4) - 31(June 12), (Nos. 31, 90, 126, 128-132, 139-147)
1899:   Jan. 7(19), (No. 7)
1900:   Dec. 31 (No. 361)
              Ref: Lisovskii 1085(v)
                    Beliaeva 5475 or 5476

NOVOSTI DNIA
        Sevastopol

1920:   June 26 (No. 23)
              Ref: LC, p. 157

NOVOSTI DNIA
        Shanghai, daily

1945:   May 7, Nov. 18-24, 27-30, Dec. 6, 10, 16, 20, 22-23
        (Nos. 121, 155-161, 164-167, 173, 177, 183, 187, 189-190)
1946:   Jan. 4-5, 7, 14-17, 19, 22, 24-26, 28-30; Feb. 7, 9, 12-16,
        18-21, 25, 27-28; Mar. 2, 4-9, 11-16, 18-23, 25-30;
        Apr. 4-6, May 3, 8, 14 (Nos. 3-4, 6, 12, 15, 17, 20, 22-24,
        26-28, 35, 37, 40-44, 46-49, 52, 54-55, 57, 59-64, 66-71,
        73-78, 80-85, 90-92, 94-99, 108-111, 118, 122, 127)

NOVOSTI DNIA
>
> Vechernii vypusk.
> Shanghai, daily

1945:　Nov. 17, 19-23, 26-27, 29, Dec. 5, 15, 19, 21-22 (Nos. 278, 279-283, 285-286, 288, 293, 302, 305-307)
1946:　Jan. 3-4, 8, 16, 21-25, 28-29, Feb. 8, May 13 (Nos. 2-3, 6, 12, 16-20, 22-23, 31, 105)

NOVOSTI VOSTOKA
>
> Kharbin, daily

1933:　Jan. 1 (No. 1(83))

NOVOSTI ZHIZNI
>
> Ezhednevnaia politicheskaia, obshchestvennaia, literaturnaia, torgovo-promyshlennaia gazeta.
> Kharbin, 1907, daily

1922:　Nov. 29 (No. 267)
1925:　Dec. 20 (No. 283)

Ref: Beliaeva 5473

NOVYI DEN'
>
> St. Petersburg, 1909, weekly

1909:　Nos. 1-15 (microfilm)

Ref: Beliaeva 5536, Columbia 311

NOVYI DEN'
>
> Continuation of Den'
> Petrograd, 1917, daily

1917:　No. 1
1918:　Nos. 1-7, 11-43 (microfilm)

Ref: LC, p. 64

NOVYI KRAI
>
> Ezhednevnaia, obshchestvenno-politicheskaia i literaturnaia gazeta.
> Lvov, 1915, daily

1915:　Apr. 22 (No. 38)

NOVYI KRAI
        Port-Artur, 1900, 3 times a week

    1902:   Sept. 27 (No. 106)
    1903:   Aug. 20 (No. 94)
    1904:   Jan. 1-3 (Nos. 1-2)
                                Ref: Beliaeva 5545; Lisovskii 2751 (2)

NOVYI LUCH
        Organ TSentral'nogo Komiteta sotsial-demokraticheskoi
rabochei partii [ob''edinennoi]. Ezhednevnaia gazeta. [Organ
of the Central Committee of the Russian Social Democratic
Workers' Party (United)]
        Continuation of Luch and Zaria. As of May 14, 1918, continued
as Nasha Gazeta.
        Petrograd, 1917, daily

    1917:   Dec. 1-30 (Nos. 1-11, 13-24)
    1918:   Nos. 2-6, 10-12, 15, 18, 20-22, 25-28
                                Ref: LC, p. 64

NOVYI MIR
        Ezhenedel'naia rabochaia gazeta. Russkii organ Kommunisti-
cheskoi partii Soed. Shtatov Ameriki, Sektsii Communisticheskogo
Internatsionala.
        New York, weekly

    1916-1917: (microfilm)
    1926:   May 1-Dec. 26 (Nos. 1-35)
    1927:   No. 70
    1928:   Apr. 21 (No. 99)
    1933:   Nos. 1-12, 14-38, 40-46, 48-52
    1934:   Nos. 1-2, 16, 20-21, 23-26, 44, 46-52
    1935:   Jan. 5-July 27 (Nos. 1-3, 6-7, 9-12, _4-15, 18-30)

NOVYI PAKHAR'
        Organ Mozhaiskogo Ukoma VKP(b) UIspolkoma i Uprofbiuro.
        Mozhaisk, twice a week

    1928:   Mar. 9 (No. 20 [291])

NOVYI PUT'

Ezhemesiachnik Biuro trudiashchikhsia khristian.
Geneva, monthly and semi-monthly

1934: Jan., Dec. (Nos. 22, 31)
1937: Mar., May (Nos. 49, 50)
Mar. 1939 - Mar. 1940 (Nos. 69-73, 75-82)

Ref: Columbia 315

NOVYI TURKESTAN see SVOBODNYI TURKESTAN

NOVYI VECHERNII CHAS

[Continuation of Vechernii chas.]
Petrograd, 1917, daily

1917: Dec. 29 - Dec. 30 (Nos. 1-2)
1918: Jan. 5-July 30(Nos. 4, 5-31, 36, 40, 48-49, 51, 57-58, 61-62,
65, 72, 74-76, 78-79, 85, 87-88, 90-91, 93-94, 98-99,
101-103, 106, 108, 122-123, 127)

Ref: Columbia 317; LC, p. 64

NOVYIA RUSSKIIA NOVOSTI DNIA

[Continuation of Russkiia Novosti Dnia.]
Petrograd, Dec. 1, 1917, daily

1917: Dec. 1(14), 3(16), 7(20) - 9(22), 17(30) (Nos. 1, 3, 6-8, 14)
1918: Jan. 5(Dec. 23), 11(Dec. 29), 17(4), 19(6), 24(11) - 26(13),
30(17), 31(18), Feb. 3(Jan. 21), 5(Jan. 23)

Ref: Columbia 318; LC, p. 65

NOVYIA VEDOMOSTI

Vecherniaia gazeta. Izdanie sotrudnikov "Birzhevykh
Vedomostei".
Petrograd, 1918, daily

1918: Nos. 3-5, 10, 13-14, 16-21, 23-28, 31-32, 34, 47, 52, 55-59,
63, 65, 68-69, 71, 73-74, 80-81, 83-87, 91, 94, 99, 101,
104-105, 113, 116-117, 121, 124-125
Continuation of Nashi Vedomosti (one of the newspapers
continuing Birzhevyia Vedomosti).

Ref: LC, p. 65

O

OB"EDINENIE
> Ezhenedel'naia politicheskaia i literaturnaia gazeta.
> St. Petersburg, 1905, weekly

    1907:   Apr. 13 (No. 20)

                             Ref: Beliaeva 5673

OBORONCHESKOE DVIZHENIE
> Izdanie rossiiskogo emigrantskogo oboroncheskogo
dvizheniia.
> Paris, 1936, irreg.

    1936:   May (No. 1, 2)

                             Ref: Columbia 320

OBOZRENIE
> Russkaia natsional'no-politicheskaia obshchestvennaia gazeta.
> Belgrad, 1934, semimonthly

    1935:   Aug. 4-18 (Nos. 13-14)

OBSHCHEE DELO
> Redaktor-izdatel' V. L. Burtsev.
> French title: La cause commune
> Paris, irreg. (Oct. 15, 1920-Dec. 31, 1921 daily; later irreg.)

    1918:   Sept. 17-Nov. 10 (Nos. 24-30)
    1919:   Jan. 1-Dec. 25 (Nos. 31-63)
    1920:   Jan. 24-July 31, Aug. 13-Aug. 20, Sept. 3-Sept 10,
            Sept. 24-Dec. 31 (Nos. 64-81, 83, 84, 86, 87, 89-159, 161-169)
    1921:   Jan. 1-Dec. 31 (Nos. 170-530)
    1922:   Jan. 1-Jan. 24, Feb. 1-Feb. 3, Feb. 8-Feb. 14, Feb. 19-
            June 23 (Nos. 531-551, 553-556, 558, 560-565)
    1929:   Feb. 15 (No. 2)
    1930:   Feb. 15-Sept. 20 (Nos. 3-8)

                             Ref: Columbia 323

OBSHCHEE DELO
            Petrograd, irreg.

    1917:   Oct. 4, 6, 8, 11, 14, 20 (Nos. 8, 10, 12, 14, 17, 22)
                                    Ref: LC, p. 65

OBYVATEL' - GRAZHDANIN
            Title also in French: Le citoyen sans parti.
            Paris, 1932, semimonthly

    1932:   Dec. 20 (No. 2)
    1934:   No. 3

                                    Ref: Columbia 324

ODESSKIE NOVOSTI see ODESSKIIA NOVOSTI

ODESSKII KUR'ER
            Odessa, 1911, daily

    1912:   Nos. 518-522 (microfilm)
    1919:   Nos. 6, 7, 8, 10 (microfilm)
                                    Ref: Beliaeva 5733

ODESSKII LISTOK
            Gazeta literaturnaia, politicheskaia i kommercheskaia.
            Odessa, 1872, daily

    1894:   Sept. 29(Oct. 11), Oct. 4(16) - Nov. 3(15) (Nos. 250, 254-283)
                                    Ref: Lisovskii 1123 (b)
                                        Beliaeva 5723; LC, p. 138

ODESSKII NABAT
            Organ Odesskoi federatsii anarkhistskikh grupp "Nabat".
            Odessa

    1919:   May 1-12, 16, June 16 (Nos. 1-2, 4, 7)
    1920:   Feb. 8 - 16 (9-10)

ODESSKIIA NOVOSTI
>Gazeta politicheskaia, literaturnaia, nauchnaia, obshchest-
vennaia i kommercheskaia.
>Odessa, Dec. 1, 1884, daily

1895: June 19, July 9 (Nos. 3324, 3343)
1919: Nos. 10, 885-10, 905; 10, 908-10, 913; 10, 915-10, 919; 10, 921-
10, 932; 10, 935-10, 942 (Jan.-March) (microfilm)
>Ref: Beliaeva 5722; Columbia 325,
LC, p. 138; Lisovskii 1689

ODNA SHESTAIA
>Dvukhnedel'naia gazeta.   Editor: N.M. Polezhaev.
>Paris, semimonthly

1928: Jan. 1, Feb. 1 (Nos. 1, 3)

OKAR'
>Organ Moskovsko-Okskogo oblastnogo komiteta.   Vykhodit
ezhednevno, krome dnei posleprazdnichnykh.   [At head of title:
Vserossiiskii soiuz rabotnikov vodnogo transporta.]
>Moscow, daily

1918: Nov. 23(10) - 28(15), (Nos. 74-78)

OLONETSKAIA KOMMUNA
>Organ Olonetskogo gubernskogo komiteta RKP, Olonetskogo
ispolnitel'nogo komiteta sovetov, Murmanskoi zheleznoi dorogi i
Politotdela N-skoi divizii.   [Organ of the Olonets Provincial Committee
of the Russian Communist Party, of the Olonets Executive Committee
of Soviets, of the Murmansk Railroad and of the Political Committee
of the ... Division.]
>Petrozavodsk, daily

1919: Nov. 7 (No. 253)
1920: May 29 - June 4 (Nos. 118-122)
>Ref: LC, p. 145

ORENBURGSKII KAZAK
>Odnodnevnaia gazeta, izdaiushchaiasia Kruzhkom revnitelei
istorii Orenburgskogo kazach'iago voiska v den' Sv. Velikomuchenika
i Pobedonostsa Georgiia-voiskovogo prazdnika orenburgskikh kazakov.
>Kharbin, 1933, 1935, one day's paper

1933: May 6 (Apr. 23) 6 p.
1935: May 6 (Apr. 23) 6 p.

ORLOVSKII VESTNIK
>Ezhednevnaia gazeta obshchestvennoi zhizni, literatury, politiki i torgovli.
>Orel, 1873, daily

1894:   May 11 (No. 128)

>Ref: Lisovskii 1252, Beliaeva 5812

OTECHESTVENNYE VEDOMOSTI
>Organ natsional'noi i gosudarstvennoi mysli.
>Ekaterenburg

1919:   Jan. 4 (Dec. 22, 1918) May 13(Apr. 30) (Nos. 3, 99)
>Ref: LC, p. 164

OTECHESTVO
>Ezhednevnaia, bezpartiinaia, obshchestvenno-politicheskaia gazeta natsional'nogo ob"edineniia.
>Arkhangelsk, Sept. 20, 1918, daily

1919:   June - Oct., (Nos. 6(103), 150(247), 175(272), 216(313))
>Ref: LC, p. 3

OTECHESTVO "PATRIE"
>Izdanie "Russkogo zarubezhnogo patrioticheskogo ob"edineniia".
>Paris, 1925

1926:   June 6 - Oct. 24 (Nos. 1, 2, 4-7, 9, 10, 13-17)
>Ref: Columbia 332

OTECHESTVO
>Ezhednevnaia politicheskaia gazeta.
>Petrograd, 1917, daily

1917:   July 25(Aig. 7), Aug. 31(Sept. 13) (Nos. 8, 40)
>Ref: Columbia 333, LC, p. 65

OTKLIKI ZHIZNI
>Izdanie Gruppy sotsialistov-revoliutsionerov.
>Paris, semimonthly

1916:   March 12, Apr. 23, May 21, June 18-July 23 (Nos. 1, 4, 6, 8-10)

P

PAMIATI G. V. PLEKHANOVA
Petrograd, one day's newspaper

1918:   June 9 (8 p.)

Ref: Columbia 335, LC, p. 63

PARIZHSKII VESTNIK
Izdanie Upravleniia delami russkoi emigratsii vo Frantsii.
Paris, weekly

1942:   June - Dec. (Nos. 1-29)
1943:   Jan. - Dec. (Nos. 30-80)
1944:   Jan. - Aug. (Nos. 81-95, 96-100, 101-112)

Ref: Columbia 336

PARUS
Ezhednevnaia bezpartiinaia demokraticheskaia gazeta.
Rostov-on-Don, 1919, daily

1919:   Nov. 24 (Dec. 7) (No. 25)

Ref: LC, p. 151

PASTYR' DOBRYI
Kharbin

1938:   Mar. 12

PERVOPOKHODNIK
Izdanie Glavnogo Pravleniia Soiuza 1-go Kubanskogo pokhoda.
(Editor: V. M. Pronin)
Belgrade

1928:   Feb. 22 (No. 1)
1933:   Feb. 22 (No. 2)
1938:   Feb. 22 (No. 3)

Ref: Columbia 342

PETERBURGSKII KUR'ER
            St. Petersburg

    1914:   July 24, 27, 28 (Nos. 178, 181, 182)

PETROGRADSKAIA GAZETA
            Politicheskaia i literaturnaia.
            Petrograd, 1867, daily

    1917:   Jan. 25, March 7, 8, 28; Apr. 5-7, 8, 12, 15, 18, 21, 22,
            25-29; May 2, 8, 31; June 21; Oct. 17
                                Ref: Lisovskii 919; Beliaeva 6029
                                Columbia 344; LC, p. 65

PETROGRADSKAIA KOOPERATSIIA
            Organ Petrogradskogo edinogo potrebitel'skogo obshchestva.
            Petrograd, 1919, 3 w.

    1921:   Dec. 10 (No. 1[372])
    1922:   Jan. 3-12 (Nos. 1[392] - 3[394])
                                Ref: LC, p. 66

PETROGRADSKAIA PRAVDA see LENINGRADSKAIA PRAVDA

PETROGRADSKAIA SVOBODNAIA PECHAT'
            Petrograd, Nov. 26, 1917
            Continued as Russkiia novosti dnia and Novyia Russkiia
    novosti dnia.
            English edition: Petrograd Free Press (No. 2, Dec. 26, 1917)

    1917:   Nov. 26(Dec. 9), 28(Dec. 11) (Nos. 2-3)
                                Ref: LC, p. 66

PETROGRADSKAIA VECHERNIAIA PECHAT'
            Petrograd

    1918:   Nos. 5-7

PETROGRADSKAIA VECHERNIAIA POCHTA
            [Continuation of Novaia vecherniaia pochta.]
            Petrograd, 1917, daily

    1917:   Nov. 25, 29, Dec. 11 (Nos. 5, 7, 17)
                                Ref: LC, p. 66

PETROGRADSKII GOLOS
Gazeta politicheskaia i literaturnaia s risunkami v tekste.
Petrograd, 1917, daily

1918:   Jan. 3(16) - July 31 (Nos. 1-3, 5-32, 73, 84, 90, 105-106, 131, 135-137, 142, 144)
Continuation of Petrogradskii listok.
Ref: Columbia 346, LC, p. 66

PETROGRADSKII KUR'ER
Petrograd, daily

1915:   May 3 (No. 457)

PETROGRADSKOE EKHO
Petrograd, daily

1918:   Jan. 1 - May 20 (Nos. 3-31, 34-47, 49-66, 68-71)
Ref: Columbia 349, LC, p. 67

PETROGRADSKII LISTOK
Gazeta politicheskaia, obshchestvennaia i literaturnaia s risunkami v tekste.
Petrograd, 1864, daily

1893:   May 13 (No. 117)
1915:   Apr. 21(May 4), (No. 107)
1917:   Nos. 55, 55a, 56, 57a, 61, 79, 159, 160, 207, 254
Continued by Petrogradskii Golos
Ref: Lisovskii 812, Beliaeva 6050
Columbia 347, LC, p. 67

PETERBURGSKII LISTOK see PETROGRADSKII LISTOK

PIATYI KRASNYI OKTIABR'
IUbileinoe izdanie v den' chetvertoi godovshchiny Oktiabr'skoi revoliutsii.
Kozlov, 1921, one day's newspaper

1921:   No. 7 (Oct. 25)

PIONERSKAIA PRAVDA

Organ Tsentral'nogo i Moskovskogo komitetov VLKSM. [Organ of the Central Committee and the Moscow Committee of the All-Union Lenin Communist Youth League.]
Moscow, 1925, S. W.

1933:   Apr. 14
1945:   May 22, June 19, July - Sept. (Nos. 22, 26, 28-53)
1946:   Mar. - May (Nos. 24-33, 42-43)
1947:   Apr. - Dec. 26 (Nos. 31-104)
1948, June (Nos. 44-104) - Dec. 1951 (Nos. 1-104)

Ref: Columbia 350; LC, p. 107

PLAMIA

Organ Tsentral'nogo komiteta Rossiiskoi sots.-dem. rabochei partii (ob"edinennoi). Ezhednevnaia gazeta.
Petrograd, daily

1917:   Nov. 24 (No. 1)
Only this number was published under the above title. Continued as Fakel.

Ref: LC, p. 67

POD RUSSKIM STIAGOM

Izdanie Rossiiskago obshchestvennago komiteta v Pol'she.
"Den' neprimirimosti" 1934.
Warsaw, 1934, one day's newspaper

PODVIG VO L'DAKH

Odnodnevnaia gazeta Prezidiuma Soiuza Osoviakhima SSSR. [Published by the Presidium of the Society for the Promotion of Defense and Aero-Chemical Development.]
Moscow, 1928, one day's newspaper

1928:   Oct. (8 p.)

Ref: LC, p. 108

POLESSKAIA PRAVDA

Organ Gomel'skikh gubernskogo i uezdno-gorodskogo revkoma. [Organ of the Gomel Provincial Committee and of the City Revolutionary Committee.]
Gomel, daily
1920:   June 21 (No. 49)
1921:   Nov. 7 (No. 438)
1922:   Mar. 12 (No. 546)

Ref: LC, p. 19

POLITICHESKIIA IZVESTIIA
Vykhodiat v Gel'singforse po ponedel'nikam.
Helsingfors, weekly

1920:   Apr. 26 - July 7 (Nos. 200-210)

POLNOCH'
Petrograd

1917:   Nov. 24 (No. 1)
Continuation of Noch (one of the papers continuing Den)
Ref: LC, p. 67

POMOSHCH
Biulleten' Vserossiiskogo komiteta pomoshchi golodaiushchim.
[Published by the All-Russian Committee for Assistance to the
Starving Population.]
Moscow, 1921, weekly

1921:   Aug. 16, 22 (Nos. 1-2) (Microfilm)
Ref: LC, p. 108

PONEDEL'NIK
Moscow, daily

1918:   July 1 (June 18) (No. 18)

PONEDEL'NIK
Ezhenedel'naia gazeta.
Tiflis, weekly

1921:   Jan. 17, 24 (Nos. 3(26), 4(27))
Ref: LC, p. 169

POSEV
Ezhenedel'nik obshchestvennoi i politicheskoi mysli.
Limberg/Lahn, Germany, weekly

1949, Jan. - to the present
Missing nos.
1957:   Oct. 27 - Nov. 24
1959:   Mar. 29
1960:   Jan. 17

POSLEDNIIA IZVESTIIA
Reval, 1920, daily

1921: Nos. 167, 171-179, 183-188, 190, 192-196, 198-200, 202-205, 207-209, 211, 213, 216-217, 219-225, 227-228, 230, 231, 237, 242, 245-246, 253-256, 259, 260, 262

1923: Nos. 5(751)-13(759), 15(761), 18(764), 20(766)-23(769), 25(771), 26(772), 28(774), 32(778)-33(779), 35(781)-58(804), 60(806)-74(820), 76(322)-79(825), 83(829)-93(839), 96(842)-97(843), 100(846)-107(853), 109(855)-110(856), 112(858)-113(859), 115(861)-121(867), 122(888)-123(889), 126(892), 142(908), 144(910)-147(913), 150(916)-152(918), 154(920), 165(931)-166(932), 176(942), 194(960)-196(962), 198(964)-200(966), 204(970)-205(971), 207(973)-209(975), 255(1021), 271(1037), 286(1052), 297(1063), 313(1079), 323(1089), 325(1091)-327(1093)

1924: No. 13(1106)

1925: Nos. 1-12, 14-17, 19-86, 88-104, 106, 108-111, 113-123, 126, 128-130, 132-134, 136-165, 167-215, 217-233, 235, 237-271, 275-279, 281-299

Ref: Columbia, 359; LC, p. 165

POSLEDNIIA NOVOSTI
Editor P. N. Miliukov.
Paris, Est. (1920)? , daily

1920, April 27 - March 11, 1940 (Nos. 1-3021, 3023-3042, 3045-3049, 3053-3060, 3062-3065, 3067-3069, 3073-3074, 3078, 3080-3086, 3088-3090, 3092, 3094-3097, 3099-3101, 3103, 3106-3110, 3113, 3330-3331, 3334, 3336-3337, 3340-3451, 3630-5090, 5092-6725, 6727-6732, 6735, 6738-6741, 6745-6746, 6748-6749, 6751-6923) Nos. 1708, 1722, 1724, 5634 (incomplete)

Ref: Columbia 361

PRAVDA
Organ TSentral'nogo Komiteta Kommunisticheskoi Partii Sovetskogo Soiuza. [Organ of the Central Committee of the Communist Party of the Soviet Union.]

From Mar. 5, 1917 to Mar. 1918 published in Petrograd and thereafter in Moscow. Title varies: from Mar. 5, 1917 (No. 1): Pravda; On July 6, 1917 (No. 100): Listok Pravdy; subsequently: Proletarii, Rabochii and Rabochii put'; from July 23, 1917 to Aug. 9, 1917: Rabochii i soldat; since Oct. 27, 1917 (No. 170): again Pravda. Name of issuing body varies: No. 1, 1917 (Mar. 5, 1917): Central Organ of the Russian Social Democratic Workers' Party (of Bolsheviks); Nos. 2-99 (Mar. 6, 1917 to July 5, 1917): Organ of the Central Committee of the Russian Social Democratic Workers' Party

(Continued on next page)

PRAVDA (Continued)
(of Bolsheviks); from Aug. 4, 1917: Central Organ of the Russian
Social Democratic Workers' Party (of Bolsheviks); from Mar. 1918:
Organ of the Central Committee and the Moscow Committee of the
Russian Communist Party (of Bolsheviks); from 1925 until 1953: Organ
of the Central Committee and the Moscow Committee of the All-Union
Communist Party (of Bolsheviks); 1953: issuing body assumed present
name.
   Moscow, March 5, 1917, daily

On Microfilm:
1917, March - Dec. 1919
1941, Jan. 1 - Oct. 31, 1947
1951, Jan. - Dec. 1953

In Original:
1917: Mar. 18 - July (Nos. 1-97)
   Rabochii i Soldat, No. 12 (Aug. 18)
   Rabochii, No. 2-10 (Sept. 8-14)
   Rabochii Put', Nos. 1-46 (Sept. 16 - Nov. 8)
    Nos. 170 (101) - 217 (148) (Nov. 9-Dec. 30)
    (Reprint of issues Mar. 18-Sept. 15 in Serial "Pravda"]
1918: Nos. 218 (149) - 227 (Jan. 1-13)
   Nos. 1 (228) - 62 (Jan. 16-Mar. 30)
   Nos. 52, 80-260 (Mar. 22, Apr. 25-Nov. 30)
1919 - 1940
1942 - to present
Missing Numbers in original set; for some of these see the microfilm set
1917: No. 24, 86, 96, 98-99
   Listok Pravdy, no numeration but called No. 100
   Rabochii i Soldat, Nos. 1-11, 13-15 (Aug. 5-17, 19-22)
   Proletarii, Nos. 1-10 (Aug. 26 - Sept. 6)
   Rabochii, Nos. 1, 5, 9, 11-12 (Sept. 7, 10, 13-15)
   Rabochii Put', Nos. 43-44
   (Nos. 172-175, 177-180, 183, 185-186, 188, 192-193, 196-203,
   205-206, 209-211, 214-216) (Nov. 11-14, 16-17, 21, 23-24, 26,
   30, Dec. 5-14, 16-18, 21-24, 27-29)
1918: Jan. 11 (No. 225); Mar. (No. 41 [267]);(Nos. 48-51, 53-79, 82-
   87, 89-90, 92, 95-96, 98-107, 109-112, 114-151, 153-154, 159-
   161, 163-164, 166-225, 233-236, 238, 254, 261 - end of year.
   Mar. 16-21, Mar. 23-Apr. 24, Apr. 27 - May 8, May 10 - 11,
   May 13, May 17 - 18, May 20 - 31, June 2 - 6, June 8 - July 22,
   July 24 - 25, July 31 - Aug. 2, Aug. 4 - 6, Aug. 8 - Oct. 18, Nov. 2,
   Dec. 1 - 31
1919: No. 1
1920: No. 293
1921: No. 221

(Continued on next page)

PRAVDA (Continued)

    Missing nos., cont'd

    1939:   No. 189

    1940:   Nos. 311-320, 322, 323, 325-335, 338-342

    1941:   All nos. missing

    1942:   Nos. 1-177, 120-123, 132-139, 141, 145, 151 - end of year

    1943:   Nos. 1-269, 273, 283, 295, 317 - end of year

    1945:   Nos. 1-22, 29, 32, 34, 43, 50-52, 65, 92-99, 179, 181,
           189-193, 197-202, 204, 206-234, 236-237, 242-252, 258-259,
           261-276, 278, 280-284, 287, 294, 296-297, 300-303, 309;
           Jan. 1-24, Feb. 3, 6-9, 20, Feb. 27 - Mar. 2, Mar. 17,
           Apr. 17-26, July 28, 31, Aug. 4-14, 18-24, 26, Aug. 28-
           Oct. 4, Oct. 9-21, Oct. 28-Nov. 20, Nov. 22, 24-29, Dec. 2,
           11, 14-15, 18-22, 29

                            Ref: Columbia 366; LC, p. 109

PRAVDA

        Organ TSentr. Sev. Oblastn. i Petrograd. Komiteta Rossiiskoi
Kommunisticheskoi Partii (bol'shevikov). Petrograd.

        See Leningradskaia pravda

PRAVDA

        Gazeta dlia russkogo naroda v Soedin. Shtatakh Ameriki.
Philadelphia, Pa., 1901 (?), twice a week

1930, 1932 - 1935

1942, Jan. - Dec. 1945

Missing Numbers:

    1932:   Nos. 35-53

    1933:   Nos. 87, 95-96

    1934:   Nos. 6-28, 31-36, 40, 41, 48-83

    1935:   Nos. 7-11, 15-17, 25, 27

                            Ref: Columbia 367

PRAVDA

        Rabochaia gazeta. [Published by Rossiiskaia sotsial-demokrati-
cheskaia rabochaia partiia, by a group headed by L. Trotsky.]

        Vienna

(All issues on microfilm)

    1908:   Oct. 3 (16), Dec. 17 (31) (Nos. 1, 2)

    1909:   Mar. 27 (Apr. 9) - Dec. 8 (21) (Nos. 3-8)

(Continued on next page)

PRAVDA (Continued)

    (All issues on microfilm)
    1910:   Jan. 1 (14) - Nov. 20 (Dec. 30) (Nos. 9-17)
    1911:   Jan. 29 (Feb. 11) - Dec. 10 (23) (Nos. 18-23)
    1912:   Mar. 14 (27) - Apr. 23 (May 6) (Nos. 24, 25)
        Supplement to No. 21: Svoboda koalitsii i petitsionnaia
kompaniia
        Supplement to May 1, 1911: Pervomaiskii listok rabochei
gazety Pravda
        Numbers 1 and 2 were published in Lvov and carried additional
subtitle: Organ Ukrainskago soiuza "Spilki".
                                 Ref: Columbia 368

PRAVDA

        Vestnik vtorogo kongressa kommunisticheskogo internatsionala.
(Supplement to Pravda, July - August 1920)
        8 issues

PRAVDA GRUZII

        Ezhednevnaia gazeta.   Organ TSentral'nogo i Tifliskogo
komitetov kommunisticheskoi partii i Revoliutsionnogo komiteta
Gruzii. [Organ of the Central and Tiflis Committees of the Communist
Party and of the Revolutionary Committee of Georgia.]
        Tiflis, 1921, daily

    1922:   Feb. 23, Mar. 1 (Nos. 295, 299)
                                  Ref: LC, p. 167

PRAVDA SEVERA

        Organ Sevkraikoma VKP(b), Kraiispolkoma, Kraisovprofa i
Arkhangel'skogo gorkoma VKP(b). [Organ of the Archangel
Provincial Committee and of the City Committee of the All-Union
Communist Party (of Bolsheviks) and of the Provincial Soviet of
Toilers' Deputies.]
        Archangel, 1920, daily

    1936:   Jan. 16, June 6, 12, July 6, Aug. 23, 24 (Nos. 11(4715), 129(4833),
           134(4838), 154(4858), 194(4898), 195(4899))
    1944:   Jan. 19 (No. 14(7112))
                                Ref: LC, p. 3

PRAVDA UKRAINY

Organ TSentral'nogo komiteta KP(b)U, Verkhovnogo soveta i
Soveta narodnykh komissarov USSR. [Organ of the Central Committee
of the Communist Party of the Ukrainian S. S. R., of the Supreme
Soviet and of the Council of Ministers of the Ukrainian S. S. R.]
Kiev, 1939, daily

1945:   July 10-12, 14-15, 17-19, 21-22, 24-26, 28-29; Aug. 1-2, 4,
        7-10, 12, 14-16, 18-19, 21-23, 25-26, 28-30; Sept. 1-3, 6-7,
        9-11, 13-14, 16-19, 21, 23-25, 27, 30-31; Nov. 1, 3-4, 6, 10-11,
        13-15, 17-18, 2022, 24-25, 27-29; Dec. 1-2, 4-5, 7-9, 11-13,
        15, 18-20, 22-23, 25-26
1949, May 17 - to the present

Missing numbers:
1950:   June 16, Nov. 17
1955:   June 12, Aug. 14 - 20, Nov. 9, 13-21
1956:   Jan. 23-24, Feb. 2, 5-8, 10-11, 25 - Mar. 2; May 26-27, 30-31,
        June 29
1962:   Feb. 13, 21, 23-27
1963:   May 14, June 15, 18-23

Ref: Columbia 369, LC, p. 33

PRAVDA VOSTOKA

Organ TSentral'nogo komiteta, Tashkentskogo oblastnogo i
gorodskogo komitetov Kommunisticheskoi partii (b) Uzbekistana i
Verkhovnogo soveta Uzbekskoi SSSR. [Organ of the Central Committee
and the Provincial and City Committees of the Communist Party (of
Bolsheviks) of Uzbekistan and of the Supreme Soviet of the Uzbek SSR.]
Tashkent, Est. 1925

1925:   Sept. 27 (No. 217 [817])
1945:   June 6-7, 18 - Dec. 23
1946:   Jan. 13, 15
1949:   May 17 - Dec. 31
1950:   Jan. 1 - Dec. 31, 1953
1954, July 1, 1954 - to the present

Missing numbers:
1945:   July 11, 25, 29; Aug. 3, 7, 11-14, 18, 22-27, 29; Sept. 2, 9-22,
        25-26, 29; Oct. 1, 9-10, 15-19, 21-25, 29 - Nov. 3, 7, 9, 13,
        17-18, 21, 25, 28, Dec. 7, 9, 11, 15, 18, 22
1949:   July 23, Aug. 2, Oct. 4, Nov. 22, Dec. 14
1951:   Aug. 31
1955:   Aug. 12-14, Nov. 15-18
1959:   Apr. 30
1960:   July 19-21
1961:   Apr. 1, June 3, Aug. 10-16, 29, Oct. 12
1962:   Mar. 17-18, Nov. 22, Dec. 22, 29
1963:   June 18, Sept. 13-14

Ref: Columbia 370, LC, p. 167

PRAVDIVYE IZVESTIIA
Ezhenedel'naia bespartiinaia gazeta, podpol'no vykhodiash-
chaia v gor. Smolenske.
Smolensk, weekly

1919:   Oct. (No. 2)

Ref: LC, p. 161

PRAVITEL'STVENNYI VESTNIK
Vykhodit ezhednevno, krome dnei posleprazdnichnykh.
Omsk, Est. 1918, daily

1919:   July 15 - Aug. 23, 31 - Sept. 6, 9-13, 16-23, 25-27, Oct. 3-4,
8-18, 21-24, Nov. 9 (Nos. 184-217, 223-228, 230-233, 235-241,
243-245, 248, 249, 252-260, 262-265, 278)
Superseded Vestnik Vremennago Vserossiiskago Pravitel'stva
Ref: Columbia 371, LC, p. 140

PRAVITEL'STVENNYI VESTNIK
Poslednie novosti.
Petrograd, daily (morning and evening edition)

1914, Aug. 5 - Nov. 16, 1915 (Nos. 1-609)

PRAVITEL'STVENNYI VESTNIK
Petrograd, daily, Est. 1869

1893:   Jan. - Dec.
1894:   Index only
1895:   Jan. 6, 8, 21, 26; Feb. 10, 15; Mar. 5, 17, 25, 28, 29, 31;
Apr. 7; May 21, 25
1899:   Jan. 1
1901:   Mar. 6, 13
1914:   Jan. 1 - Dec. 31
1915:   Jan. 3 - 1916, Dec. 31
Missing numbers:
1893:   Nos. 149, 168, 202, 207, 208, 214-216, 266-269, 275-276
1915:   Nos. 1, 6, 7, 14, 21, 23-25, 34-37, 41, 54, 61, 63-69, 80, 93,
95, 97-108, 110-116, 118, 120, 122, 124-140, 142-146, 150-162,
164-171, 173-177, 180-182, 185-191, 200, 212
1916:   Nos. 4, 26-28, 30, 32, 38, 51, 53, 55, 56, 59, 61, 69-81, 84,
85, 87, 107-111, 116, 127, 138, 139, 172-185, 142, 199, 208, 223-
225, 230, 231, 243
1917:   Jan. 1 - Feb. 25
As of March 5(18), 1917, continued as Vestnik Vremennago
Pravitel'stva

Ref: Beliaeva 6288; Columbia 372;
LC, p. 68; Lisovskii 1005

PRAVOSLAVNAIA KARPATSKAIA RUS'
>TSerkovno-narodnyi organ pravoslavnago dvizheniia na Karpatskoi i Priashevskoi Rusi.
>S. Vladimirova, 1928, semimonthly

1928:   Apr. 17 (No. 2)
1929:   Nov. 15 (No. 22)
1932:   Feb. - May, June - Dec. (Nos. 2-10, 12-24)
1933   - June 1939
Missing numbers:
1936:   Nos. 22(204) - 24(206)
>Title varies: Jan. 1935 - Pravoslavnaia Rus'.
>>Ref: Columbia 373

PRAVOSLAVNAIA RUS' see PRAVOSLAVNAIA KARPATSKAIA RUS'

PRAVOSLAVNYI SIBIRIAK
>Gazeta politicheskaia i literaturnaia, vykhodit v gor. Krasnoiarske, Eniseiskoi gubernii.
>Krasnoiarsk, 1906, 3 times a week

1906:   Oct. 22 - Dec. 24 (Nos. 1-18)
>>Ref: Beliaeva 6307

PRIAMURSKIIA VEDOMOSTI
>Khabarovsk, 1894, weekly

1895:   Jan. - Dec. 17 (Nos. 53-103)
>>Ref: Lisovskii 2392
>>Beliaeva 6334

PRIAZOVSKII KRAI
>Ezhednevnaia gazeta politicheskaia, ekonomicheskaia i literaturnaia. Osnovana S. Kh. Artiunovym.
>Rostov-on-Don, 1891, daily

1918:   Dec. 21(Jan. 3) (No. 226)
1919:   Jan. 10(23), 22(Feb. 4), Mar. 23(Apr. 3), May 18(31), Sept. 18 (Oct. 1), 21(Oct. 4), Oct. 27 (Nov. 9) - 31(Nov. 13), Nov. 29 (Dec. 12) - Dec. 5(18), 10(23) (Nos. 8, 18, 68, 112, 211, 214, 243-246, 270-275, 278)
>>Ref: Beliaeva 6329; LC, p. 151;
>>Lisovskii 2128

PRIBOI

Organ sevastopol'skogo i krymskogo oblastnogo komiteta
R. S. D. R. P. [Organ of the Sevastopol and Crimean Provincial
Committee of the Russian Social Democratic Workers Party.]
Sevastopol, Est. 1917, daily

1919: May - Aug.

Ref: Columbia 374; LC, p. 158

PRIKARPATSKAIA RUS'

Ezhednevnaia politicheskaia, obshchestvennaia i literaturnaia
gazeta; organ Russkoi narodnoi organizatsii v Galichine.
Lvov, daily

1915: Apr. 13 (No. 1614)

PRIKARPATSKAIA RUS'

Organ Russkago Ispolnitel'nago Komiteta vo L'vove.
Lvov, 1919

1920: Jan. 23 (No. 46)

PRIMORSKAIA ZHIZN'

Organ nezavisimoi demokraticheskoi mysli. Gazeta
ezhednevnaia, vnepartiinaia, posviashchennaia interesam russkago
D. V. i zhizni sopredel'nykh s nami stran.
Vladivostok, 1918, daily

1918: July 25(Aug. 7) (No. 1)

Ref: LC, p. 182

PRIURAL'SKAIA PRAVDA

Organ Miasskogo ukoma, Uispolkoma i Gorsoveta. [Organ of
the Miass District Committee, of the District Executive Committee
and of the City Soviet.]
Miass, Cheliabinskaia gub., 3 w.

1922: Mar. 12 (No. 27[116])

Ref: LC, p. 13

PRIZYV
>
> Ezhednevnaia gazeta.
> Kharbin, daily

1918: June 4-7, 9-18, 20-26, 28 - July 14, 16, 19-20, 24-26, 31,
Aug. 14-15, 21-23, 25, 28 - Sep. 4, 6 - 10, 14, 17, 19 - 21, 25 -
Oct. 12, 16, 17, 20 - 22, Nov. 1, 3 - 24 (Nos. 68-71, 73-79,
81-85, 87-100, 102, 104, 105, 108-110, 114, 125, 126, 130-132,
134, 136-141, 143-146, 148, 150, 152-154, 156-170, 172, 173,
176-177, 186, 188-205)

PROBUZHDENIIA ROSSII; GOLOS ROND'a
>
> Organ Rossiiskogo osvoboditel'nogo narodnogo dvizheniia
> (Rossiiskoe natsional-sotsialisticheskoe dvizhenie trudiashchikhsia)
> Berlin, weekly

1933: June 25 (No. 3)

Ref: Columbia 378

PRODOVOL'STVENNAIA GAZETA
>
> [Published by the People's Commissariat for Food Supply]
> Moscow, 1921

1921, Jan. 13 - May 27, 1922
Missing numbers:
>
> 3, 5, 9, 66, 69-94, 112, 118, 128, 140, 142, 143, 156, 161-
> 176, 192

Ref: LC, p. 112

PROFESSIONAL'NOE DVIZHENIE
>
> Izdanie Vserossiiskogo tsentral'nogo i Moskovskogo sovetov
> professional'nykh soiuzov. [Published by the All-Russian Central
> Soviet and the Council of Labor Unions.]
> Moscow, 1919

1919: August 1 (No. 22)

Ref: LC, p. 112

PROGRESS
>
> Ezhenedel'naia gazeta.
> New York, 1892

1892: March 4, 18 (No. 13, 15)

Ref: Columbia 380

PROLETARII
Tsentral'nyi organ Rossiiskoi sotsial-demokraticheskoi rabochei
partii.
Geneva, irreg., weekly

1905:   May 27(14) - Nov. 25(12) (Nos. 1-26)
Ref: Columbia 381

PROLETARII
Organ Mosk., SPB., Mosk., okr., Kazansk., Kursk. i Permsk.
komitetov, R.S.D.R.P.
Moscow

1907:   Oct. 20 (No. 17)

PROLETARII
Organ Biuro Moskovskikh organizatsii Rossiiskoi sotsial-
demokraticheskoi rabochei partii.
Moscow, 1917, daily

1917:   June 17(29) (No. 44)
Ref: LC, p. 109 (Pravda)

PROLETARII
Organ S. Peterburgskago i Moskovskago komitetov R.S.D.R.P.
Paris, weekly

1906 - 1909 : Nos. 1, 4-7, 9, 11-13, 16-19, 21-50
Subtitles vary: Nos. 1-20 - Organ Mosk., Spb., Mosk. okr.,
Kazansk., Kursk. i Permsk. komitetov R.S. - D.R.P.
Nos. 1-20 have been published in Vyborg; Nos. 21-40 - in
Geneva; Nos. 41-50 - in Paris.

PROLETARII see also PRAVDA

PROLETARSKAIA MYSL'
Ezhednevnaia rabochaia gazeta, organ Zlatoustovskogo
okruzhkoma VKP(b), Okrispolkoma, Okrprofbiuro i raikoma V.S.R.M.
Zlatoust, 1928, daily

1928:   Apr. 27, May 9, 13, 20, 22, 25, 26, 27; June 1, 6, 7, 21;
Nov. 14, 15-17 (Nos. 98(1822), 106(1820), 110(1834), 116(1840),
117(1841), 120(1844)-122(1846), 126(1850), 129(1853), 130(1854),
142(1866), 263(1987)-266(1990))

PROLETARSKAIA PRAVDA

Ezhednevnaia gazeta Kievskogo gubkoma KRPU i Gubprofsoveta.
[Published by the Kiev Provincial Committee of the Communist Party
(of Bolsheviks) of the Ukrainian S. S. R. and the Provincial Labor
Union Council]

Kiev, 1921, daily

1922:   March 11 (No. 56(169))

Ref: LC, p. 33

PROMYSLOVYI VESTNIK

Ezhednevnaia rabochaia obshchestvenno-ekonomicheskaia i
literaturnaia gazeta, posviashchennaia vyiasneniiu i zashchite
interesov promyslovo-zavodskogo proletariata.

Baku, 1907, daily

1907-1908: Nos. 1-3, 7-10, 26-27 (microfilm)

Ref: Beliaeva 6466

PROSTAIA GAZETA SOTSIALISTOV-REVOLIUTSIONEROV DLIA GORODA I
DEREVNI

Petrograd, 1917, daily

1917:   Oct. 23, (No. 13)
Continued as Novaia prostaia gazeta as of Dec. 1917

Ref: LC, p. 68

PSKOVSKII NABAT

Ezhednevnaia gazeta Okruzhkoma VKP(b), Okrispolkoma i
Okrprofbiuro

Pskov, 1917, daily

1928:   Nov. 15, 16, 18, 20, 29, 30; Dec. 21, 22, 28 (Nos. 265-266,
268, 269, 277-278, 296, 297, 299)

PSKOVSKII PAKHAR'

Pskov, twice a week

1928:   Apr. 14-24, May 12 (Nos. 30(264) - 33(267), 37(271))

PUT'

Helsinki, daily

1921, Feb. 1-Jan. 8, 1922 (Nos. 1-267)

PUT'

Ezhednevnaia politicheskaia, obshchestvennaia i literaturnaia gazeta.

Moscow, 1906, daily

1906: Nos. 1-4; 6-16; 18-41; 43-48; 50-60, 62-75; 77-78; 80; 83-94; 96-100; 102-107 (Microfilm)

Ref: Beliaeva 6610

PUT' BEDNIAKA

Organ El'ninskogo ukoma R. K. P. (b) i uezdnogo ispol. komit. Sov. rab., kr. i kr. dep.

El'nia, Smolenskoi gub.

1921: Nov. 7 (No. 31)

PUT' OKTIABRIA

Organ Okruzhkoma VKP(b), Okrispolkoma i Okrprofsoveta. St. -Oskol, 1929, 3 times a week

1930: May 24 (No. 53(60))

PUT' RABOTNITSY I KREST'IANKI

Odnodnevnaia gazeta otdela rabotnits i krest'ianok pri Peterburgskom gubernskom komitete RKP. [One day newspaper. Published by the Section of Women Workers and Peasants of the Petersburg Provincial Committee of the Russian Communist Party.]

Petrograd, 1920, Nov. 7 (4 p.)

Ref: LC, p. 68

PUT' REVOLIUTSII

Organ Alatyrskogo uispolkoma i ukoma RKP(bol'sh.). [Organ of the Alatyr' District Executive Committee and of the District Committee of the Russian Communist Party (of Bolsheviks).]

Alatyr', Simbirskoi gub., 1918

1921: Nov. 6 (No. 162(261))

Ref: LC, p. 1

R

R. N. S. D.

Osvedomitel'nyi vestnik Otdela propagandy R. N. S. D. Ezhemesiachnaia gazeta Rossiiskago natsional'nago fronta.
Berlin, 1937, monthly

1938:   March, May-Dec. (Nos. 16, 18-26)
1939:   Jan. - Aug.

RABOCHAIA GAZETA

Ezhednevnaia gazeta TS K Vsesoiuznoi Kommunisticheskoi Partii (b-v). [Published by the Central Committee of the All-Union Communist Party (of Bolsheviks.]
Moscow, 1922, daily

1923:   Sept. 20 (No. 211)
1926:   (No. 278)
1927:   Jan. 1-4 (Nos. 1-2)

Ref: LC, p. 113

RABOCHAIA GAZETA

Organ Tsentral'nago komiteta Rossiiskoi sotsial'demokraticheskoi rabochei partii.
Paris, 1910

1910, Nov. 12 (Oct. 31) - Aug. 12 (July 30), 1912 (Nos. 1-9)
Ref: Columbia 387

RABOCHAIA GAZETA

Organ Ts. K. Rossiiskoi Sotsial-Demokraticheskoi Rabochei Partii (Ob"edinennoi). [Organ of the Central Committee of the Russian Social Democratic Workers' Party (United).]
Continued as <u>Luch'</u> as of Nov. 19, 1917.
Petrograd, 1917, daily

1917:   March - Dec. (Microfilm)
Also in original:
1917:   Nos. 1-148, 158, 169, 175-181, 186, 189-194, 195, 196-206, 211

(Continued on next page)

RABOCHAIA GAZETA (Continued)

    1926:   279(1421) - 303(1445)
    1927:   1(1446) - 15(1460), 17(1462) - 18(1463), 20(1465) - 24(1469),
            26(1471) - 27(1472)
                              Ref: Columbia 388, LC, p. 69

RABOCHAIA GAZETA
       Organ nezavisimoi sotsial'noi rabochei partii.
       St. Petersburg, 1906, daily

    1906, 1908 (Microfilm)
                        Ref: Beliaeva 6648

RABOCHAIA I KREST'IANSKAIA KRASNAIA ARMIIA I FLOT
       Organ Narodnogo komissariata po voennym i morskim delam.
    [Organ of the Council of People's Commissars for the Army and Navy.]
       Continuation of Armiia i flot rabochei i krest'ianskoi Rossii.
       As of May 1, 1918, continued as Krasnaia armiia.
       Petrograd, daily

    1918:   Jan. 31 - Apr. 30 (Nos. 1(46) - 74(119)
                        Ref: Columbia 389, LC, p. 69

RABOCHAIA MOLVA
       Izd. sots.-dem. (bol'shevikov).
       St. Petersburg, 1906

    1907:   March 1 (No. 1)
                     Ref: Beliaeva 6651, Columbia 390

RABOCHAIA MOSKVA
       Organ MK VKP(b) Mosk. soveta RK i K Dep. i MGSPS. [Organ
    of the Moscow Committee of the All-Union Communist Party
    (of Bolsheviks) of the Moscow Soviet of Workers', Soldiers' and
    Peasants' Deputies and of the Moscow City Council of Labor Unions.]
       Continuation of Kommunisticheskii trud. Continued as
    Moskovskii bol'shevik as of Mar. 1, 1939.
       Moscow, 1922, daily

    1922 - 1923
    Missing numbers:
    1922:   (Nos. 33, 139)
    1923:   (Nos. 1(273), 22(294), 46(318), 48(320), 107(380))
                        Ref: Columbia 391, LC, p. 113

RABOCHAIA MYSL'

Gazeta Peterburgskikh rabochikh, organ St. Peterburgskago komiteta Rossiiskoi sotsial-demokraticheskoi partii - St. Pet. Soiuza bor'by za osvobozhdenie rabochago klassa.
St. Petersburg

1898:   Nos. 4-16
1900:   No. 8

RABOCHAIA MYSL'

Sotsial'no-ekonomicheskaia, obshchestvenno-literaturnaia, politicheskaia i illiustrirovannaia gazeta.
St. Petersburg, 1906, 1-3 times a week

1906:   Jan. 21 (No. 1)

Ref: Beliaeva 6652

RABOCHAIA ZHIZN'

Ezhednevnaia gazeta.
Moscow, daily

1918:   Sept. 16 (No. 28)

Ref: LC, p. 113

RABOCHAIA ZHIZN'

Ezhemesiachnaia sotsial-demokraticheskaia gazeta.
Paris

1911:   Nos. 1, 2, 3 (Microfilm)

Ref: Columbia 392

RABOCHEE UTRO

Obshchestvenno-politicheskaia i literaturnaia gazeta.
St. Petersburg, 1915, 1-6 times a week

1915:   Nos. 1-3, 5 (Microfilm)

Ref: Beliaeva 6658

RABOCHEE ZNAMIA

Organ russkikh anarkhistov-kommunistov.
Lausanne

1915:   March-June (No. 1-3)

RABOCHII
Organ TSentral'nogo komiteta Rossiiskoi kommunisticheskoi partii. [Organ of the Central Committee of the Russian Communist Party.]
Moscow, daily

1922: March 12 (No. 11)
Ref: LC, p. 114

RABOCHII
Izd. partii sotsialistov-revoliutsionerov.
Paris

1911: Nov. (No. 1)

RABOCHII
Gazeta Partii russkikh sotsial-demokratov (blagoevtsev).
St. Petersburg, 1885

1885: Jan. - July (Nos. 1-2) (this is a 1928 reprint of the original)

RABOCHII
Organ TSentral'nogo biuro professional'nykh soiuzov g. Vladivostoka. [Organ of the Central Bureau of the Vladivostok Labor Unions.]
Vladivostok, 1918, daily

1918: July 14(1), 21(8), 23(10) (Nos. 2, 6, 7)
Ref: LC, p. 182

RABOCHII GOLOS
Organ gruppy rabochikh sotsial-demokratov, posviashchennyi preimushchestvenno prakticheskim zadacham rabochego dvizheniia.
St. Petersburg, 1905, weekly

1905: Nov. 26 (Microfilm)
Ref: Beliaeva 6665

RABOCHII I ISKUSSTVO
Massovaia gazeta po voprosam iskusstva.
Moscow, weekly

1929: Nov. 30, Dec. 21/27 (Nos. 1-4, 7)
Ref: LC, p. 114

RABOCHII I KREST'IANIN
>   Organ TSentral'n. biuro prof. soiuzov. [Organ of the Central
> Bureau of Labor Unions.]
>   Vladivostok, 1918, daily

>   1918: July 26(13), Aug. 9(June 27) (Nos. 1(9), 12(20)
> Ref: LC, p. 182

RABOCHII I PAKHAR'
>   Organ Rybinskogo ukoma VKP(b), Uispolkoma Uprofbiuro.
>   Rybinsk, daily

>   1928:   Apr. 29 (No. 100)

RABOCHII I SOLDAT
>   Ezhednevnaia gazeta.
>   [One of the continuations of Pravda, preceeded by Listok Pravdy,
> and superseded by Proletarii. For complete history see Pravda; organ
> tsentral'nogo i MK VKP(b).]
>   Petrograd, daily

>   1917:   Aug. 18 (No. 12)

> Ref: Columbia 398

RABOCHII-KHIMIK
>   Ezhenedel'naia gazeta TSentral'nogo komiteta Vserossiiskogo
> soiuza rabochikh khimicheskoi promyshlennosti. [Published by the
> Central Committee of the All-Russian Union of Chemical Industry
> Workers.]
>   Moscow, 1921, weekly

>   1921:   June 28 - Oct. 10 (Nos. 1-11)
> Ref: LC, p. 114

RABOCHII KLICH
>   Organ Riazanskogo gubkoma VKP(b), Gubispolkoma i Gub-
> profsoveta.
>   Riazan

>   1928:   Mar. 2 (No. 53)

RABOCHII KRAI
>   Ezhednevnaia gazeta Ivanovo-Voznesenskogo gubkoma VKP(b),
> Gubispolkoma, Gorsoveta i Gubprofsoveta. [Organ of the Ivanovo-
> Voznesensk Provincial and City Soviets of Toilers' Deputies and of the
> Provincial Committee.]
>   Ivanovo-Voznesensk, 1917, daily

(Continued on next page)

RABOCHII KRAI (continued)

    1922: Mar. 10 (No. 59)
    1928: Mar. 6, 9-11, 15-17, 21-25, 27, 29, Apr. 10 (Nos. 56(2959),
          57, 59(2962) - 61(2964), 63(2966) - 65(2967), 68(2971) -
          73(2976), 75(2978), 85(2988)
                                 Ref: LC, p. 22

RABOCHII NAROD
        Organ Revoliutsionnoi sotsial-demokraticheskoi (bol'shevistskoi)
    rabochei organizatsii.
        Winnipeg, Man., weekly

    1918: Jan. 4, Mar. 9, Apr. 13, 20, July 13 (Nos. 2, 10, 15, 16, 28)

RABOCHII PUT'
        Professional'naia gazeta.
        Chita

    1922: No. 86 (Microfilm)

RABOCHII PUT'
        Organ Omskogo gubispolkoma i Gubkoma RKP (bol'shevikov).
    [Organ of the Omsk Provincial Executive Committee and of the
    Provincial Committee of the Russian Communist Party.]
        Omsk, 1921

    1921: Nov. 6 (No. 123)
    1922: Mar. 12 (No. 59)
                            Ref: LC, p. 140

RABOCHII PUT'; Tsentral'nyi organ RSDRP. (Petrograd.) see PRAVDA;
Organ tsentralnogo komiteta i MK VKP(b)

RABOCHII PUT'
        Ezhednevnaia gazeta Smolenskogo Gubkoma RKP i Gubispol-
    koma S. r., k. i k. d. [Organ of the Smolensk Provincial and City
    Committees of the All-Union Communist Party (of Bolsheviks) and of
    the Provincial and City Soviets of Workers' Deputies.]
        Smolensk, 1918, daily

    1922: Mar. 12 (No. 55)
    1928: Mar. 1, 17-20, 22, 27, Apr. 14-18, 20-22, 25-27, May 11, 29,
          31, June 8-13 (Nos. 52, 65-67, 69, 73, 89, 90, 91, 93-95, 97-
          99, 108, 123, 125, 131-135)
                            Ref: LC, p. 161

RABOTNIK

Gazeta dlia russkikh rabochikh. (Organ russkikh bakunistov N. Zhukovskogo, Ralli i dr.)

Geneva, 1875

1876: Jan. - Mar. (No. 13-15)

RADIOGRAMMY VSESOIUZNOGO RADIOKOMITETA PRI SOVNARKOME SOIUZA SSR.

Moscow, weekly

1938: Jan. - Dec. (Nos. 1(18) - 21(182) (Nos. 4(184) - 60(140))
1939: Jan. - Apr. 11 (Nos. 3(243) - 7(247), 9(249) - 15(255), 17(257))

RANNEE UTRO

Vykhodit ezhednevno, krome dnei posleprazdnichnykh. Bol'-shaia ezhednevnaia politicheskaia, obshchestvennaia i literaturnaia gazeta. Izdanie Moskovskago T-va izdatel'stva i pechati "Pechatnoe slovo".

Moscow, 1889, daily

1917: June 17 (No. 136(9242))
1918: Apr. 4(Mar. 22), 6(Mar. 24), 10(Mar. 28), 11(Mar. 29), 17(4) (Nos. 55(9439), 57(9441), 60(9444), 61(4445), 66(4450))

Ref: Beliaeva 6698, LC, p. 114

RANNEE UTRO

New York, daily

1932, Dec. 28-Feb. 1, 1933 (Nos. 1-36)

Ref: Columbia 404

RASSVET

Ezhednevnaia gazeta rossiiskikh rabochikh organizatsii Soedinennykh Shtatov i Kanady.

Continued as Vse novosti.

Chicago, New York, 1918, daily

1924: Nos. 166, 172-176
1925: Nos. 180-181, 184-186, 188-193, 196-197, 201, 204, 205, 208, 212-213, 216-218, 221, 223, 224, 259, 265, 292-294, 298, 300-302, 307, 310-312, 320, 322, 323, 325, 328-329, 342, 350, 359, 363, 366-368, 371, 373-374, 383-384, 393-394, 397, 441, 449, 445
1926: Nos. 540-541, 546, 550, 563, 577, 580, 587-591, 593, 596, 598-602

(Continued on next page)

RASSVET (continued)

    1927
    1929 - 1934
    1935: (Jan. - July 27) Nos. 1-176
    1940: Nos. 191-308 (Aug. 13 - Dec. 31)
    Missing Numbers:

    1927: Nos. 8, 11, 13, 52, 68, 72, 78, 99, 110, 111, 132, 204, 210,
            229, 242, 255, 261, 295, 301
    1929: Nos. 1-77, 80, 230
    1931: Nos. 180, 238, 299, 303
    1933: Nos. 39, 83, 136, 138, 165, 167, 169, 176, 189, 192, 207, 209,
            212, 220, 225, 246, 252
    1934: Nos. 19-45, 47-90, 93, 97-113, 125-128, 147-148, 154-174,
            176-246, 248-253, 261, 263, 291-293
    1935: Nos. 3, 5, 7-8, 18-19, 21, 23, 26, 28-30, 43, 47, 48, 50, 55,
            59, 60, 69-71, 75-78, 80, 82-83, 169
                                   Ref: Columbia 406

RAZA

    Organ independent al unniunei clerului din Basarabia.
    See SVET; izdanie soiuza bessarabskago dukhovenstva.

RAZSVIET

    Ezhednevnaia gazeta.
    Helsinki, daily

    1919: Nov. 14 - Dec. 16 (Nos. 1-28)
    1920: Jan. 5 - Feb. 11 (Nos. 1, 3-5, 7-11, 24-33)

RAZSVIET

    Vladivostok, weekly

    1921: Apr. 11 (No. 20) (Microfilm)
                             Ref. LC, p. 182

RECH'

    Politicheskaia, literaturnaia i ekonomicheskaia gazeta,
    izdavaemaia v St. Peterburge V. D. Nabokovym i Petrunkevichem pri
    blizhaishem uchastii P. N. Miliukova i I. V. Gessena.
    St. Petersburg, Mar. 1906, daily

    1906: Mar. 2(15), May 2(15), Aug. 16(29) - 31(Sept. 13), Nov. 29(D. 12),
            30(13), Dec. 6(18) (Nos. 8, 62, 139-152, 229, 230, 235)
    1913: Sept. 5 - Nov. 16, 1917

(Continued on next page)

RECH' (continued)
Missing Numbers:

1913: Jan. 1 - Sept. 5, 8, 11, 15, 22, Oct. 27, 29, Nov. 24 (Nos. 1-
241, 245, 248, 250, 252, 259, 294, 296, 322)
1914: Aug. 16, Sept. 14, 21, Oct. 30 (Nos. 218, 247, 254, 293)
1915: Feb. 2-10, 13, 22, March 13, Apr. 19, May 11, 12, 18, July 1,
7, 17, Sept. 1, 13, 18, Nov. 1, 2, 29, Dec. 1-6, 11, 17, 18, 20,
24 (Nos. 33-39, 42, 51, 70, 106, 127, 128, 123, 178, 184, 194,
240, 252, 257, 301, 302, 329, 331-336, 341, 347, 348, 350, 354)
1916: Feb. 4, 5, 11, 17, Mar. 6, 7, Apr. 15, 18, July 18, Nov. 12,
Dec. 6, 7, 24 (Nos. 34, 35, 41, 64, 65, 102, 105, 205, 312,
336, 337, 354)
1917: Jan. 1-11, 15-18, 20, 22, 26-29, Feb. 2-11, 15, 16, 18, 19,
21-24, 16, Oct. 26 - to end of the year. (Nos. 1-9, 12-15, 18, 20,
22, 24-27, 29, 31-39, 43, 44, 46, 47, 49, 51-54, 253 - to end of
the year.)
Continued under the following titles:
Nasha rech', Nov. 16, 1917
Svobodnaia rech', Nov. 19, 1917
Novaia rech', Nov. 28, 1917

Ref: Beliaeva 6743; Columbia 407;
LC, p. 70

RECHNOI TRANSPORT
Organ Narodnogo komissariata rechnogo flota SSSR i TS K
Profsoiuza rabochikh rechnogo transporta. [Organ of the Ministry
of the Ocean and River Fleet of the U.S.S.R. and of the Central
Committee of the Labor Union of River Transportation Workers.]
Moscow, 1932, weekly, semiweekly

1945: July 3017, Aug. 3, 10-24, Sept. 7-8, 25 (Nos. 36-52, 55-6)
Ref: LC, p. 115

REFORMA
St. Petersburg, 1906, daily

1906: Apr. - May (Nos. 1, 4, 11, 12, 13, 16, 18, 20, 35)
Ref: Beliaeva 6740

REVEL'SKOE SLOVO
Ezhednevnaia obshchestvenno-politicheskaia gazeta.
Revel, 1917, daily

(Continued on next page)

REVEL'SKOE SLOVO (Continued)

1917:   Nos. 50, 61, 66-69, 71, 76-77, 99-100, 105-106, 109-113, 115-
116, 118-123, 126-131, 133-134, 136-142 (Mar. 2(15), 16(29),
22(Apr. 4)-27 (Apr. 9), 29 (Apr. 11), Apr. 7(20) - 8(21),
May 5(18) - 6(19), 13(26) - 15(28), 18(31) - 25 (June 7), 27 (June 9)-
29 (June 11), 31 (June 13), June 1 (14) - 6 (19), 9 (22) - 15 (23),
17 (30) - 19 (July 2), 21 (July 4) - 29 (July 12)

1918:   Nos. 1-4, 13-15, 17

1919:   Nos. 41, 54, 68-70, 72-74, 80, 82-84, 86-97, 99-120

Ref: LC, p. 165

REVOLIUTSIONNYI NAROD

Gazeta Petrogradskoi voennoi organizatsii partii sotsialistov-
revoliutsionerov.

Petrograd

1917:   July 4-9, 18, 21

REVOLIUTSIONNYI VOSTOCHNYI TURKESTAN

Tashkent

1946:   July 30, Dec. 26, 28 (Nos. 22, 140, 141, 493, 611, 612)

1947:   Jan. 15, 18, Mar. 30, Apr. 26 (Nos. 9, 11, 72, 90, 624, 626,
687, 705)

RODINA

Lausanne

1920:   Feb. 5 - Oct. 23 (Nos. 1-12)

RODINA

Moscow, 1918, daily

1918:   Apr. 9(Mar. 27), May 10(Apr. 27) (Nos. 2, 24)

Ref: LC, p. 115

RODINA

Ezhednevnaia obshchestvenno-politicheskaia i literaturnaia
gazeta pod redaktsiei E. A. Efimovskago.

Paris, daily

1925:   Feb. 1 - Mar. 29 (Nos. 1, 2, 5-6)

Ref: Columbia 414

RODNAIA ZEMLIA
>   Le pays natal.
>   [Editor: G. A. Aleksinskii]
>   Paris, 1925, semimonthly

>   1925:   Feb. 1 - Oct. 5 (Nos. 1-9, 12-24, 26-34)
>   1927:   Aug. 1 - Dec. 15 (Nos. 1-10)
>   Ref: Columbia 415

ROSSIIA
>   Izdanie Soiuza russkikh pisatelei i zhurnalistov.
>   Belgrad, 1926, irregular

>   1934:   Nov. 17 (No. 31)
>   1935:   Nov. 3 (No. 33)

ROSSIIA
>   Obshchestvennaia, literaturnaia, politicheskaia i profess.
>   gazeta. Vykhodit ezhednevno, krome dnei posleprazdnichnykh.
>   Kharbin, 1921, daily

>   1922:   Apr. 21 (No. 83(248))

ROSSIIA
>   Stavit svoei tsel'iu obshcherusskoe natsional'no-narodnoe
>   ob"edinenie i osvoboditel'nuiu bor'bu.
>   New York, 1933, daily

>   1954, Jan.-Dec. 31, 1960

ROSSIIA
>   Parizhskaia ezhednevnaia gazeta. La Russie.
>   Paris, 1919, daily

>   1919, Dec. 17-Mar. 24, 1920 (Nos. 1-4, 6-10, 13, 19(def), 20 (def),
>   22, 26-27, 29, 33-34, 36, 42, 45, 51
>   Ref: Columbia 419

ROSSIIA
>   Ezhenedel'naia gazeta pod redaktsiei Petra Struve.
>   Continued as Rossiia i slavianstvo.
>   Paris, weekly

>   Aug. 28, 1927 - May 26, 1928 (Nos. 1-37)
>   Ref: Columbia 420

ROSSIIA

Ezhednevnaia gazeta.
Petrograd, 1918, daily

1918:   Jan. 26, 27 (Feb. 8-9) (Nos. 2, 3)
                                Ref: LC, p. 70

ROSSIIA

Russkaia natsional'naia gazeta pod redaktsiei N. V. Kolesnikova.
Shanghai, 1924, weekly

1925:   July 21 - Oct. 25 (Nos. 171, 203, 237-239, 579-581)
1927:   Dec. 3-4, 7
1928:   Nov. 18, Dec. 2, 9 (Nos. 1018, 1020-1021)
1929:   Jan. 1 (No. 1023)
                                Ref: Columbia 422

ROSSIIA I SLAVIANSTVO

Organ natsional'no-osvoboditel'noi bor'by i slavianskoi
vzaimnosti. Ezhenedel'naia gazeta pri blizhaishem uchastii Petra
Struve.
Continuation of Rossiia.
Paris, weekly

1928, Dec. 1-June 1933 (Nos. 1-233)
Missing no. :
1931:   Feb. (No. 116)
                                Ref: Columbia 423

ROSSIIA ZA RUBEZHOM

Organ Kraevogo pravleniia Soiuza russkago sokol'stva vo
Frantsii. Ezhemesiachnaia gazeta-zhurnal pod redaktsiei I. A.
Kirilova.
Paris, monthly, irregular

1935, March-May 1936 (Nos. 1-6)
                                Ref: Columbia 424

ROSSIISKAIA RESPUBLIKA

Ezhednevnaia politicheskaia, obshchestvennaia, literaturnaia
i ekonomicheskaia gazeta. [Publication of the Joint-Stock Company
"Svobodnaia Pechat' ".]
Petrograd, 1917, daily

1917:   Apr. 11, 12 (Nos. 5, 6)
                                Ref: Columbia 425, LC, p. 70

RUL'

Vykhodit ezhednevno v Berline.   Osnovan I. V. Gessenom,
Prof. A. I. Kaminka i V. D. Nabokovym.
Berlin, 1920, daily

1920-1931: Nos. 28, 31-102, 104-205, 207-228, 230-252, 254-265, 267-270,
272-273, 275-279, 281-285, 287, 289-370, 374-375, 377-392,
394,420, 422-490, 493-497, 499, 503-515, 517-519, 603-607,
1082, 1157-1207, 1209-1213, 1215-1367, 1369-1379, 1383, 1391-
1425, 1428-1436, 1439-1442, 1496-1499, 1502, 1505-1507, 1509-
1510, 1515-1516, 1520, 1545-2461, 2486, 2741, 2800, 2931, 2933-
2985, 2987-3091, 3093-3127, 3129-3309)
Ref: Columbia 427

RUL'

Ezhednevnaia natsional'no-demokraticheskaia gazeta.
Omsk, 1919, daily

1919:   Nov. 1 (No. 95)

RUL'

Vecherniaia gazeta.
Vladivostok

1922:   June 3, 5, 7, 8 (Nos. 104-105, 107, 108)
Ref: LC, p. 182

RUPOR

Ezhednevnaia vecherniaia demokraticheskaia gazeta.
Kharbin, 1921, daily

1929:   Feb. 23 - Dec. 13 (Nos. 7, 40-60, 62-65, 67, 70-74, 77-79,
85-86, 89-91, 93-96, 98-114, 117-130, 133-146, 148, 150-154,
157-159, 163, 165, 230, 248, 257, 325, 330)
1932:   July 26 - Aug. 26 (Nos. 202, 206-209, 217-226, 231-233)
1933:   Jan. 1-7, 15 - Feb. 7, 11-24, Mar. 1 - Apr. 16, 22-25, May
3-5, 10-23, June 28 - July 4, 26 - Aug. 4, 13-19, 27 - Sept.
2, 17 - 19, 26-30, Oct. 7-10, 21-31, Nov. 29 - Dec. 1, 6-14,
16-23, 25 (Nos. 1-5, 12-35, 39-52, 57-101, 105-108, 116-118,
123-136, 171-177, 199-201, 203-208, 217-223, 231-237, 252-254,
261-265, 272-275, 286-296, 325-327, 332-338, 342-349, 351
1934:   Apr. 30 - May 27, Aug. 27 - Sept. 8, Oct. 8-28, Nov. 19 -
Dec. 23 (Nos. 113-118, 127-132, 134-140, 231-243, 273-285,
287-294, 316-322, 344-350)
1935:   Feb. 6 - May 25 (Nos. 32-34, 85-87, 113, 135-318)

RUS'
___

        Russkaia natsional'naia gazeta.
        Buenos Aires, 1936

1937:   Jan. 7, Mar. 6 (Nos. 13 17)
                              Ref: Columbia 428

RUS'
___

        Ezhednevnaia utrenniaia gazeta, organ russkoi obshchestvennoi
mysli.
        Kharbin, daily

1932:   Nov. 10 (No. 15)
1933:   Jan. 1 (No. 58)

RUS'
___

        Ezhednevnaia natsional'no-demokraticheskaia gazeta. [Pub-
lished by the Union of Siberian Butter-Making Artels and the Union
of Siberian Credit Associations.]
        Subtitle varies: July 8 - Sept. 8, 1919, Demokraticheskii organ
sel'sko-khoziaistvennoi kooperatsii, izdavaemyi Soiuzom sibirskikh
maslodel'nykh artelei.
        Omsk, 1919, daily

1919:   July 8-12, 16 - Aug. 13, 16-21, 24, Sept. 2-23, 25 - Nov. 2
        (Nos. 1-5, 7-31, 34-37, 40, 46-63, 65-90)
                              Ref: LC, p. 140

RUS'
___

        Izdatel' V. P. Gaideburov.
        St. Petersburg, 1897, daily

1898:   Nov. 26(Dec. 8), 29(Dec. 11), 30(Dec. 12), Dec. 3(15) (Nos.
        152, 155, 156, 159)
                            Ref: Lisovskii 2593
                            Beliaeva 6999

RUS'
___

        Sofia, three times a week

1922:   Nov. 15 (No. 50)
1923:   Apr. 4, June 6, 12, 22 (Nos. 71, 99, 102, 107)
                            Ref: Columbia 434

RUS'

Ezhenedel'nyi organ russkoi natsional'noi mysli v Bolgarii.
Sofia, 1934, weekly

1934, Apr. 8- Dec. 1936 (Nos. 1-32, 37-69, 75-84, 86, 88-99)

RUSSKAIA ARMIIA

Gazeta voennaia, obshchestvennaia i literaturnaia. [Published
by the Information Department of the Staff of the Supreme Commander-
in-Chief.]
Omsk, 1918, daily

1919:   June 1 - July 16, 18-20, 25, 27, 30 - Aug. 3, 6-7, 9-17, 21-22,
        24-26, Sept. 2-3, 5-9, 11-21, 25, 27 - Oct. 4, 7-12, 16, 18-26,
        30-31, Nov. 2 (Nos. 137-149, 151-153, 157, 159, 162-165, 167-
        168, 170-177, 179-180, 182-183, 188-189, 191-194, 196-204, 207,
        209-214, 216-221, 223, 225-232, 235-236, 238)
                                Ref: Columbia 437, LC, p. 140

RUSSKAIA ARMIIA

Odnodnevnaia gazeta, posviashchennaia russkomu belomu
voinstvu.
Tientsin, 1929, one day's newspaper

1929:   June 29 (July 12)

RUSSKAIA GAZETA

Organ nezavisimoi mysli.
Belgrade, daily

1920:   Sept. 4, 5, 8, 11, Oct. 7, 16 (Nos. 89, 90, 92, 95, 117, 125)
                                Ref: Columbia 438

RUSSKAIA GAZETA

Periodicheskii organ. Izdatel' - Soiuz rossiiskikh patriotov.
Redaktor O. Lomot'.
Buenos Aires, 1937

1937:   Jan. - May (Nos. 1-6)
1942:   Sept. - Oct. (Nos. 7-8)
                                Ref: Columbia 439

RUSSKAIA GAZETA

Published by the Russian Press Publishing Co.
New York, N. Y.

1931, Nov. 29-Mar. 1934 (Nos. 1-108, 110-133)

RUSSKAIA GAZETA
>Ezhednevnaia gazeta pod redaktsiei A. I. Filippova.
>Paris, 1923, daily

1923:   June 4, July 16 (Nos. 5, 11)
1924:   Feb. 11 (No. 6)
1925:   Jan. 4, 6, Feb. 7, 21, 25 (Nos. 215-216, 244, 256, 259)
>>>>>Ref: Columbia 441

RUSSKAIA GAZETA
>San Francisco, 1921, weekly

1921:   Mar. 23 - Apr. 16, May 21 (Nos. 1-4, 9)

RUSSKAIA GAZETA
>Saõ Paulo, Brazil, 1928, weekly

1932, Dec.-Oct. 1934 (Nos. 347-348, 351-356, 358-403, 405-409,
411-439, 441-442)

RUSSKAIA MYSL'
>Belgrade, daily

1920:   Nov. 25 (No. 1)

RUSSKAIA MYSL'
>Paris

1949 - 1962: Nos. 194-202, 205, 229-230, 232-620, 623-628, 631-845,
847-1296, 1298-1361, 1363-1936
>>>>>Ref: Columbia 444

RUSSKAIA VECHERNIAIA POCHTA
>Ezhenedel'naia literaturnaia, ekonomicheskaia i nauchno-
populiarnaia gazeta.
>New York, weekly

1931:   Apr. 5-26, Nov. 8-22 (Nos. 1-4, 32-34)

RUSSKAIA VOLIA
>Editor N. D. Smirnov
>Petrograd, daily

1916:   Nos. 1-26, 28-53
(Continued on next page)

RUSSKAIA VOLIA (Continued)

    1917:   Nos. 2-10, 12, 14-18, 20-22, 23, 24-32, 34-36, 38-44, 46,
           48-50, 52,54, 56, 58, 60, 62, 64, 66-67, 71, 73, 75, 79, 81,
           83, 85, 87, 91, 93, 95, 97, 99, 101, 103, 105, 107, 111, 113,
           115, 117, 118, 120-130, 134, 136-137, 139, 142-143, 146, 147,
           148, 150, 153, 156-206, 208-215, 217-226, 228-232, 234, 236-
           251, 253

                                 Ref: Columbia 448, LC, p. 70

RUSSKAIA ZEMLIA
           Ezhenedel'naia narodnaia gazeta.
           Uzhgorod, 1919, weekly

    1932: Nos. 3-4, 35-37
    1933, Jan.-March 1935
                           Ref: LC, p. 175

RUSSKAIA ZHIZN'
           Ezhednevnaia gazeta. (Editor P. I. Leont'ev).
           Continued as Novaia russkaia zhizn'.
           Helsinki, daily

    1919:   Aug. 11, Oct. 16, 17, 25, Nov. 1-2 (Nos. 45-47, 131, 188, 189,
           196, 202-203)

RUSSKAIA ZHIZN'
           Russian life; Russian daily morning news.
           San Francisco, 1921, daily

    1927: July 15 (No. 28)
    1931: Dec. 25 (No. 52)
    1932: Jan. 15, 29, Feb. 12, Apr. 1, 29 (Nos. 3, 5, 7, 14, 18)
    1937, Apr. 28 - Nov. 1941 (Nos. 1-19, 30, 35-38, 41-77, 79-97,
           99-115, 117-215, 217-237)
    1944: Nos. 1-110, 112-246
    1945: Nos. 2-34, 36-242
    1946: Nos. 1-19, 21-164, 166-247
    1947: Nos. 1-12, 14-116
           Title varies: v. 1-16 (1921-1936), Russkaia zhizn'; v. 17-21
    (1937-1941), Russkie novosti; v. 22- (1942-), Russkaia zhizn'.
                         Ref: Columbia 449

RUSSKAIA ZHIZN'
           Gazeta vykhodit ezhednevno.
           St. Petersburg, 1890, daily

    1894: Dec. 19(31) (No. 338)
                       Ref: Lisovskii 2133

RUSSKAIA ZHIZN'
>Ezhednevnaia gazeta.
St. Petersburg, 1907, daily

1907:   Nos. 1-52   (Microfilm)
>>Ref: Beliaeva 6847

RUSSKAIA ZHIZN'
>Ezhenedel'naia politicheskaia, obshchestvennaia i literatur-
naia gazeta.
>Sofia, 1925, weekly

1925:   Aug. 2-9 (Nos. 7-8)

RUSSKIE NOVOSTI
>Paris, weekly

1945:   May 18 - Dec. (Nos. 1-33)
1946:   Jan. - Nov. (Nos. 34-80)
1947,   Jan. - Dec. 31, 1954 (Nos. 86-131, 133-289, 291-500)
>>Ref: Columbia 450

RUSSKIE NOVOSTI
>Continuation of Russkaia zhizn'; continued as Russkaia zhizn'.
San Francisco, weekly

1937,   Apr. 28 - Nov. 1941 (Nos. 1-19, 30, 35-38, 41-77, 79-97, 99-
115, 117-215, 217-237)
>>Ref: Columbia 451

RUSSKII AVANGARD
>Ezhenedel'nyi organ russkoi natsional'noi mysli na Dal'nem
Vostoke.
>Shanghai, 1936, weekly

1936:   Aug. 16-30 (Nos. 32-34)
1937:   June, Nov. 14, 28 - Dec. 12 (Nos. 75, 89, 91-93)
1938:   July 5 (No. 118)
>>Ref: Columbia 452

RUSSKII EKONOMIST
>Posviashchennyi finansam, promyshlennosti, torgovle i
narodnomu khoziaistvu. Vykhodit 3 raza v nedeliu pod redaktsiei
A. IA. Gutmana (Anatolii Gan).
>Vladivostok, 1919, 3 times a week
(Continued on next page)

RUSSKII EKONOMIST (Continued)

    1919:   May 8, 11, 15, 22, 26, June 2, 16, 23, 30, July 7, Aug. 20, 25,
               Sept. 2, 12, 22 (Nos. 2-4, 6-8, 10-13, 19-26)
    1920:   Jan. 6, 19 (Nos. 34(1), 35(2))

                             Ref: Columbia 455, LC, p. 183

RUSSKII EZHENEDEL'NIK V BEL'GII
           Brussels, 1927, weekly

    1932,   Dec. 22 - Oct. 1939 (Nos. 274 [145] - 617 [488])

RUSSKII GOLOS
           Natsional'naia obshchestvennaia i voennaia ezhenedel'naia
gazeta.
           Belgrade, weekly

    1931,   Apr. 12 - June 9, 1940 (Nos. 1-355, 357-393, 394-429, 431-433,
           435-455, 457, 459-469, 471-479)

RUSSKII GOLOS
           Ezhednevnaia gazeta.
           Kharbin, daily

    1923:   Mar. 1, June 11 (Nos. 760, 843)
    1924:   Jan. 1 - 12 (Nos. 1010-1017)

                             Ref: Columbia 456

RUSSKII GOLOS
           Organ russkoi obshchestvennoi mysli.
           Lwow, 1922, weekly

    1933,   June - Jan. 13, 1939 (Nos. 612-629, 631-895)

RUSSKII GOLOS
           Pod redaktsiei Ivana K. Okuntsova.
           New York, 1917, daily

    1917:   July 16 - Sept. 22 (Nos. 142-147, 149-169, 171-183, 186-201)
    1918:   Nos. 306, 308
    1921:   No. 1336
    1923:   No. 2892
    1927:   July 23 (Nos. 4266-4271, 4273-4289, 4291-4386, 4388-4401,
           4404-4417, 4419-4424, 4426
    1928:   Jan. 1 - Mar. 16 (Nos. 4428-4429, 4431-4440, 4442-4464, 4466-
           4484, 4486-4496, 4499

(Continued on next page)

RUSSKII GOLOS   (Continued)

 1931-1932: Nos. 5697, 5813, 5820, 5827, 5841-5842, 5845-5846, 5848-
      5862, 5877-5883, 5887-5893, 5895-5909, 5911, 5913-5916, 5918-
      5919, 5921-5925, 5951, 5953, 5955, 5960, 5964-5966, 5971-
      5972, 5974-5982, 5984-5987, 5989-5998, 6000, 6001, 6010-
      6024, 6026-6131, 6033, 6035-6037
 1933: Feb. 6 - Aug. 30 (Nos. 6291-6299, 6301-6468, 6470-6487,
     6492-6494, 6497)
 1934: Nov. 18 (No. 6947)

RUSSKII GOLOS
    Pervaia progressivnaia gazeta v Amerike.
    New York, 1908, weekly

 1909: Sept. 30 (No. 102)

RUSSKII INVALID
    Gazeta voennaia. Odnodnevnyi vypusk.
    Paris, 1925, annual

 1927 - 1929: (Nos. 3-5)
           Ref: Columbia 459

RUSSKII INVALID
    Voenno-nauchnaia i literaturnaia gazeta. 1813 - 1917 g. v.
 Sankt-Peterburge, s 22 fevralia 1930 g. v Parizhe.
    Paris, 1930, twice a month

 1930, Feb. 22 - May 1940 (Nos. 1-151)

RUSSKII INVALID
    Organ russkikh voennykh invalidov v Bolgarii.
    Sofia, irregular

 1933, Sept. - July 1936 (Nos. 1-13)

RUSSKII INVALID V BEL'GII
    Brussels

 1938: Aug. 1 (No. 14)

RUSSKII INVALID V MAN'CHZHU-DI-GO
    Izdanie Soi uza voennykh russkikh invalidov v Man'chzhu-Di-Go.
    Kharbin, annually

 1934, May 22 - May 1939 (Nos. 1-6)

RUSSKII KLICH

> Organ tserkovnoi, natsional'noi i gosudarstvennoi mysli.
> Los Angeles, irregular

1937: July 14 (No. 1)
1938: Aug. 28 - Sept. 10 (No. 2)
1940: Oct. 16 (29) (No. 3)

> Ref: Columbia 460

RUSSKII LISTOK

> Ezhednevnaia gazeta bez predvaritel'noi tsenzury.
> Moscow, 1889, daily

1899: Feb. 1, Mar. 3, 29, May 1 (Nos. 3303-3329, 3331, 3353-3358, 3387)

> Ref: Beliaeva 6924, Lisovskii 2067

RUSSKII MEDVED'

> Organ russkago natsional'nago studencheskago obshchestva.
> Vykhodit ezhegodno v Tat'ianin den'.
> Berkeley, annual

1930: Jan.
1931: Jan.
1934: Jan.

RUSSKII NARODNYI GOLOS

> Obshchestvenno-vnepartiinaia gazeta.
> Uzhgorod, 1934

1936: Mar. - Oct. (Nos. 34-36, 99-101)

RUSSKII NATSIONAL'NYI KOMITET G. N'IU IORKA
> New York

1935: Apr., Biulleten' No. 1

RUSSKII PATRIOT

> Patriote russe. Organe de L'Union des patriotes russes en
> France paru en clandestinite.
> Paris
> See SOVETSKII PATRIOT, Paris.

RUSSKII PECHATNIK
> Organ Professional'nogo o-va rabochikh pechatnogo proiz-
vodstva imeni pervopechatnika Ivana Fedorova.
> Moscow, 1909, 2-4 times a month

1909 - 1910:   Nos. 9, 12-20 (Microfilm)
> Ref: Beliaeva 6937

RUSSKII PUT'
> Ezhenedel'nyi organ natsional'noi russkoi mysli.
> Tientsin, weekly

1937:   June 21 - Sept. 20 (Nos. 1-14)

RUSSKII SOLDAT-GRAZHDANIN VO FRANTSII
> Izdaetsia pri podderzhke Amerik. Khrist. o-va molod. liudei.
Osnovan Otriadnym komitetom russkikh voisk vo Frantsii.

1917:   Nos. 1-2, 4-23, 26-27, 30-31, 33, 35-36, 38-42, 45-50, 56,
63, 66, 71-73, 77-80, 86, 88-89, 92-93, 96, 98-99, 102, 103,
105-107, 110-119, 121-124, 126-128

1918:   Nos. 139, 147-150, 153-156, 159-164, 166, 170-174, 178-181,
185, 188-198, 200-201, 203-205, 210-220, 222-234, 237-246,
248-254, 257-269, 271, 273, 275-285, 287, 291-298, 300-302,
304-305, 306-325, 327-332

1919:   Nos. 333-337, 339-345, 347-349, 351-354, 356, 358, 363-
367, 369-374, 376-381, 383-404, 406-427, 429-438, 440-445,
447, 449)

1920:   Nos. 459, 463, 464

RUSSKII STIAG
> Za Veru, TSaria i Otechestvo.
> Novyi Sad, 1925

1925:   Dec. 27(14) (No. 6)

RUSSKII TSENTR
> Informatsionnaia odnodnevnaia gazeta Komissii po sozdaniiu
Russkago TSentra v San Francisco.
> San Francisco, one day's newspaper

1939:   Jan. (4 p.)

RUSSKII V ANGLII
>
Obshchestvo severian v Velikobritanii.
London, 1936, semimonthly

1936, Jan. - 1939, Aug. (Nos. 1-88)

Ref: Columbia 467

RUSSKII V ARGENTINE
>
Buenos Aires, 1930, weekly

1933, Jan. - 1943: Nos. 129-597
1945 - 1946: Nos. 753-831, 833-852

RUSSKII VESTNIK
>
Gazeta dlia russkikh voennoplennykh v Germanii.
Berlin, 1915, twice a week

1915, Dec. 4-Mar. 31, 1917 (Nos. 1-98, 100-138)
1918:   Mar. 28 (No. 264)

RUSSKII VESTNIK
>
Organ Rossiiskikh professional'nykh soiuzov i kul'turno-
prosvetitel'nykh organizatsii Soedinennykh Shtatov i Kanady.   (Russian
Daily Herald.)
Chicago, 1917, daily

1926:   Feb. 6 - Nov. 10 (Nos. 20, 113, 115, 116, 117, 120-122, 129,
147, 154-155, 173, 190-193, 217, 227, 242, 253, 260, 262-263)
In 1926, May 15, consolidated with Rassvet (from New York)
and assumed the name of the latter.

Ref: Columbia 469

RUSSKII VESTNIK
>
Obshchestvenno-literaturnyi zhurnal Russkago ob"edinennago
o-va vzaimopomoshchi v Amerike (ROOVA) i Federatsii molodezhi.
New York, 1933, semimonthly

1934:   Oct. 21 - Nov. 11 (Nos. 7, 8)
1935:   Apr. 14 - May 15, June 15 (Nos. 19, 20, 21, 23)
1936:   May 15 (No. 45)

RUSSKII VESTNIK
>
Uriadnyi organ soedineniia russkikh pravoslavnykh bratstv v
Amerike.
Pittsburgh, Pa., 1918, weekly

1933 - 1941: Vols. 16-24

RUSSKII VOENNYI VESTNIK
> Continued as TSarskii Vestnik.
>
> Belgrade

 1925, Jan. 7 - Aug. 12, 1928 (Nos. 1, 3, 5-73, 75-97, 98, 99-134,
   136-149, 153-157)

RUSSKIIA IZVESTIIA
> Bezpartiinaia neitral'naia gazeta na russkom i nemetskom

iazyke.
> Berlin, twice a week

 1915: Aug. 7(No. 41) 16/3 Nov. (No. 70)

RUSSKIIA NOVOSTI DNIA
> Special edition of the English paper Daily News. Continued

as Novyia russkiia novosti dnia as of Dec. 1, 1917.
> Petrograd, daily

 1917: Nov. 7(2), 19(Dec. 2), 21(Dec. 4), 24(Dec. 7) (Nos. 744, 755-
   756, 758)

           Ref: LC, p. 70

RUSSKIIA VEDOMOSTI
> Moscow, 1863, daily (microfilm)

 1890: Jan. - Dec.
 1894: July 1 - July 15
 1895: Jan. - Dec.
 1897-1916
 1917: Jan. 1 - Sept. 1, Sept. 3 - Dec. 3, Dec. 5-31 (Nos. 1-200, 202-
   265, 268-279)
 1918: Jan. 3, 10 - Mar. 27 (Nos. 1, 3-46)
Missing numbers:
 1899: Jan. 1 (p. 1-2), June 25, Sept. 23
 1904: July 1-30

        Ref: Beliaeva 6880; Columbia 471;
          LC, p. 115; Lisovskii 815

RUSSKOE DELO
> Belgrade, 1936

 1936: Apr. (No. 2)

RUSSKOE DELO
>   Omsk, 1919, daily

1919:   Oct. 5-10 (Nos. 1-5)

>   Ref: LC, p. 140

RUSSKOE DELO
>   Vykhodit 3 raza v nedeliu po vtornikam, chetvergam i
subbotam.
>   Prague, 1919, 3 times a week

1919:   Nos. 1-95
1920:   Nos. 1(96) - 68(163), 70(165), 73(168) - 76(171), 78(173) - 84
>   (179), 86(181), 91(186) - 92(187), 94(189), 96(191), 99(194), 99
>   (194), 101(196) - 102(197)

>   Ref: Columbia 473

RUSSKOE DELO
>   Izdatel'stvo "Natsional'noe vozrozhdenie".
>   Sofia

1921:   Dec. 4-14, 23 (Nos. 45-49, 53)
1922:   Feb. 19, 22, Mar. 10-17 (Nos. 76, 77, 83-116, 118-132)

RUSSKOE EKHO
>   Ezhednevnaia, demokraticheskaia, obshchestvenno-politiches-
kaia, torgovo-promyshlennaia i literaturnaia gazeta, organ zashchity
russkikh interesov v Kitae.
>   Shanghai, 1920, daily

1920:   Oct. 14, 17 (Nos. 87, 90)

>   Ref: Columbia 475

RUSSKOE OBOZRENIE
>   Russian review.
>   Chicago, weekly

1929-1947
Missing numbers:
1929:   Nos. 1-8
1930:   Nos. 3, 27, 35
1931:   Nos. 2-5, 48-52
1932:   Nos. 31-51
1933:   Nos. 7, 11-13, 17, 24, 26-27, 40
1937:   Nos. 37, 38
1939:   No. 41 (was never published)
1947:   No. 25

RUSSKOE SLOVO
        Ezhednevnaia gazeta.
        Kharbin, daily

1928:   Nos. 603-613, 616-620, 622-651, 653-654, 686-691, 693,
        695-703, 705-708, 711-722, 725, 728, 730-742, 744-746,
        804, 805, 807-820, 822, 842-848, 850-855
1931:   No. 1451 (Jan. 1)
1932:   Nos. 2001, 2005, 2041-2049 (Nov. 3, 9, Dec. 21-30)
1933:   Nos. 2085-2114, 2119-2147, 2149-2196, 2198-2217, 2220-2237,
        2239-2258, 2260-2266, 2268-2304, 2306-2323, 2325-2331,
        2333-2345 (Jan. 1 - Dec. 24)
1934:   Nos. 2354-2356, 2358-2390, 2392-2420, 2422-2429, 2431,
        2437, 2439, 2441-2487, 2489-2499, 2501-2536, 2538-2539,
        2546-2618, 2621-2642, 2645-2649 (Jan. - Dec.)
1935:   Nos. 2650-2659, 2661-2688, 2690-2717, 2719-2737, 2745-
        2763, 2765, 2767-2774, 2776-2783, 2791-2869, 2871-2872,
        2874-2893 (Jan. - Sept. 21)

                    Ref: Columbia 478

RUSSKOE SLOVO
        Gazeta politicheskaia, obshchestvennaia, ekonomicheskaia i
literaturnaia. Vykhodit ezhednevno (bez predvaritel'noi tsenzury).
        Moscow, 1894, daily

1895:   Jan. 31, Feb. 1, June 14-17 (Nos. 30, 31, 159-162)
1914:   Jan. 1, Aug. 26 (Nos. 1, 195)
1915:   Jan. 1, Mar. 22, Dec. 25 (Nos. 1, 67, 296)
1916:   July 1 - Dec. (Nos. 151-302)
1917:   Jan. - Nov. (Nos. 2, 4-5, 7-78, 80-85, 87-107, 109, 117-130,
        132-136, 138-139, 140, 143-150, 152-154, 156-160, 193-216,
        218-259)

             Ref: Lisovskii 2441, Beliaeva 6986
                Columbia 479, LC, p. 115

RUSSKOE SLOVO
        Narva, 1932, twice a week

1932:   Dec. 1 (No. 9)

RUSSKOE SLOVO
        Ezhednevnaia narodno-obshchestvennaia gazeta.
        New York, 1911, daily

1917:   Aug. 21 (No. 1670)

RUSSKOE SLOVO
        Tian'tszin-Pekinskaia ezhednevnaia liberal'naia gazeta.
        Tientsin, daily

1921:   May 24-27 (Nos. 174-177)

RUSSKOE SLOVO
        Ezhednevnaia obshchestvenno-politicheskaia gazeta.
        Warsaw-Vilno, 1932, daily

1938:   Feb. 26 (No. 45)
                         Ref: Columbia 480

RUSSKOE VOSKRESENIE
        La resurrection russe. Natsional'no-gosudarstvennaia nad-
partiinaia gazeta.
        Paris, twice a week

1956:   May 6 - Nov. 15 (Nos. 46-71)
1957:   Oct. 30 - Dec. 28 (Nos. 73-90)
1958:   Jan. 1 - Apr. 5 (Nos. 91-107)
                         Ref: Columbia 482

RUSSKOE VREMIA
        Pod redaktsiei Aleksandra Filippova.
        Paris, weekly

1926:   Oct. 10 (No. 347)
                         Ref: Columbia 483

RUSSKOE VREMIA
        Rostov-on-Don, 1919

1920:   Jan. 19 (No. 15)
                         Ref: LC, p. 151

RZHEVSKAIA PRAVDA
        Organ Rzhevskogo uispolkoma i uezdkoma RKP(b). [Organ of
the Rzhev District Executive Committee and of the District Committee
of the Russian Communist Party.]
        Rzhev, 1920, 3 times a week

1922:   Mar. 12 (No. 20)
1928:   Apr. 11 (No. 44(2092))
                         Ref: LC, p. 153

RZHEVSKOE EDINSTVO
        Organ revoliutsionno-demokraticheskii. Vykhodit pri
blizhaishem uchastii Soveta soldatskikh deputatov i drugikh
obshchestvennykh organizatsii, ezhednevno.
        Rzhevsk, 1917, daily

1917:   June 18, 22 (Nos. 22, 25)
                              Ref: LC, p. 153

S

SAKHALINKA

Ezhenedel'naia obshchestvennaia, populiarnaia i maloizvest-
naia, bezpartiinaia i uzko-partiinaia gazeta.

[N.p.], weekly

1919, Dec. 28 - Apr. 1, 1920: (Nos. 1-12, 45)

SARATOVSKII LISTOK

Gazeta politicheskaia, obshchestvennaia i literaturnaia.
Vykhodit ezhednevno, krome dnei posleprazdnichnykh.

Saratov, 1863, daily

1917:   Nov. 5-16, 19-23 (Nos. 238-243, 246-248)

Ref: Lisovskii 1439, Beliaeva 7140

LC, p. 154

SARATOVSKII VESTNIK

Saratov, 1907, daily

1917:   Nov. 5, 11, 14, 15, 18-24 (Nos. 241, 242, 244, 245, 248-252)

Ref: Beliaeva 7129, LC, p. 154

SEGODNIA VECHEROM

Riga, daily

1926:   Jan. 2-18, Mar. 1, Dec. 24 (Nos. 1-13, 47)
1928:   Oct. 27 (No. 245)
1939:   Aug. 30 (No. 197)
1940:   Apr. 22-24 (Nos. 90-92)

SEL'SKO-KHOZIAISTVENNAIA ZHIZN'

Gazeta Narodnogo komissariata zemledeliia i TS K Vserabot-
zemlesa. [Published by the People's Commissariat of Agriculture
and the Central Committee of the Central Union of Agricultural and
Forestry Workers.]

Moscow, 1921, weekly, semiweekly

(Continued on next page)

SEL'SKO-KHOZIAISTVENNAIA ZHIZN' (Continued)

    1921:   Aug. 2 (No. 3)
    1922:   Feb. 28 - Mar. 17 (Nos. 16(57) - 21(62))
                                 Ref: LC, p. 116

SEL'SKOE KHOZIAISTVO

        [Organ of the Ministry of Agriculture and Supply of the
U. S. S. R.]
        Formed by merger of Sotsialisticheskoe zemledelie,
Sovetskoe khlopkovodstvo, and Sovkhoznaia gazeta.
        Moscow, 1953, daily

    1953:   Apr. 3 - Dec. 31 (Nos. 1-51, 53-151, 153-208, 211-218, 220,
           222-224, 229-230)
    1954:   Jan. - Dec. (No. 1-310)
    1955:   Jan. 1 - June 23 (No. 1-145)
                          Ref: Beliaeva 491, LC, p. 116

SEL'SKOE KHOZIAISTVO MOSKOVSKOI GUBERNII

        Listok Moskovskogo zemel'nogo otdela. [Published by the
Moscow Agricultural Department.]
        Moscow, 1921

    1922:   Jan. 29 (No. 4)
                         Ref: LC, p. 116

7 DNEI V ILLIUSTRATSIIAKH

        Ezhenedel'naia literaturnaia illiustrirovannaia gazeta.
Redaktor M. P. Mironov.
        Paris, weekly

    1934,   Sept. 29 - Feb. 1935 (Nos. 1-21)
                       Ref: Columbia 492

SEMENOVETS

        Gazeta kul'turno-prosvetitel'noi komissii gvardii Semenovs-
kago reservnago polka.
        Petrograd

    1917:   Oct. 9 (No. 6)

SENATSKIE VEDOMOSTI

        Petrograd, 1809, semiweekly

    1917:   June 27 (No. 48)
                  Ref: Lisovskii 187, Beliaeva 7527

SERET see GAZETA "SERET"

SERP I MOLOT
   Organ Kuznetskogo (Sar. gub.) ispolnitel'nogo komiteta
Sovetov raboch., krest'. i krasnoarmeiskikh deputatov i komiteta
R. K. P. [Organ of the Kuznetsk Executive Committee of the Soviet
of Workers', Peasants', and Red Army Deputies and of the
Committee of the Russian Communist Party.]
   Kuznetsk

1921: Nov. 7 (No. 246)
           Ref: LC, p. 45

SERP I MOLOT
   Organ Serdobskogo uispolkoma Sov. r., kr. i kr. dep. i
Komiteta RKP. [Organ of the Serdobsk District Executive Committee
of Soviets and of the Committee of the Russian Communist Party.]
   Serdobsk, 1919, semiweekly

1921: Nov. 7 (No. 157)
1922: Mar. 12 (No. 30)
           Ref: LC, p. 155

SEVERNAIA KOMMUNA
   Izvestiia tsentral'nogo ispolnitel'nogo komiteta sovetov
krest'ianskikh rabochikh i krasnoarmeiskikh deputatov severnoi
oblasti i petrogradskogo soveta rabochikh i krasnoarm. deputatov.
Petrograd. (1918-1919)
   See Izvestiia petrogradskogo soveta rabochikh i krasnoarmeiskikh deputatov. 1918-

SEVERNAIA PRAVDA
   Organ Kostromskogo gubkoma VKP(b), Gubispolkoma i
Gubprofsoveta.
   Kostroma

1928: Apr. 29 (No. 100(2646))

SEVERNAIA RABOCHAIA GAZETA
   St. Petersburg, 1914, daily

1914: Nos. 1-59, 61-69 (Microfilm)
        Ref: Beliaeva 7354; Columbia 494

SEVERNAIA ZARIA
Vologda

1918:   Nos. 12-14   (Microfilm)

SEVERNAIA ZHIZN'
Ezhednevnaia gazeta russkago naseleniia v Finliandii.
Helsinki, weekly

1918:   Nov. 26 - Dec. 31 (Nos. 1-12)
1919:   Jan. 3 - Feb. 28 (Nos. 1-47)

SEVERNOE SLOVO
Revel, 1942

1944:   Feb. 13 (No. 18)

SEVERNOE UTRO
Arkhangelsk, 1911, daily

1918:   Dec. 4(Nov. 21) - 8(Nov. 25), 10(Nov. 27), 12(Nov. 29), 14(1),
         16(8), 18(5), 20(7) - 31 (Nos. 245(2141) - 248, 250, 252, 254,
         256, 258, 260-271)
1919:   Jan. 1, 3-11(Dec. 29), 13(Dec. 31), July 12 (June 29), Aug. 25
         (12), Dec. 22(9) (Nos. 1(2160), 3 - 8(2167), 10, 177(2335), 220,
         335(2492))

SEVERNYI GOLOS
Rossiiskaia sotsial-demokraticheskaia rabochaia partiia.
St. Petersburg, 1905, daily

1905:   Nos. 1-3   (Microfilm)

Ref: Columbia 495, Beliaeva 7376

SEVERNYI KUR'ER
St. Petersburg, 1899, daily

1899:   Nov. 1(13), Dec. 14(26) (Nos. 1, 44)

Ref: Lisovskii 2779

SEVERNYI RABOCHII
Ezhednevnaia gazeta IAroslavskogo Gubkoma VKP(b), Gub-
ispolkoma i Gubprofsoveta.
IAroslavl', daily

1928:   Apr. 29 (No. 100(1742))

SHANGHAISKAIA ZARIA
>Shanghai, 1924, daily

1928: May 13-15 (Nos. 1066-1067, vneochered. No. 8)
1932: Apr. 1 - Dec. 21 (Nos. 1957-1967, 1969-1983, 1985, 1988-2000,
2001-inc. , 2002, 2003-inc. , 2004-inc. , 2005-2010, 2011-inc. ,
2012-2017, 2018-inc. , 2019-2029, 2030-inc. , 2037-2040, 2042-
2047, 2048-inc. , 2049-2053, 2054-inc. , 2055-2060, 2062-
2079, 2084-2092, 2094-2095, 2098-2099, 2101-2150, 2152,
2154-2156-2165, 2166-inc. , 2167-2172, 2174-2175, 2177-2179,
2181-2195, 2197-2199, 2200-2202, vneocherednye Nos. 68, 70,
72-74, 75-inc. , 76-80, 82-99. Also incomplete 2177, 2171,
2170)
1933: Jan. 1 - 7 (Nos. 2197-inc. , 2198-2199)

>Ref: Columbia 496

SHTANDART
>Odnodnevnaia legitimno-monarkhicheskaia gazeta.
Kharbin, 1934, one day's newspaper

1934: July 28 (10 p.)

SIBIR'
>Ezhednevnaia progressivnaia vnepartiinaia gazeta.
Irkutsk, 1906, daily

1917: Nov. 18 (No. 254)

>Ref: Beliaeva 7618, LC, p. 21

SIBIR'
>Gazeta politicheskaia, obshchestvennaia i literaturnaia.
Krasnoiarsk, 1906

1906: Apr. 19 (No. 1)

>Ref: Beliaeva 7619

SIBIR'
>Gazeta politichesko-obshchestvennaia i literaturnaia, posviash-
chennaia interesam vsei Sibiri i sopredel'nykh s neiu mestnostei.
Izdaetsia v S. Peterburge bez predvaritel'noi tsenzury.
St. Petersburg, 1897, twice a week

1898: Jan. 25 (No. 8)

>Ref: Lisovskii 2603

SIBIRSKAIA RECH'
        [Published by the Omsk Committee of the People's Freedom
Party.]
        Omsk, 1917, daily

  1919:   July 17 - Aug. 10, 13-15, 17-19, 26-27, 30, Sept. 2-18, 20 -
           Oct. 16, 18, 22-25, 28, 30 - Nov. 4 (Nos. 152-173, 175-177,
           179-180, 185-186, 188, 190-203, 205-227, 230-233, 235, 237-
           241)
                               Ref: Columbia 499, LC, p. 144

SIBIRSKAIA TORGOVAIA GAZETA
        Ezhednevnaia obshchestvennaia i kommercheskaia gazeta.
        Tiumen', Tobol'skoi gub., 1897, daily

  1897:   July 26(No. 16)
  1898:   Jan. 20, July 11 (Nos. 15, 150)
                  Ref: Lisovskii 2606, Beliaeva 7564

SIBIRSKAIA ZHIZN'
        Gazeta politicheskaia, literaturnaia i ekonomicheskaia.
    Osnovana P.I. Makushinym.
        Tomsk, 1897, daily

  1900:   Nov. 28-30 (Nos. 257-259)
  1902:   Mar. 3, 31 (Nos. 50, 73)
  1903:   Aug. 1, 3 - Oct. 8 (Nos. 166, 168-218)
  1904:   Feb. 6 (No. 29)
  1905:   Jan. 23, Sept. 7 (Nos. 18, 185)
  1919:   Oct. 11 (No. 215)
                  Ref: Lisovskii 2601, Beliaeva 7542
                  LC, p. 171

SIBIRSKII DEN'
        Odnodnevnaia gazeta.
        Shanghai, 1938, one day's newspaper

  1938:   Aug. 15, (12 p.)

SIBIRSKII KAZAK
        Kharbin, annual

  1932:   Dec. 6 (19)
  1933:   Dec. 6 (19)

SIBIRSKII VESTNIK POLITIKI, LITERATURY I OBSHCHESTVENNOI
ZHIZNI

Tomsk, 1885, daily

1895:   Aug. 2-26, Sept. 1-22 (Nos. 89-99, 102-111)
1900:   Nov. 28, 30 (Nos. 260,262)
1901:   Feb. 17, Mar. 2, 30, May 4-6, 9 (Nos. 37, 49, 72, 96, 98,
        100)
1902:   Jan. 1, Nov. 29 (Nos. 1,258)
1905:   Feb. 9 (No. 31)

Ref: Lisovskii 1770, Beliaeva 7582

SIBIRSKOE OBOZRENIE

Gazeta politicheskaia i literaturnaia.
Irkutsk, 1906, daily

1906:   June 15 (No. 108)

Ref: Beliaeva 7611

SIGNAL

Organ russkago natsional'nago soiuza uchastnikov voiny.
Redaktor N. V. Piatnitskii.
Paris, 1937, semimonthly

1937,   Feb. 20-July, Oct. - July 1939 (Nos. 1-10, 16-58)

Ref: Columbia

SILA ZEMLI

Ezhednevnaia gazeta.
Petrograd, 1917, daily

1917:   July 12 (No. 1)

Ref: LC, p. 71

SKANDINAVSKII LISTOK

Torgovo-promyshlennaia gazeta.
Stockholm

1917,   Jan. 13 - Oct. 19, 1918 (Nos. 248, 259, 297-384)

SLAVIANSKAIA ZARIA

Progressivnaia gazeta, posviashchennaia kul'turno-politiches-
koi i ekonomicheskoi zhizni.
Prague, 1920

1920:   Feb. 2 (No. 58)

SLAVIANSKII VESTNIK; WIESCI SLOWIANSKIE; SLOVANSKY VESTNIK;
SLAVENSKI GLASNIK
          Kiev, 1917, weekly

    1917:   Jan. 8, 15, Apr. 23 - June 18, July 2, Aug. 27 (Nos. 2, 3,
            17-23, 25, 28)
                                      Ref: LC, p. 35

SLOVO

          Organ nezavisimoi russkoi mysli.
          Buenos Aires, 1949, weekly

    1949,   July 3 - Jan. 18, 1950 (Nos. 1-30)

SLOVO

          Shanghai, 1929, daily

    1932:   May 4 - July 1 (Nos. 1111-1113, 1115-1162, 1164-1169)
    1933:   June 6 (No. 1504)
    1934:   June 4-9, Aug. 6-26 (Nos. 1862-1867, 1925-1928, 1930-1931,
            1939-1945)
    1935:   Apr. 28, June 2 (Nos. 2186, 2220 (incomplete)
    1936:   Jan. 20-26, Feb. 11, Apr. 14-26, July 13-19, Nov. 2 (Nos.
            2450-2455, 2471, 2533-2545, 2623-2629, 2735)
            Nos. 1112-1113, 1118-1119, 2220 are incomplete.

   ----   Bezplatnoe voskresnoe illiustrirovannoe prilozhenie.

    1931:   May 10, 31, July 19, August 23
    1932:   Dec. 18

SLOVO

          Ezhednevnaia gazeta.
          Tiflis, daily

    1920:   Nov. (No. 265)
    1921:   Jan. 1 - Feb. 17 (Nos. 3-10, 16-37)
                            Ref: LC, p. 170

SLOVO

          Illiustrirovannaia tserkovnaia, obshchestvennaia i literatur-
naia gazeta.
          Warsaw, 1931, twice a week

    1933:   Nos. 6-7, 9-11, 13-19, 21-29, 31-38, 40, 42-76, 78-104
    1934:   Nos. 1-42, 47-64, 66-67
    1935:   Nos. 30-31

SLOVO NARODA
>Izdaetsia pri blizhaishem uchastii S. P. Mel'gunova, V. A. Miakotina, A. B. Petrishcheva i A. V. Peshehonova.
>Moscow, 1918, daily

>1918:   June 6 (No. 10)

>>>Ref: LC, p. 116

SMELAIA MYSL'
>Krest'ianskaia i rabochaia gazeta.
>St. Petersburg, 3 times a week

>1914:   May 14 - June 6 (Nos. 1-9)

>>>Ref: Beliaeva 7707

SMENA
>Gazeta raboche-krest'ianskoi molodezhi Izdatel'stvo Peterburgskogo gubernskogo komiteta Rossiiskogo kommunisticheskogo soiuza molodezhi. [Published by the Petersburg Provincial Committee of the Russian Communist Union of Youth.]
>Petrograd

>1919:   Dec. 18 (No. 1)

>>>Ref: LC, p. 71

SMYCHKA
>Organ Orenburgskogo gubkoma VKP (b), Gubispolkoma i Gubprofsoveta.
>Orenburg, 1926

>1928:   Apr. 27 (No. 99(203))

SMYCHKA
>Ezhednevnaia gazeta Verkhne-Kamskogo okruzhnogo komiteta VKP(b), Okruzhnogo ispoln. k-ta sovetov i Okruzhnogo biuro prof. soiuzov.
>Usol'e, Ural'sk. obl., 1926, daily

>1928:   Apr. 8, 27 (Nos. 84(684), 98(698))

SMYCHKA: GORODA S DEREVNEI
>Ezhenedel'nyi organ Krasnoslobodskogo ukoma V. K. P. (b), Uispolkoma i Profsoiuzov.
>Krasnoslobodsk, Penzenskoi gub., weekly

>1928:   Feb. 29 - Mar. 17, May 31 (Nos. 6(129) - 8(131), 16(139))

SNABZHENIE, KOOPERATSIIA, TORGOVLIA
Organ Narkomsnaba SSSR, TSentro-soiuza i TSK Soiuza rabotnikov kooperatsii i gostorgovli. [Organ of the People's Commissariat of Supplies, of the Central Union of Consumers' Cooperatives and of the Central Committee of the Union of Workers of Cooperatives and State Trade Enterprises.]
Continued as Sovetskaia torgovlia (a journal) as of Sept. 6, 1934.
Moscow

1933:   May 30 (No. 123(2163))
Ref: LC, p. 117

SOKHA I MOLOT
Ezhednevnaia gazeta. Organ Eletsk. uispolkoma Sov. rab., k. kr. dep. i UKRKP. [Organ of the Yelets District Executive Committee of the Soviet of Toilers' Deputies and of the District Committee of the Russian Communist Party.]
Yelets, 1918, daily

1922:   Mar. 12 (No. 59(903)
Ref: LC, p. 187

SOLDAT
Ezhednevnaia gazeta.
Petrograd, 1917, daily

1917:   Aug. 18 (No. 4)

SOLDAT-GRAZHDANIN
Organ Moskovskago soveta soldatskikh deputatov. [Organ of the Moscow Soviet of Soldiers' Deputies.]
Moscow, 1917, daily

1917:   Jan. - Oct. (Microfilm)
Ref: LC, p. 117

SOLDAT I RABOCHII
Izdanie Kozlovskago soveta rabochikh i soldatskikh deputatov. [Published by the Kozlov Soviet of Workers' and Soldiers' Deputies.]
Kozlov, 1917, 3 w.

1917:   Sept. 24 (No. 65)
Ref: LC, p. 83

SOLDATSKAIA MYSL'
>Ezhednevnaia voenno-politicheskaia gazeta. Izd. soldat-zhurnalistov.
>Petrograd, 1917, daily

1917:   Apr. 22(May 5) (No. 4)
>>Ref: Columbia 511, LC, p. 72

SOLDATSKAIA PRAVDA
>Organ voennoi organizatsii pri TSentral'nom Komitete Rossiiskoi Sotsial-Demokraticheskoi Rabochei partii. Ezhednevnaia gazeta. [Organ of the Military Organization of the Central Committee of the Russian Social Democratic Workers' Party.]
>Petrograd, 1917, daily

1917:   April (No. 1)
>>Ref: Columbia 512, LC, p. 72

SOLDATSKII GOLOS
>Organ Vserossiiskago tsentral'nago ispolnitel'nago komiteta sovetov sol. i rab. dep. (pervago sozyva). [Organ of the All-Russian Central Executive Committee of Soviets of Soldiers' and Workers' Deputies (of the First Assembly).]
>Continuation of Golos soldata. Subsequently published as Iskry, Soldatskii krik. Revoliutsionnyi nabat, Mira. Khleba. Svobody , and Nabat revoliutsii.
>Petrograd, 1917, daily

1917:   Oct. 27 (No. 1)
>>Ref: Columbia 513, LC, p. 72

SOLDATSKOE SLOVO
>Gazeta revoliutsionnoi armii. [Published by the Group of Military Journalists.]
>Petrograd, 1917, daily

1917:   Mar. 4 - Oct. 5 (Nos. 4-18, 20-32, 35, 37-43, 45, 47-68, 70-79, 124-138, 140-141, 143-150, 152, 154-158)
>>Ref: Columbia 514, LC, p. 72

SOTSIAL-DEMOKRAT
>Organ Mosk. oblastnogo biuro, Mosk. komiteta i Mosk. okruzhnago komiteta R. S. -D. R. P. [Organ of the Moscow Provincial Bureau, of the Moscow Committee and of the Moscow District Committee of the Russian Social Democratic Workers' Party.]
>Moscow, 1917, daily

(Continued on next page)

SOTSIAL-DEMOKRAT (Continued)

    1917:   May 30(June 12), 31(June 13), June 1(14) - 4(17)   (Nos. 68-73)

    1918:   Mar. 6(Feb. 21)   (No. 40)

                              Ref: Columbia 515; LC, p. 117

SOTSIALDEMOKRAT

          Polnyi tekst pod obshchei redaktsiei N. L. Meshcheriakova...

          Moskva, Partiinoe izdatel'stvo, 1933.   Reprint

    1908 - 1917: Nos. 1-58

          Includes also reprints of the Paris newspaper Sotsialdemokrat.

    Nos. 1-9, Feb. 1908-9

SOTSIALDEMOKRAT

          Tsentral'nyi organ Rossiiskoi sotsialdemokraticheskoi

    rabochei partii.

          Vilna, Paris; since Nov. 1914 Geneva

    1904:   Nos. 1-3

    1906:   .Nos. 1-76

    1908:   Feb. (No. 1)

    1909:   Feb. 28/10 - Nov. 31-13 (Nos. 1-9)

    1910:   Jan. 24/6 - Nov. 16/29 (Nos. 10-18)

    1911:   Jan. 13/26 - Dec. 8/21 (Nos. 19/20 - 25)

    1912:   May 8/25 - Nov. 5/18 (Nos. 26 - 28/29)

    1913:   Jan. 12/25 (No. 30), Nov. 15/28 (No. 31), Dec. 15/28(No. 32)

    1914:   Nov. 1 - Dec. 12 (Nos. 33-36)

    1915:   Feb. - July 26, Oct. 11 - Dec. 21 (Nos. 37-43, 45-46, 49)

    1916:   Feb. 18 - June 10 (Nos. 50 - 54-55), Dec. 30(No. 57)

          H. I. has also supplements to Nos. 19-20 (1911), 27-29 (1912), 42

    (1915). Nos. 50-52 (1916) of the library set are photographic copies.

SOTSIALISTICHESKOE ZEMLEDELIE

          Organ Narkomzema SSSR i Narkomzema RSFSR.   [Organ of the

    Ministry of Agriculture of the USSR.]

          Appeared from 1929 to Jan. 29, 1930 as Sel'skokhoziaistven-

    naia gazeta.   Merged with Sovetskoe khlopkovodstvo and Sovkhoznaia

    gazeta as of Apr. 3, 1953 to form Sel'skoe khoziaistvo.

          Moscow, 1929, irregular, daily

    1933:   Jan. - Dec. (Nos. 1-300)

    1934:   Sept. 15-21, Oct. 28 - Dec. 30 (Nos. 213-218, 249, 252, 256-

          260, 262-275)

    1935:   Nos. 12, 150

(Continued on next page)

SOTSIALISTICHESKOE ZEMLEDELIE (Continued)

    1936:   Jan. - Dec. (Nos. 17, 18, 20, 22-24, 26-39, 44-49, 52, 55, 62, 73, 75-189, 191, 193, 214-215, 218-225, 227-237, 239, 241-246, 259)

    1937:   Jan. 27 - Dec. (Nos. 21-34, 36-39, 41, 43-68, 70, 74-88, 90-93, 95-274, 276-278, 280, 282-283, 285-292, 294-298)

    1938 - 1947

    1948:   July - Dec. (Nos. 128-310)

    1949:   Jan. 1 - Dec. 31 (Nos. 1-154, 156-309)

    1950:   Jan. - Dec. (Nos. 1-309)

    1951:   Jan. - Dec. (Nos. 1-305)

    1952:   Jan. - Dec. (Nos. 1-308)

    1953:   Jan. - Apr. (Nos. 1-78)

Missing numbers:

    1939:   No. 197

    1940:   Nos. 1, 3-6, 10-22, 27-82, 84, 86, 88, 96, 98-101, 103, 105-106, 108, 112-116, 261

    1942:   Nos. 1, 7, 11

    1943:   Nos. 91, 97

    1944:   Nos. 1, 34, 111

    1945:   Nos. 4, 127

    1946:   Nos. 26, 37-120

Ref: LC, p. 118

SOVET RABOCHIKH I KREST'IAN

    Organ Klinskogo raionnogo kom. Ross. kommunisticheskoi partii i Klinskogo uezdnogo ispolnit. kom. S. R. I K. D. [Organ of the Klin District Committee of the Russian Communist Party and of the Klin District Executive Committee of the Soviet of Toilers' Deputies.]

    Klin, 1918, weekly

    1919:   Nov. 7 (No. 30)

    1921:   Nov. 5 (No. 37)

Ref: LC, p. 38

SOVET TURKMENISTANY

    Ashkhabad, daily

    1945:   July 17, 20-21, 27 - Aug. 7, 10-17, 21 - Sept. 11, 15 - Oct. 31, Nov. 4-7, 13 - Dec. 4, 8 - 30 (Nos. 143, 145-146, 150-158, 160-165, 168-182, 185-218, 221-223, 226-241, 244-260)

SOVETSKAIA BELORUSSIIA
Organ TSK KP(b) Belorussii, Sovnarkoma i Prezidiuma Verkhovnogo soveta BSSR. [Organ of the Central Committee of the Communist Party of Belorussia, of the Supreme Soviet and of the Council of Ministers of the Belorussian SSR.]
Continuation of Rabochii.
Minsk, 1937, daily

1945: Oct. 26, 27 (Nos. 205-206)
1946: Jan. 12 (No. 9)
Ref: Columbia 519; LC, p. 84

SOVETSKAIA DEREVNIA
Organ Verkhne-Kamenskogo okruzhnogo komiteta Vsesoiuznoi kommunisticheskoi partii (bol'shevikov) i Okruzhnogo ispolnitel'nogo komiteta Sovetov r., k. i kr. deputatov. Ezhenedel'noe platnoe prilozhenie k gazete "Smychka". Vykhodit po voskreseniiam.
Solikamsk, weekly

1928: Dec. 9-23 (Nos. 38-40)

SOVETSKAIA KIRGIZIIA
Organ TSentral'nogo komiteta Frunzenskogo obkoma KR(b) Kirgizii i Verkhovnogo soveta Kirgizskoi SSSR. [Organ of the Central Committee, of the Provincial Committee of the Communist Party of Kirgiziia and of the Supreme Soviet of the Kirgiz SSR.]
Frunze, 1925, daily

1945: July 1-3, 14-15, 24 - Aug. 12, 17-22, 25, 29, Sept. 1-8, 11-14, 17 - Dec. 3 (Nos. 128-131, 133-140, 144-158, 161-165, 167, 170, 172, 177, 179-224, 226-239, 241-258)
Ref: Columbia 521; LC, p. 18

SOVETSKAIA KUL'TURA
Organ Ministerstva kul'tury SSSR.
Moscow, 1953, three times a week

1953: July 4 - Sept. 26, Oct. 1 - 31, Nov. 24 - Dec. 3, 8 - 24, 29 - 31 (Nos. 1-37, 39-52, 62-66, 68-75, 77-78)
1954: Jan. 1 - 7, 12, 16, 23 - Feb. 16 (Nos. 1(79) - 3(81), 5(83), 7(85), 10(88) - 20(98))
Ref: Columbia 522

SOVETSKAIA MYSL'
Organ S.-Dvinskikh gubispolkoma i gubkoma RKP. [Organ of the Northern Dvina Provincial Executive Committee and of the Provincial Committee of the Russian Communist Party.]

(Continued on next page)

SOVETSKAIA MYSL'   (Continued)
Velikii Ustiug

1922:   Mar. 12 (No. 57)

Ref: LC, p. 176

SOVETSKAIA PRAVDA
Organ Cheliabinskogo gubernskogo k-ta RKP i Cheliabinskogo
Gubisplkoma. IUbileinyi nomer. [Organ of the Cheliabinsk
Provincial Committee of the Russian Communist Party and of the
Cheliabinsk Provincial Executive Committee.]
Cheliabinsk, 1920, one day's newspaper

1920:   Nov. 7 (6 p.)

Ref: LC, p. 13

SOVETSKAIA SIBIR'
Organ Novosibirskogo obkoma i gorkoma vsesoiuznoi kommunisticheskoi partii (bol'shevikov), oblastnogo i gorodskogo sovetov
deputatov trudiashchikhsia. [Organ of the Novosibirsk Provincial and
City Committees of the All-Union Communist Party (of Bol'sheviks)
and of the Provincial and City Soviets of Toilers' Deputies.]
Novosibirsk, 1919, daily

1921:   Nov. 6 (No. 263(603))
1922:   Mar. 12 (No. 57(707))
1928:   Apr. 26-27, May 15 (Nos. 98(2539) - 99(2540), 111(2552))
1945:   July 17 (No. 118(7823))

Ref: LC, p. 136

SOVETSKAIA TORGOVLIA
Organ of Ministerstvo torgovli SSSR.
Moscow, 1934, weekly

1957,   Jan. 1 - to present
Missing numbers:
Jan. 1, 1961; Aug. 1965

Ref: Columbia 527

SOVETSKII PAKHAR'
Organ Severo-Kavkazskogo kraevogo i Donskogo okruzhnogo
komitetov Vsesoiuznoi kommunisticheskoi partii (b).
Rostov-on-Don, 1924, three times a week

1928:   Apr. 28, Dec. 6, 8, 11, 13, 20 (Nos. 50(880), 141(971) - 144(974),
146(976), 147(977)

SOVETSKII PATRIOT
Continuation of Russkii patriot.
Paris, 1943, weekly

1944: Oct. - Dec. 9 (Nos. 14-22)
1945: Jan. - Dec. (Nos. 11-62)
1946: Sept. 27 - Nov. 15, Nov. 29 - Dec. 27 (Nos. 90-108, 110-114)
1947: Jan. 3 - Nov. 14 (Nos. 115-166)
1948: Jan. 2 - Jan. 16 (Nos. 167-169)

Ref: Columbia 462

SOVETSKII SPORT
Organ Vsesoiuznogo komiteta po delam fizkul'tury i sporta
pri Sovete Ministrov SSSR i V TS SPS. [Organ of the Ministry of
Health of the U. S. S. R. and the All-Union Central Council of Labor
Unions.]
Continuation of Krasnyi sport.
Moscow, 1946, twice a week

1946: Mar. 23 - Apr. 9, 16 (Nos. 13-18, 20)

Ref: Columbia 529, LC, p. 119

SOVETSKOE ISKUSSTVO
Organ Narkomprosa RSFSR
Moscow, 1930, every six days

1934: Dec. 11 (No. 57)
1935 - 1937
1939: Jan. 4 - Dec. (Nos. 2(582) - 23(603), 25(605) - 53(633), 55
(635) - 64(644), 66(646) - 77(657), 79(659), 81(661) - 89(669))

SOVETSKOE ISKUSSTVO
Organ Komiteta po delam iskusstva pri SNK SSSR, Komiteta
po delam kinematografii pri SNK SSSR i Komiteta po delam arkhitek-
tury pri SNK SSSR. [Organ of the U. S. S. R. Ministry of Culture.]
From Jan. 6, 1942 to Nov. 1944 published jointly with Literaturnaia gazeta under the title Literatura i iskusstvo.
Moscow, 1931, weekly, irregular

1945: June 29 - July 27, Aug. 31, Sept. 14 - Dec. 21 (Nos. 26-30, ·35,
37-51)
1950: Aug. 19 - Sept. 12, Sept. 26 - Oct. 3, Oct. 17 - Nov. 4 (Nos.
54-61, 65-67, 71-76)
1951: Jan. 22, 27, Feb. 3, 6, 13, Mar. 10, 17, May 8-29, June 12-
July 3, Aug. 11 - Aug. 22, Sept. 19, 22, Nov. 24 - Dec. 15
(Nos. 7, 8, 10, 11, 13, 20-22, 37-43, 47-53, 64-67, 75, 76,
94-100)

Ref: Columbia 530, LC, p. 119

SOVETSKOE STROITEL'STVO
> Organ Kustanaiskogo gubkoma RKP (bol'shevikov) i Gubispol-
koma. [Organ of the Kustanai Provincial Committee of the Russian
Communist Party and of the Provincial Executive Committee.]
> Kustanai, 1921

1921:   Nov. 7 (No. 56)

> Ref: LC, p. 44

SOVKHOZNAIA GAZETA
> Organ Narodnogo komissariata zernovykh i zhivotnovodches-
kikh sovkhozov. [Organ of the Ministry of State Farms of the
U. S. S. R.]
> Merged with Sotsialisticheskoe zemledelie and Sovetskoe
khlopkovodstvo as of Apr. 3, 1953, to form Sel'skoe khoziaistvo.
> Moscow, 3 times a week, semi-weekly

1936:   Aug. 26, 30 (Nos. 122(872), 124(874)
1945:   July 3 - Aug. 2 7 - 28, Sept. 1, 6, 11 - Oct. 9, 13 - Nov. 15,
         29 - Dec. 29 (Nos. 64-77, 79-88, 90, 92, 94-106, 108-126,
         128-141)

> Ref: LC, p. 120

SOVREMENNOE SLOVO
> (Published also as Sovremennyia vesti and Sovremennost' in
Nov. 1917)
> Petrograd, 1917, daily

1917:   March 5-7, Aug. 8 (Nos. 3274, 3275, 3277, 3282, 3291, 3292,
         3302, 3304, 3308, 3309, 3311, 3322, 3327, 3335, 3374-3375,
         3398, 3443)
1918:   Jan. 28, June 13(May 31) - 16(3), July 13(June 30), 20(7),
         24(11), 26(13) - 28(15), 31 (Nos. 3462, 3491, 3551-3554, 3576,
         3582, 3585, 3587-3589, 3591)

> Ref: Beliaeva 7768, Columbia 532,
> LC, p. 73

SOVREMENNOST'
> Bol'shaia ezhednevnaia politicheskaia, obshchestvennaia i
literaturnaia gazeta.
> Continuation of Sovremennoe slovo.
> Petrograd, 1917, daily

1917:   Nov. 23 (No. 1)

> Ref: LC, p. 73

SOVREMENNYIA VESTI
        Petrograd, 1917, daily (discontinued in 1917)

1917:   Dec. 16 (No. 15)

                            Ref: LC, p. 73

SREDNE-VOLZHSKAIA DEREVNIA
        Oblastnaia krest'ianskaia gazeta. Organ Obkoma VKP(b)
Sredne-Volzhskoi oblasti i Samarskogo okruzhkoma.
        Samara, 1926, twice a week

1928:   Dec. 23, 30 (Nos. 200, 202)

STALINSKII KOMSOMOL'SK
        Organ Komsomol'skogo-na-Amure gorodskogo komiteta
vsesoiuznoi kommunisticheskoi partii (bol'shevikov) i gorodskogo
soveta deputatov trudiashchikhsia. [Organ of the Komsomol'sk-na-
Amure City Committee of the All-Union Communist Party (of Bolsheviks) and of the City Soviet of Toilers' Deputies.]
        Komsomol'sk-na-Amure, 1932, daily

1945:   Apr. 15, 29 (Nos. 73, 83)

                            Ref: LC, p. 39

STANITSA
        Informatsiia Sofiiskoi kazach'ei stanitsy.
        Sofia, 1927

1927:   Jan. (6 p.)

STAROE VREMIA
        Organ Russkoi Natsional'no-Gosudarstvennoi Mysli.
        Belgrad, weekly

1923,   Oct. 8 - Jan. 1925 (Nos. 1, 33, 54-56, 58-61, 63, 65-66, 68-70,
        76, 78, 79, 81-88)

STARYI NARVSKII LISTOK
        Osnovan I. K. Griuntal'
        Narva, 1905 (?), three times a week

1934:   Feb. 8 (No. 17)

                          Ref: Columbia 536

STENNAIA GAZETA GLAVPOLITPROSVETA A. S. S. R.
Baku, 1921

1921:   Apr. 20 (No. 20)

Ref: LC, p. 9

STENNAIA GAZETA LUZHSKOGO OTDELENIIA PETERBURGSKOGO BIURO ROSTA
Luga, Petrogradskoi gub.

1921:   Nov. 6 (No. 168(298))

Ref: LC, p. 83

STENNAIA GAZETA ROSTA
Moscow

1920:   Dec. 16 (No. 411)

Ref: LC, p. 121

STEPNAIA ZVEZDA
Organ Akmolinskogo gubkoma VKP(b), Gubispolkoma i Gubprofsoveta.
Petropavlovsk, 1921

1928:   Apr. 26 (No. 64(2108))

STEPNOI KRAI
Obshchestvenno-literaturnaia gazeta.
Continuation of Stepnoi listok.
Omsk, 1893, twice a week

1893:   Dec. 2 (No. 45)
1894:   Jan. 2 (No. 1)
1946:   June 27 (No. 49)
1897:   Jan. 3 (No. 1)

Ref: Beliaeva 7995, Lisovskii 2375

STEPNOI LISTOK
Continued as Stepnoi krai.
Omsk, 1893, twice a week

1893:   July 11 (No. 4)

Ref: Lisovskii 2273

STRANA

   Politicheskaia, ekonomicheskaia i obshchestvennaia gazeta
pod redaktsiei Maksima Kovalevskago i professora I. Ivaniukova.
   St. Petersburg, 1906, daily

  1906: July 2(15), 4(17), 6(19) - 8(21) (Nos. 103, 114-115, 117-119)
            Ref: Columbia 539, Beliaeva 8042

STRANA

   Ezhednevnaia utrenniaia obshchestvenno-politicheskaia i
literaturnaia gazeta.
   Petrograd, 1918, daily

  1918: Mar. 28 - May 3 (Nos. 1-21, 23-31)
            Ref: LC, p. 73

SUVOROVETS

   Organ russkogo voenno-natsional'nogo dvizheniia.
   Subtitle varies: up to Apr. 1950 "Ezhenedel'nik sviazi i
informatsii".
   Buenos Aires, 1948, weekly

  1948: Sept. 24 - Dec. 31 (Nos. 1-3, 5-15)
  1949: Jan. 7 - Dec. 30 (Nos. 1(16) - 50(65))
  1950: Jan. 6 - Dec. 30 (Nos. 1(66) - 52(117))
  1951: Jan. - Dec. (Nos. 1(118) - 52(169))
            Ref: Columbia 543

SVET

   Gazeta obshchestvennaia i politicheskaia (organ nezavisimoi
mysli)
   Kharbin, 1919

  1919: Apr. 9 (No. 29)
  1924: Apr. 2-12 (Nos. 1424, 1425) (No. 1433?)

SVET

   Izdanie Soiuza Bessarabskago dukhovenstva.
   Kishenev, 1931, weekly, two times a week

  1933, Jan. 1 - May 1935 (Nos. 99-103, 106-111, 123-171, 173-188,
     190-214, 216-251)

SVET

Gazeta politicheskaia, ekonomicheskaia i literaturnaia.
Moscow, daily

1890: Apr. 4-27 (Nos. 75-95)
1901: Mar. 3, Oct. 30 (Nos. 58, 287)

SVET DETEI

(Supplement to Amerikansky Russky Viestnik)
Homestead, Pa.

1941: Mar. 13 - Dec. 18 (No. 2-19)
1942: Apr. 2 (No. 4)

SVETOCH

Moscow, 1906, daily

1906: Nos. 2, 5-9, 11-13, 15-17 (Microfilm)
Ref: Beliaeva 7264

SVIET

Russkaia ezhenedel'naia gazeta.
Wilkes-Barre, Pa., 1897, weekly

1918: Sept. 12 (No. 34)
1923: Feb. 1, 15 - Mar. 1, 9, Apr. 5, 19, 26, May 10, June 21,
       Nov. 8 (Nos. 3, 5-7, 9, 12, 14, 15, 17, 21, 41)
1924: Jan. 31, Feb. 7, 28, Apr. 3-17, May 1-29, Aug. 14 - Oct. 9,
       23, Nov. 6-20 (Nos. 5, 6, 9-14-16, 18-22, 33-41, 43, 45-47)
1925: Mar. 5, 11 (Nos. 10-1o)
1932: Oct. 14 - Dec. 29
1933 -1945

Ref: Columbia 545

SVOBODA

Ezhenedel'naia demokraticheskaia gazeta.
Landshut, weekly

1948: June, Aug. - Nov. (Nos. 1, 6-10)
Ref: Columbia 547

SVOBODA
> Gazeta politicheskaia, literaturnaia i obshchestvennaia.
> Warsaw

    1921:   Nos. 1(140) - 2(141), 19(149) - 61(200), 63(202) - 104(243),
            106(245) - 109(248), 111(250) - 121(260), 125(264) - 138(277),
            140(279) - 158(297), 160(299) - 183(322), 185(324) - 186(325),
            188(327) - 190(329), 192(331) - 193(332), 195(334), 200(339),
            202(341), 205(344) - 214(353), 216(355) - 219(358), 222(361) -
            247(386), 259(398) - 260(399)

SVOBODA ROSSII
> Moscow, 1918, daily

    1918:   Nos. 1-38, 41-65
> Ref: LC, p. 121

SVOBODA ROSSII
> Literaturno-politicheskaia gazeta; organ nezavisimoi
> demokraticheskoi mysli.
> Revel, 1919

    1919:   Sept. 20 - Dec. 31 (Nos. 2, 4, 8, 31-32, 44-58, 60-61, 75,
            76, 82, 85-86)
    1920:   Jan. 15 - Mar. 25 (11(97) - 15(101), 18(104), 26(112), 33(119),
            35(121) - 37(123), 51(137), 53(139), 68(154), 69(155))
> Ref: Columbia 548, LC, p. 165

SVOBODNAIA BOLGARIIA
> Obshchestvenno-politicheskaia i literaturnaia gazeta.
> Sofia, twice a month

    1947:   Mar. 9 (No. 1)
    1948:   Sept. 8 - Nov. 23 (Nos. 1-6)

SVOBODNAIA KOMMUNA
> Organ Petrogradskikh ob"edinennykh grupp anarkhistov-
> kommunistov. [Organ of the Petrograd United Groups of Anarchists
> and Communists.]
> Petrograd, 1917, weekly

    1917:   Oct. 2(15) (No. 2)
> Ref: LC, p. 73

SVOBODNAIA MYSL'
          Petrograd, 1917, weekly

1917:   Mar. 7 - Apr. 10 (Nos. 1-6)
                              Ref: LC, p. 73

SVOBODNAIA RECH'
          Ekaterinodar, Rostov-on Don, 1918, daily

1919:   June 19/2, July 10/23, Aug. 15/28, Sept. 17/30, Nov. 5/18 -
          8/21, 19(Dec. 2) - 21(Dec. 4) (Nos. 131, 149, 175, 200, 239-
          242, 251, 252-253)
                              Ref: LC, p. 151

SVOBODNAIA RECH'
          Continuation of Nasha rech'. Continued as Vek as of Nov. 23,
     1917.
          Petrograd, 1917, daily

1917:   Nov. 19 (No. 1)
                              Ref: LC, p. 73

SVOBODNAIA ROSSIIA
          Literaturno-politicheskaia gazeta.   Organ nezavisimoi
     demokraticheskoi mysli.
          Revel, daily

1919:   Aug. 27 (No. 2)
                              Ref: LC, p. 165

SVOBODNAIA SIBIR'
          Gazeta politicheskaia, ekonomicheskaia i literaturnaia.
     Vykhodit ezhednevno, krome dnei posleprazdnichnykh.
          Krasnoiarsk, 1917, daily

1919:   Aug. 1-7, 9, 12, 14, 15, 17, 19, 22, Sept. 3, 6, 10, 11, 13,
          16-20, 23, 24, Oct. 2, 4, 7-17, 22-24, 26, Nov. 7, 11-12,
          14-16, 23, 26, 28, 30 (Nos. 167(563) - 172(568), 174(570),
          176(572), 178(574), 179(575), 181(577), 182(578), 184(580) -
          193(589), 196(592), 199(595), 200(596), 202(598), 204(600) -
          208(604), 210(606), 211(607), 217(613), 219(615), 221(617) -
          229(625), 233(629) - 235(631), 237(633) - 247(643), 240(646) -
          251(647), 254(650) - 255(651), 257(653), 261(657), 263(659),
          265(661), 267(663))
                              Ref: LC, p. 42

SVOBODNAIA TSERKOV'
Petrograd, 1917, weekly

1917:   Mar. 15 (No. 1)

Ref: Columbia 554, LC, p. 74

SVOBODNAIA ZHIZN'
Ezhednevnaia politicheskaia, obshchestvennaia i literaturnaia gazeta.

Moscow, 1906, daily

1906:   Nos. 1-20 (Microfilm)

Ref: Columbia 555, Beliaeva 7286

SVOBODNOE SLOVO
Landshut, weekly

1948:   Apr., May (Nos. 1, 4)

Ref: Columbia 557

SVOBODNOE SLOVO
Gazeta obshchestvenno-politicheskaia i literaturnaia.
Moscow

1917:   Dec. 11 (No. 36)

Ref: Columbia 558

SVOBODNOE SLOVO
Ezhednevnaia demokraticheskaia natsional'naia gazeta.
Revel, 1921, daily

1921:   Apr. 17, May 31 (Nos. 1, 35)

SVOBODNYI KRAI
Gazeta ezhednevnaia krome dnei posleprazdnichnykh.
Irkutsk, 1918, daily

1919:   June 7, 26; July 1, 2, 6, 8, 16, 17, 19, 23-26, 31; Aug. 6, 8-12, 14, 17-25, 30, 31; Sept. 2, 4, 5, 7, 10-12, 16, 17, 19-21, 26, 30; Oct. 6, 7, 16, 17 (Nos. 246, 261, 265, 270, 271, 277, 278, 280, 283, 284, 286, 291, 295, 297-300, 302, 305-312, 314-316, 318, 319, 321, 323-325, 328, 329, 331-333, 337, 341, 345, 347, 349, 351-355, 363-366, 370, 372, 374, 377, 380, 387, 394, 395, 401, 402)

Ref: LC, p. 21

SVOBODNYI NAROD

Ezhednevnaia gazeta partii narodnoi svobody. [Published by the People's Freedom Party.]
Petrograd, 1917, daily

1917:   June 27 (No. 23)

Ref: LC, p. 74

SVOBODNYI TURKESTAN

Organ nezavisimoi sotsialisticheskoi mysli. Gazeta politi-chesko-ekonomicheskaia, obshchestvennaia i literaturnaia. [Organ of independent socialist thought.]
Title changed to Novyi Turkestan as of Feb. 19, 1918.
Tashkent, 1918, daily

1918:   Jan. 15 - Apr. 7 (Nos. 8-57)

Ref: LC, p. 167

SVOBODNYIA MYSLI

Politicheskaia, obshchestvennaia i literaturnaia ezhenedel'-naia gazeta, zakrytaia tsarskim pravitel'stvom v 1908 g. Redaktor I. Vasilevskii (Ne-Bukva). Izdanie "Zhurnala-zhurnalov".
Petrograd, 1907-1908, 1911 - , weekly

1917:   Mar. 7, 20, Apr. 3, 10, May 17 (Nos. 1, 3, 5, 6, 9)

Ref: LC, p. 74, Columbia 561

SYN OTECHESTVA

Vykhodit ezhednevno (bez predvaritel'noi tsenzury)
St. Petersburg, 1811, daily

1897:   July 8(20), Sept. 22(Oct. 4) (Nos. 182, 257)

Ref: Lisovskii 537

T

TAKSI

Organ Sindikata shofferov taksi departamenta Seny (S. ZH, T.).
Paris

1930, Dec. - Nov. 1932 (Nos. 13, 15-21)

TALLINSKII RUSSKII GOLOS
Tallin

1932: Dec. 4 (No. 4)

TAMBOVSKAIA PRAVDA

Organ Gubispolkoma i gubkoma RKP(b). [Organ of the Provin-
cial Executive Committee and of the Provincial Committee of the
Russian Communist Party.]
Tambov, 1922, daily

1922: Mar. 12 (No. 10)

Ref: LC, p. 166

TEATRAL'NYI KUR'ER
Moscow, 1918, daily

1918: Nov. 26/28 (No. 49)

Ref: LC, p. 121

TEKUSHCHII MOMENT
Petrograd, 1917, one day's newspaper

1917: Nov. 1-2 (2-3)

Ref: Columbia 565, LC, p. 74

TELEGRAF

Ezhenedel'naia gazeta.
Vyborg, 1917, weekly

1917: May 22 (No. 3)

TELEGRAMMY PETROGRADSKAGO AGENSTVA
Zmeinogorsk

1914:   Aug. 21, 23, 25 (Nos. 18, 20, 22)

TELEGRAMMY ROSSIISKAGO I PETERBURGSKAGO TELEGRAFNYKH AGENSTV
Krasnoiarsk, 1916, daily

1906:   Oct. 17 - Nov. 9 (Nos. 1-24)

TEREK
Ezhednevnyi organ Terskogo ispolkoma i Gubkoma RKP(b).
[Organ of the Terek Provincial Executive Committee and of the
Provincial Committee of the Russian Communist Party (of Bolsheviks.]
Piatigorsk, daily

1922:   Mar. 12 (No. 43)

Ref: LC, p. 147

TERNISTYI PUT'
Vladivostok, one day's newspaper

1921

Ref: LC, p. 183

TETKA SAKHALINKA
Satiriko-ser'eznaia ezhenedel'no-subbotniaia gazeta.
1920

1920:   Feb. 1 (No. 1)

TOMSKII LISTOK
Tomsk, 1894, daily

1895:   Jan. 5, Sept. 20, Dec. 24 (Nos. 4, 201, 278)
1897:   Aug. 6 (No. 169)

Ref: Lisovskii 2379

TOMSKII SPRAVOCHNYI LISTOK see TOMSKII LISTOK

TORGOVAIA GAZETA see CHERNAIA METALLURGIIA

TORGOVO-PROMYSHLENNAIA GAZETA see CHERNAIA METALLURGIIA

TORGOVO-PROMYSHLENNAIA GAZETA
    Finansy, torgovlia, promyshlennost', sel'skoe khoziaistvo.
    Continued as Finansy i narodnoe khoziaistvo as of Sept. 24,
  1918·
    Petrograd, 1893, daily

  1894: Dec. 11(23) (No. 267)
  1899: July 6(18) (No. 145)
  1902: Mar. 21(Apr. 3) (No. 67)
  1917: March 31, Apr. 13 (Nos. 57, 66)
           Ref: Columbia 569, LC, p. 75
           Beliaeva 8417, Lisovskii 2277

TORGOVO-PROMYSHLENNYI BIULLETEN' KIEVSKOI TOVARNOI BIRZHI I
KOMITETA KONTRAKTOVOI IARMARKI
    Vykhodit ezhednevno, krome posleprazdnichnykh dnei.
    Kiev, daily

  1923: Mar. 31 (No. 190)

TORGOVYI BIULLETEN' see CHERNAIA METALLURGIIA

TOVARISHCH
    Politicheskaia, literaturnaia i ekonomicheskaia gazeta.
  Osnovana Prof. L. V. Khodskim.
    St. Petersburg, 1906

  1906: Aug. 3(16) (No. 25)
           Ref: Beliaeva 8388, Columbia 571

TOVARISHCH
    [Published by the Military Organization of the People's
  Socialist Labor Party.]
    Petrograd, 1917, daily

  1917: Nov. 14 (No. 1)
           Ref: LC, p. 75

TOVARISHCH

Organ Viazemskogo komiteta RKP i Soveta raboch., krest'ian, i krasnoarm. deputatov. [Organ of the Viazma Committee of the Russian Communist Party and of the Soviet of Toilers' Deputies.]
Viazma, 1919

1921: Nov. 7 (No. 169)
1929: June 23 (No. 46(145))

Ref: LC, p. 185

TOVARISHCH

Eta gazeta presleduet tsel' oznakomit' chitatelia s vazhnei-shimi sobytiiami, sopriazhennymi s voinoiu. Glavnym obrazom pechataiutsia offitsial'nyia izvestiia, krome togo vypiski iz gazet vsekh partii, kak oboikh vrazhdebnykh soiuzov, tak i neitral'nykh derzhav.
Vilna

1917, June 6 (13) - March 10 (Feb. 25), 1918 (No. 1-133)

TREZVOE SLOVO

Po vsem voprosam zhizni lichnoi, semeinoi, obshchestvennoi i gosudarstvennoi.
St. Petersburg, 1907

1907: Apr. (No. 1)

Ref: Beliaeva 8458

TRUD

Izdanie Dal'biuro partii sotsialistov-revoliutsionerov. [Published by the Far Eastern Bureau of the Party of Social Revolutionaries.]
Chita, 1921

1922: Apr. 7 - July (Nos. 38(99), 42(103), 45(106), 73(134), 74(135))
Ref: LC, p. 15

TRUD

Organ Mosk. komiteta partii sots-rev.
Moscow

1917: June 17 (No. 75)

TRUD
>
>Ezhednevnaia gazeta VTSSPS. [Organ of the All-Union Central Council of Labor Unions.]
>>Moscow, 1921, daily

1921 - 1923
1933 - 1940
1944, Mar. - Dec. 1947
1948:   Apr. 16, 17, June - Dec.
1949, Jan. - Mar. 30, 1955

Missing numbers:
1921:   Nos. 6, 21, 180, 229-251
1922:   Nos. 24-25, 29, 61, 144, 184
1923:   Nos. 4, 46, 154
1938:   No. 143
1940:   Nos. 1-47, 55-86, 88-90, 92-97, 99-105, 108
1948:   No. 134
>>>>>Ref: Columbia 573; LC, p. 123

TRUD
>
>Organ Petrogradskogo Soveta Professional'nykh Soiuzov. Ezhenedel'naia gazeta. [Organ of the Petrograd Council of Labor Unions.]
>>Petrograd, 1919, weekly

1919:   Nos. 3, 5, 6, 13, 20-22, 25, 27, 28-30, 32-33, 37
1920:   Nos. 3(40), 8(45), 13(50), 17(54), 21(58)
>>>>Ref: LC, p. 75

TRUD
>
>Dvukhnedel'nyi organ Russkago obshche-trudovogo soiuza v Bolgarii.
>>Sofia, 1932, semimonthly

1932,   May 22 - Feb. 18, 1933 (Nos. 1-19)
>With No. 20 this newspaper consolidated with Golos and formed Golos truda.

TRUD I VOLIA
>
>Ezhenedel'naia gazeta. Organ Soiuza anarkho-sindikalistov-kommunistov g. Moskvy. [Organ of the League of Anarchists, Syndicalists and Communists of the City of Moscow.]
>>Moscow, 1919, weekly

1919:   Apr. 14 (No. 3)
>>>>Ref: LC, p. 124

TRUD I VOLIA
>   Ezhednevnaia politicheskaia gazeta.
>   Petrograd, 1917, daily

1917:   Sept. 1(14) (No. 95)

>>   Ref: LC, p. 75

TRUDIASHCHAIASIA BEDNOTA
>   Organ ispolkomov i uezdkomov RKP Kovrovskogo, Viaznikovsko-
go i Gorkhov. u. Vladimirskoi g. [Organ of the Executive and
District Committees of the Russian Communist Party of the Kovrov,
Viaznikov and Gorokhov Distircts.]
>   Kovrov, Vladimirskoi gub., 1918, semiweekly

1922:   March 12 (No. 18)

>>   Ref: LC, p. 39

TRUDOVAIA MYSL'
>   Organ russkogo otdela Latviiskoi sotsial-demokraticheskoi
rabochei partii s profsoiuznym otdelom "Trudovaia zhizn' ".
>   Riga, 1928, weekly

1933:   Feb. 26 - Dec. (No. 9(233) - 19(243), 22(246) - 53(277)
1934:   Jan. - May 16 (Nos. 1(178) - 19(296))

TRUDOVAIA PRAVDA
>   Ezhednevnaia gazeta Penzenskogo gubkoma V. K. P. (b),
Gubispolkoma i Gubprofsoveta.
>   Penza, 1918, daily

1926:   Dec. 24 (No. 293)
1928:   June 1 (No. 124)
1923:   June 7 (126)

TRUDOVAIA ROSSIIA
>   Ezhednevnaia narodnaia gazeta, izdaiushchaiasia pri uchastii
mnogikh deputatov, chlenov "Trudovoi gruppy".
>>   Supersedes Izvestiia Soveta Rabochikh Deputatov.
>   St. Petersburg, daily

1905:   June 4, 9, 10 (Nos. 3, 7, 8)

>>   Ref: Beliaeva 8504; Columbia 576

TRUDOVAIA ZHIZN'
>   Organ Olonetskogo gubkoma R. K. P. (b) i Olonetskogo Gub-
ispolkoma. [Organ of the Olonets Provincial Committee of the
Russian Communist Party and of the Olonets Provincial Executive
Committee.]

(Continued on next page)

TRUDOVAIA ZHIZN' (continued)
        Petrozavodsk, 1921, 4 times a week

    1921:   Nov. 7 (No. 15)
    1922:   Mar. 12 (No. 37(83))
                  Ref: LC, p. 145

TRUDOVAIA ZHIZN'
        Izdanie tsentral'nago biuro professional'nykh soiuzov Latvii.
        Riga, 1923, forthnightly

    1923, May 1 - Apr. 16, 1926 (Nos. 1, 25, 28, 29, 34, 35, 46, 55-59)

TRUDOVOE SLOVO
        Ezhednevnaia politicheskaia i literaturnaia gazeta. Organ
    TSentral'nogo Komiteta Trudovoi Narodno-Sotsialisticheskoi Partii.
        Petrograd, daily

    1917:   Nos. 4, 5 (Microfilm)

TRUDOVOI GOLOS
        Krest'ianskaia i rabochaia gazeta.
        St. Petersburg, 1913, twice a week

    1913:   Feb. 17 - July 23 (Nos. 1, 6-23)
                  Ref: Beliaeva 8509; Columbia 580

TRUDOVOI NABAT
        Ezhednevnaia gazeta Tiumenskogo gubernskogo komiteta Ross.
    kom. partii (bol'shevikov) i Gubernskogo ispolkoma. [Published by
    the Tiumen Provincial Committee of the Russian Communist Party
    and the Tiumen Provincial Executive Committee.]
        Tiumen

    1921:   Nov. 6(No. 56(826))
                  Ref: LC, p. 173

TRUZHENIK
        Organ Pochinkovskogo uezdkoma RKP(b) i Pochink. uezdnogo
    ispolnitel'nogo komiteta soveta rab. i kr. deputatov. [Organ of the
    Pochinki District Committee of the Russian Communist Party (of '
    Bolsheviks) and of the Pochinki District Executive Committee of the
    Soviet of Workers' and Peasants' Deputies.]
        Pochinki, Nizhegorodskoi gub. 1920, semiweekly

    1922:   Mar. 12 (No. 19)
                  Ref: LC, p. 145

TSAR'-KOLOKOL

      Golos russkoi mysli, russkikh slez i russkago smekha.
Sevastopol, 1920, weekly

1920:   Aug. 24, Sept. 27, Oct. 5 (Nos. 1, 5, 6)

                            Ref: LC, p. 158

TSARSKII VESTNIK

      Za vozstanovlenie Prestola pravoslavnago TSaria-Samoderzhtsa.
Organ narodnago dvizheniia.
      Continuation of Russkii voennyi vestnik.
      Belgrad, 1928

1928 - Mar. 1934 (Nos. 2, 4, 6, 7, 9, 11, 13, 15, 16, 17, 20, 21, 24,
      36-39, 42, 43, 46, 48-50, 58, 60, 80, 82, 134-386)
1937:   Oct. 24(11), Nov. 14(1) (Nos. 576, 579)

                            Ref: Columbia 582

TURKESTANSKIIA VEDOMOSTI

      Organ Turkestanskago komiteta Vremennago pravitel'stva.
Tashkent, 1870

1917:   May 31 (June 13) (No. 56(114))

                    Ref: Beliaeva 8815; Lisovskii 1060;
                    LC, p. 168

TVERSKAIA PRAVDA

      Organ Gubispolkoma i gubkoma RKP. [Organ of the Provincial
Executive Committee and of the Provincial Committee of the Russian
Communist Party (of Bolsheviks).]
      Tver, 1919, daily

1919:   Nov. 7 (No. 122)
1921:   Nov. 7 (No. 232)
1922:   Mar. 12 (No. 58)

                    Ref: LC, p. 23

U

UCHITEL'SKAIA GAZETA
        Organ Narkomprosov soiuznykh respublik i tsentral'nykh komitetov profsoiuzov rabotnikov nachal'noi i srednei shkoly i nauchno-issledovatel'skikh uchrezhdenii, politiko-prosvetitel'nykh uchrezhdenii i doshkol'nykh rabotnikov. [Organ of the Ministries of Public Instruction of the Union Republics and of the Central Committees of the Labor Unions of Employees of Elementary and Secondary Schools.]
        Continuation of Za kommunisticheskoe prosveshchenie.
Moscow, 1937, weekly

1944:   May 14, 31 - June 7, July 5 - 12, Aug. 17 (Nos. 21(3045), 12(3047) - 24(3048), 28(3052) - 29(3053), 35(3059))
1945:   June 27, July 4, 18, 25, Aug. 1 - 8, 15, 29, Sept. 12 - Nov. 21, Dec. 12 - 16 (Nos. 27 - 8, 30 - 33, 35 - 6, 38 - 48, 50 - 52)
1946:   Apr. 3 - 10, Oct. 6, Nov. 16 (Nos. 17, 18, 46, 52)
1947:   Mar. 8, 29, Apr. 19 - May 1 (Nos. 11, 14, 17 - 19)
1949, Jan. - March 30, 1955

                        Ref: Columbia 587; LC, p. 125

URAL
        Gazeta politicheskaia, obshchestvennaia i literaturnaia.
Ekaterinburg, 1897, daily

1897:   Jan. 1 (No. 2)

URAL'SKAIA ZHIZN'
        Gazeta obshchestvennaia, literaturnaia i torgovo-promyshlen-
naia.
        Ekaterinburg, 1899, daily

1899:   May 3 - 9, 11 - 14, 16 - 21, Aug. 9 (Nos. 2-8, 10-12, 15-21, 99)
                    Ref: Lisovskii 2784; Beliaeva 8873

URAL'SKII NABAT

Ezhenedel'nyi organ feratsii anarkhistskikh grupp Urala.
[Organ of the Federation of Ural Anarchist Groups.]
Ekaterinburg, 1918, weekly

1918:   June 30 (No. 8)

Ref: LC, p. 164

URAL'SKII RABOCHII

Organ Ekaterinburgskogo gub. komiteta Rossiiskoi kommunisticheskoi partii (bol'shevikov) i Gub. ispolnitel'nogo komiteta
Sovetov raboch., krest'. i krasnoarmeiskikh deputatov. [Organ of
the Sverdlovsk Provincial and City Committee of the All-Union
Communist Party (of Bolsheviks), and of the Sverdlovsk Provincial
and City Soviets of Toilers' Deputies.]
Ekaterinburg, 1917, daily

1919:   Nov. 7 (No. 81(433))
1927:   Aug. 25 (No. 192)

Ref: LC, p. 164

URGINSKAIA GAZETA see IZVESTIIA ULAN-BATOR-KHOTO

URGINSKIE IZVESTIIA see IZVESTIIA ULAN-BATOR-KHOTO

USTIUZHANIN

Organ Ustiuzhinskogo uispolkoma i uezdnogo komiteta RKP.
[Organ of the Ustiuzhna Executive Committee and of the District
Committee and the Russian Communist Party.]
Ustiuzhna, Cherepovetskoi gub. 1918, twice a week

1919:   Nov. 7 (No. 54)

Ref: LC, p. 175

UTRO

Ezhednevnaia politiko-ekonomicheskaia i literaturnaia
gazeta.
New York, daily

1922:   Jan. 2 - Mar. 14 (Nos. 1-10, 14, 16-19, 21-24, 26-62)

UTRO
>Politicheskaia, obshchestvenno-ekonomicheskaia i literatur-
naia gazeta.
>Petrograd, 1915

>1915:   Nos. 1, 2 (Microfilm)
>>Ref: Beliaeva 8917

UTRO MOSKVY
>Vykhodit po ponedel'nikam utrom. Gazeta izdaetsia
Moskovskim professional'nym soiuzom rabochikh pechatnago dela
s tsel'iu okazaniia pomoshchi bezrabotnym pechatnikam.
>Moscow, 1918, weekly

>1918:   Nos. 2-5, 7-17, 19-22 (Microfilm)
>>Ref: LC, p. 125

UTRO PETROGRADA
>Vykhodit v ponedel'nik utrom. Izdanie Petrogr. soiuza rab.
pechatnago dela. [Published by the Union of Printers.]
>Petrograd, 1918, weekly

>1918:   Apr. 8 (No. 2)
>>Ref: Columbia 603, LC, p. 76

UTRO PRIURAL'IA
>Gazeta bezpartiinaia, demokraticheskaia, vykhodit ezhednevno.
Zlatoust, daily

>1919:   Feb. 5 (No. 27)
>>Ref: LC, p. 189

UTRO ROSSII
>Moscow, 1910, daily

>1917:   Mar. 2, 4 - 10, 12, 15, Nov. 10 - Dec. 31 (Nos. 59, 61-67,
>>69, 71, 148, 259, 261-266, 269, 277, 279-289)
>1918:   Jan. 3 - Apr. 4 (Mar. 22) (Nos. 1-5, 7-13, 16, 18, 21-23,
>>26-33, 43, 46-49, 52-53)
>>Ref: Beliaeva 8932, Columbia 604
>>LC, p. 125

V

V DEN' VSEROSSIISKOI NATSIONAL'NOI KATASTROFY

Biuro po delam rossiiskikh emigrantov v Man'chzhurskoi imperii.

Harbin, 1938, one day's paper

1938: March 15 (8 p.)

V GLUBOKUIU NOCH'

Sotsialisticheskaia gazeta.
Petrograd

1917: Nov. 26 (No. 2)

V POMOSHCH' PARTIINOI UCHEBE

Izdanie TSK VKP(b). Ezhedekadnik.
Moscow, 1936, once in 10 days

1936: June (No. 16)

V TEMNUIU NOCH'

Sotsialisticheskaia gazeta.
Petrograd, 1917, one day's newspaper

1917: Nov. 25 (No. 1)
Only one number was published. Continuation of Polnoch'
(one of newspapers continuing the newspaper Den') Continued as
Vol'naia glukhaia noch' Nov. 26, 1917.

Ref: LC, p. 76

VARSHAVSKOE SLOVO

Organ demokraticheskoi mysli. Vykhodit ezhednevno.
Warsaw, 1920, daily

1920: Jan. 24 (No. 17)

VECHE
Obshchestvennaia, politicheskaia i literaturnaia gazeta s portretami, risunkami i karrikaturami.
Moscow, 3 times a week

1906: Nos. 63, 64, 68
1907: Mar. 6 (No. 26)
Ref: Beliaeva 1237; Columbia 606

VECHER
Continuation of Vechernee vremia which later continued as Vechernee slovo.
Petrograd, 1917, daily

1917: Nov. 11 (24), 15 (28) (Nos. 1, 3, 5)
Ref: LC, p. 76

VECHER
Organ vnepartiinyi, demokraticheskii, pod redaktsiei S. F. Znamenskago, L. A. Korolia. V. I. Moravskago, M. N. Pavlovskago.
Vladivostok, daily

1920: Oct. 30, Dec. 7 (Nos. 144, 174)
Ref: Columbia 607, LC, p. 183

VECHER MOSKVY
Vykhodit po voskresen'iam vecherom. Gazeta izdaetsia Moskovskim professional'nym soiuzom rabochikh pechatnago dela s tsel'iu okazaniia pomoshchi bezrabotnym pechatnikam. [Published by the Moscow Labor Union of Typographical Workers.]
Moscow, 1918, weekly

1918: Nos. 3, 8, 10, 11, 15, 17, 18, 20 (Microfilm)
Ref: LC, p. 126

VECHERNEE RADIO
Kharkov, 1924

1928: Dec. 31 (No. 360)

VECHERNEE SLOVO
Izdaetsia gruppoi sotrudnikov "Vecherniago vremeni" i pechatnikami.
Continuation of Vecher, which in turn is one of the newspapers continuing Vechernee vremia.
Petrograd, 1918, daily

(Continued on next page)

VECHERNEE SLOVO (Continued)

1918:   Mar. 26(13), 27(14), 29(15), Apr. 1(Mar. 19), 2(Mar. 20),
6(Mar. 24), 8(Mar. 26), 9(Mar. 27), 11(Mar. 29), 17(4),
19(6), June 3(May 21), 6(May 24), 8(May 26), 10(May 28),
15(2), 17(4), 20(7), 22(9), 25(12), 26(13), 28(15), July 1(June 18),
3(June 20), 4(June 21), 9(June 26), 10(June 27), 16(3), 19(6),
25(12), 29(16), 30(17), Aug. 2(July 20), 3(July 21); (Nos. 4, 5,
7, 9-10, 13-15, 17, 22, 24, 47, 50, 52, 58, 59, 62, 64-66, 68,
70, 72-73, 77, 78, 83, 86, 91, 94-95, 98-99)

Ref: Columbia 609;
LC, p. 76

VECHERNEE VREMIA

Continued as Vecher as of Nov. 11, 1917.
Petrograd, 1911, daily

Nov. 26(Dec. 9), 1911 - Dec. 31(Jan. 13), 1912, (Nos. 1-340)
1913:   Jan. 1(14) - Dec. 31(Jan. 13), (Nos. 341-649)
1914:   Aug. 3-6, 11-12 (Nos. 822 - 825, 830, 831)
1915:   Jan. 1(14) - June 30(July 13) (Nos. 985-1163)
1917:   Feb. - Sept. (Nos. 1716, 1717, 1752, 1764 - 1770, 1773, 1775 -
1777, 1779 - 1783, 1786, 1788, 1790, 1792 - 1795, 1797, 1799 -
1802, 1804 - 1808, 1835, 1839 - 1840, 1842, 1843, 1847, 1868 -
1869, 1871 - 1872, 1881, 1913)

Ref: Beliaeva 1244, Columbia 614,
LC, p. 76

VECHERNEE VREMIA

Rostov-na-Donu, daily

1919:   Aug. 28, 31 - Sept. 4, 12-16, Oct. 14, 16, 18, 19, 24, 26, 29,
Nov. 1-16, 19 - Dec. 4, 7, 10-11 (Nos. 349, 351 - 354, 361 -
363, 386, 388, 390d, 391, 394, 396, 398, 401-414, 416-427,
429, 431-432)

Ref: Columbia 613, LC, p. 152

VECHERNEE VREMIA

Editor: B. A. Suvorin.
Shanghai, 1931, daily

1931:   July 3 - 18 (Nos. 1-14)

VECHERNIAIA GAZETA
Samara, daily

1921:   Sept. 27 - 29 (Nos. 1-3)

VECHERNIAIA GAZETA
Vladivostok, daily

1921:   Sept. 13, 15, 16, Oct. 18, 20, 29 - Nov. 2, 4, 5, 18 (Nos. 90,
92-93, 117, 119, 127 - 128, 130, 132-133, 144)
Ref: LC, p. 183

VECHERNIAIA GAZETA "NAROD"
Organ Petrogradskoi gruppy sotsialistov-revoliutsionerov-
oborontsev. [Organ of the Petrograd Group of the Anti-Defeatist
Social Revolutionaries.]
Petrograd

1917:   Nov. 8 (No. 18)
Ref: LC, p. 77

VECHERNIAIA GAZETA OBSHCHEE DELO see OBSHCHEE DELO

VECHERNIAIA KRASNAIA GAZETA
Izdanie Leningradskogo soveta rab. i kr. deputatov.
Leningrad, 1921, daily

1935:   May 21 (No. 115(5025))

VECHERNIAIA MOSKVA
Gazeta Moskovskogo gorodskogo komiteta VKP(b) i Mossoveta.
[Published by the Moscow City Committee of the Communist Party of
the Soviet Union and by the Moscow Soviet.]
Moscow, Est. 1923, daily

1927:   Aug. 23 (No. 190 (1101)
1934:   Feb. 9 - Dec. 31 (Nos. 33(3062) - 42, 46, 50-52, 54-57, 59-64,
66-67, 70-92, 94-300(3229)
1945:   June 30 - July 23, Aug. 17-18, Sept. 8-10, 17, 22, 26, Oct. 9-13,
17, 19-26, 29-Nov. 3, 7-10, 16, 21-22, 24, 27, 29, Dec. 6-10,
12, 15, 19-20; (Nos. 152-171, 193-194, 212-123, 219, 224, 227,
238-242, 245, 247-253, 255-260, 263-264, 269, 273-274, 276,
278, 280, 285-288, 290, 293, 296, 297)
Ref: Columbia 615, LC, p. 126

VECHERNIAIA POCHTA
> Vecherniaia demokraticheskaia gazeta.
> Moscow, daily

    1917:   Mar. 14 (No. 5)

VECHERNIAIA POCHTA
> Continued as Novaia vecherniaia pochta with the Nov. 11, 1917
issue; later continued as Petrogradskaia vecherniaia pochta as of Nov.
21, 1917.
> Petrograd, March 14, 1917, daily

    1917:   Nov. 2, 4, 7, 9 (Nos. 2, 4, 6, 8) n. s. Nov. 23-24 (Nos. 3-4)
> > Ref: LC, p. 77

VECHERNIAIA ZARIA
> Organ ob"edinennoi sotsialisticheskoi mysli. Ezhednevnaia
obshchestvenno-politicheskaia i literaturnaia gazeta.
> Omsk, daily

    1918:   Jan. 19 (No. 13)

VECHERNIAIA ZARIA
> Continuation of Vechernee vremia.
> Petrograd, 1918

    1918:   May 14(1) (No. 1)
> > Ref: LC, p. 77

VECHERNIAIA ZARIA
> Shanghai, 1931, daily

    1932,   Nov. 22 - Jan. 5, 1933 (Nos. 109-111, 113, 115-118, 120-121,
123, 126, 128-130, 133, 135, 137-144)

VECHERNIAIA ZVEZDA
> Sotsial-demokraticheskaia gazeta. [Published by the
Cooperative of Social Democratic Journalists "Avangard".]
> Petrograd, daily

    1918:   Jan. 27 - May 22 (Nos. 6, 7, 12-13, 19-24, 26-27, 30, 32, 34,
35, 37, 38-39, 44, 46-62, 64-65, 66, 68-73)
> > Ref: Columbia 617, LC, p. 77

VECHERNIE IZVESTIIA
Organ Moskovskogo soveta rabochikh i krasnoarmeiskikh deputatov i Oblastnogo ispolnitel'nogo komiteta sovetov.
Moscow, 1918, daily

1918:   Oct. - Dec. (Nos. 65-80, 82-92, 94, 96-103, 106-111, 124-128)
Ref: LC, p. 126

VECHERNIE OGNI
Petrograd, daily

1918:   March 21(8) - July 24(11) (Nos. 1-6, 8-19, 21-30, 36-38, 40, 43-44, 46-50, 52-77, 79)
Ref: Columbia 618

VECHERNII CHAS
Petrograd, 1917, daily

1917:   Nov. 28 - Dec. 27 (Nos. 2-12, 14-24)
Continued as Novyi Vechernii Chas.
Ref: LC, p. 77

VECHERNII EKSTRENNYI VYPUSK
IAponskie osvedomitel'nye biulleteni.
Tientsin

1932:   Mar. 5, 7, 8-12, 14-15, 17-19, 21-22, 24-26, 28-29, 31, Apr. 1

VECHERNII KUR'ER
[Democratic and socialist newspaper.]
Moscow, 1914, daily

1917:   Mar. 2-5, 8-9, 13-14 (Nos. 891-894, 897-898, 901-902)
Ref: Beliaeva 1272, Columbia 619
LC, p. 127

VECHERNII ZVON
Petrograd, 1917, daily

1917:   Dec. 7, 9, 14-16, 18, 20, 21, 27-30, (Nos. 2, 4, 8-11, 13-14, 16-19)
1918:   Jan. 4, 5 (Nos. 22, 23)

VECHERNIIA VEDOMOSTI
        Politicheskaia, obshchestvennaia i literaturnaia gazeta.
        Petrograd, 1917, daily

    1917:   Nov. 30(17) (No. 2)
        Continuation of Birzhevyia vedomosti. Continued as Vedomosti.
                         Ref: LC, p. 78

VEDOMOSTI
        Vecherniaia politicheskaia, obshchestvennaia i literaturnaia
gazeta.
        Petrograd, 1917, daily

    1917:   Nov. 20 (Dec. 3), No. 1
        Continuation of Vecherniia vedomosti (one of newspapers
continuing Birzhevyia vedomosti) . Continued as Nashi vedomosti.
                         Ref: LC, p. 79

VEDOMOSTI VERKHOVNOGO SOVETA SOIUZA SOVETSKIKH
SOTSIALISTICHESKIKH RESPUBLIK
        Moscow, 1938, irreg.

    1940:   Feb. 1 (No. 4(67))
    1945:   June - Dec. (Nos. 35-82)
    1946:   Dec. 17 (No. 44)
    1947:   Apr. - Dec. (Nos. 13-45)
    1948:   Feb. 13, 18, Mar. 5, 10, 14, Apr. 4-13, June 2 - Dec. 26
        (Nos. 6, 7, 9, 10, 12-14, 21-48)
    1949 - 1953
    1954 — issued as a serial publication
                       Ref: LC, p. 127

VEK
        Ezhednevnaia politicheskaia, obshchestvennaia i literaturnaia
gazeta.
        Moscow, daily

    1906:   Nov. 17-19, 23-24, 29 - Dec. 5, 8, 9, 12, 14, 16, 22, 23, 28, 29,
        30 (Nos. 48-50, 52-53, 55, 57-62, 65, 66, 68, 70, 72, 77, 78,
        81, 82, 83)

VEK
        Continuation of Svobodnaia rech'. Continued as Novaia rech' on
Nov. 28, 1917; and as Nash vek as of Nov. 30 (Dec. 13) 1917.
        Petrograd, 1917, daily

    1917:   Nov. 23 (Dec. 6) - Nov. 24 (Dec. 7) (Nos. 1, 2)
                   Ref: Columbia, 621, LC, p. 79

VELIKAIA ROSSIIA

Organ russkoi gosudarstvennoi mysli. Osnovatel' V. V. Shul'gin.
Subtitle slightly varies. Continuation of Rossiia.
Rostov-on-Don, Novorossisk, Sebastopol, 1918, daily

1919: Nos. 234, 237, 241-242, 249, 273-289, 295-299, 303, 305,
309, 313-315, 317-321, 323, 324, 327, 330-331, 333-346,
348-355, 357-361, 365
1920: 1(412)-4(416), 28(440), 30(442), 42(454), 44(456), 45(457),
89(501), 95(507), 100(512), 107(519), 109(521), 111(523)-
114(526), 119(531)-120(532), 122(534), 123(535), 131(543)-
145(557)

Ref: Columbia 623; LC, p. 41

VELIKII OKEAN

Vykhodit ezhednevno, krome dnei posleprazdnichnykh.
Sumy, 1910, daily

1917: Sept. 1(14) (No. 39)

Ref: LC, p. 163

VERA V POBEDU

Organ N'iu Iorkskago otdela Rossiiskago imperskago soiuza i
2-go otdela Soiuza Ego Vysochestva Kniazia Nikity Aleksandrovicha
mushketerov v g. San Francisco. Ezhemesiachnoe izdanie.
New York, monthly

1941: Feb. (No. 3)

VERNAIA MYSL'

Krest'ianskaia i rabochaia gazeta.
St. Petersburg, 1914, twice a week

1914: Feb. 26 - Apr. 16 (Nos. 1-22)

Ref: Beliaeva 726; Columbia 625

VESTNIK ANARKHII
Organ Brianskoi federatsii anarkhistov. [Organ of the Bryansk Federation of Anarchists.]
Bryansk, 1918, weekly

1918:   July 14, 25. (Nos. 10-11)
Ref: LC, p. 12

VESTNIK GORODSKOGO SAMOUPRAVLENIIA
Vestnik Petrogradskago gradonachal'stva.
Petrograd, 1917, daily

1917:   Nov. 3, 12 (Nos. 109(194), 118(203))
Ref: LC, p. 79

VESTNIK MAN'CHZHURII
Ezhednevnaia gazeta posviashchennaia politike, ekonomike, kul'ture i interesam professional'no-trudovoi zhizni. Vykhodit v Kharbine ezhednevno, krome posleprazdnichnykh dnei.
Kharbin, 1918, daily

1919:   Sept. 4, 5, 9, 26, 30; Oct. 8 (Nos. 167, 168, 171, 184, 186, 193)

VESTNIK NARODA
Kuldja, Sinkiang, China

1947:   May 1-6, 10-24, 30-31, June 12-13, 19-23 (Nos. 1-4, 7-19, 24, 34-35)

VESTNIK OBSHCHESTVENNO-POLITICHESKOI ZHIZNI, ISKUSSTVA TEATRA I LITERATURY (ORGAN TSENTRAL'NOGO SOVETA PROFESSIONAL'NYKH SOIUZOV RABOTNIKOV TEATRA I ZRELISHCH)
[Organ of the Central Soviet of the Labor Unions of Theatre and Entertainment Workers.]
Petrograd, 1918

1918:   Sept. 25 (No. 7)
Ref: LC, p. 79

VESTNIK PETROSOVETA
Izdanie Otdela upravleniia Petrogradskogo gubernskogo ispolnitel'nogo komiteta.
Petrograd, 1921, twice a week

(Continued on next page)

VESTNIK PETROSOVETA   (Continued)

    1922:   Apr. 22, 29, May 3, 13, 31, June 3, Aug. 19 - Sept. 2, 9
           (Nos. 31-32(104-105), 34(107), 38(111), 43(116), 44(117), 66(139) -
           70(143), 72(145)

VESTNIK POLTAVSKOGO GUBERNSKOGO OBSHCHESTVENNOGO KOMITETA
        Poltavskiia eparkhial'nyia diela.   (Iz Vestnika P. Gub.
Obshch. Komiteta)
        Poltava

    1917:   June 7, 8 (Nos. 37, 38)

VESTNIK PRIVOLZHSKAGO RAIONA
        Vykhodit ezhednevno, za iskliucheniem dnei posleprazdnich-
nykh.
        Saratov, 1917, daily

    1917:   Dec. 16, 20, 21 (Nos. 2, 5, 6)
                              Ref. LC, p. 154

VESTNIK RUSSKOI NATSIONAL'NOI OBSHCHINY V G. TIAN'TSZINE
        Tientsin, China, weekly

    1928,   Oct. 22 - Feb. 11, 1929 (Nos. 11, 14-20, 24-27)
    1932:   June 10 (No. 33)

VESTNIK SEVERO-ZAPADNOI ARMII
        Narva, daily

    1919:   Oct. 24(11) - Nov. 20(7) (Nos. 101 - 113, 115-124)

VESTNIK TEATRA I ISKUSSTVA
        Organ Petrogradskogo otdela soiuza rabotnikov iskusstv.
[Organ of the Petrograd Section of the Union of Artists.]
        Petrograd, 1921

    1922:   Jan. 1 (No. 1)
                           Ref: LC, p. 78

VESTNIK VERKHOVNAGO UPRAVLENIIA SEVERNOI OBLASTI
        Continued as Vestnik Vremennago pravitel'stva severnoi
oblasti.
        Arkhangelsk, 1918, irreg.

    1918:   Aug. 15 (No. 5)
                           Ref: LC, p. 4

VESTNIK VREMENNAGO PRAVITEL'STVA
>Continuation of Pravitel'stvennyi vestnik. Continued as
Gazeta Vremennago rabochago i krest'ianskago pravitel'stva as of
Nov. 1917.
>Petrograd, 1917, daily

1917:   Jan. 31, Feb. 1, 5, 7, 10, 14, 15, Mar. 20, June 5, Aug. 23
>(Nos. 9, 14-16, 25, 26, 29, 30, 33, 35, 36, 59, 96, 137)
>Mar. 5(18) - Oct. 26 (Nov. 8) (Nos. 1(46) - 186(232)
>Ref: Columbia 631, LC, p. 79

VESTNIK VREMENNAGO PRAVITEL'STVA AVTONOMNOI SIBIRI
>Vladivostok, 1918, irreg.

1918:   July 28(No. 4)
>Ref: LC, p. 184

VESTNIK VREMENNAGO PRIAMURSKAGO PRAVITEL'STVA
>Vestnik Vremennago Priamurskago pravitel'stva zameniaet
soboi Sobranie uzakonenii i rasporiazhenii pr-va, Senatorskiia
vedomosti, Priamurskiia vedomosti, Vestnik Vrem. pr-va Prim.
oblasti, Zemskoi upravy i Vestnik Primorskoi oblasti.
>Vladivostok, 1921, irreg.

1921:   June 30 - July 21, Aug. 9 - Aug. 17 (Nos. 2-5, 8-10)
>(Microfilm)
>Ref: LC, p. 184

VESTNIK ZARUBEZHNOI KAZNY
>Obshchestvo vzaimnykh sberezhenii s otdelom blagotvoritel'-
nosti.
>Paris

1931:   April (No. 14)
1932,   Nov. - Sept. 1933 (No. 18-21)
>Ref: Columbia 630

VIATSKAIA GAZETA
>Ezhenedel'noe izdanie Viatskago gubernskago zemstva.
>Viatka, 1894, weekly

1902:   Nos. 1-52
>Ref: Beliaeva 1755; Lisovskii 2314

VIKHR'

        Ezhenedel'naia satiricheskaia gazeta.
        Moscow, 1906

    1907:   No. 18

                      Ref: Beliaeva 1349

VISTI

        [Published by the Poltava Executive Committee of the Soviet
of Workers', Peasants' and Red Army Deputies and by the Poltava
Provincial Committee of the Communist Party of Bolsheviks.]
        Poltava

    1922:   Mar. 12 (No. 57(507))

                      Ref: LC, p. 146

VISTNIK UKRAINS'KOI NARODNOI RESPUBLIKI

    1919:   Nos. 34-44   (Microfilm)

VLADIVOSTOK

        Obshchestvenno-literaturnaia i morskaia gazeta.
        Vladivostok, 1883, weekly

    1890-1891
        Missing nos.: 1890, No. 25; 1891, No. 12
                Ref: Beliaeva 1350; Lisovskii 1613

VLAST' NARODA

        Gazeta demokraticheskaia i sotsialisticheskaia.
        Moscow, 1917, daily

    1917:   Apr. 28, July 1-15, 18-30, Aug. 4, 23, Sept. 3, 20, Oct. 1-7,
           10-12, 14-19, 21, Nov. 7, 18-19, 24, 30, Dec. 1, 5, 14, 15,
           17-21, 23-29 (Nos. 1-35, 38-161, 164-165, 168, 173-174, 177,
           185-186, 188-191, 193-199)
                Ref: Columbia 636, LC, p. 127

VLAST' SOVETOV

        Ezhednevnaia gazeta Stavropol'skogo gubkoma RKP(b) i
Gubispolkoma Sov. raboch., krest'ian. i krasnoarm. deputatov.
[Published by the Stavropol' Provincial Committee of the Russian
Communist Party (of Bolsheviks) and the Provincial Executive
Committee of the Soviet of Toilers' Deputies.]
        Stavropol, 1920, daily

    1922:   Mar. 12 (No. 580)

                      Ref: LC, 163

VLAST' TRUDA
>   Organ Irkutskogo okruzhkoma VKP(b), Okrispolkoma i
Okrprofsoveta. [Organ of the Irkutsk District Committee of the All-
Union Communist Party (of Bolsheviks), the District Executive
Committee and the District Council of Labor Unions.]
>   Irkutsk, 1917, daily

1928:   Mar. 30 (No. 76 (2481))
>   Ref: LC, p. 21

VLAST' TRUDA
>   Gazetu izdaiut Minusinskii i Khakasskii okruzhnye komitety
VKP(b) i Okruzhnye ispolnitel'nye komitety.
>   Minusinsk

1928:   May 22-23 (Nos. 117(1365) - 118(1366)

VLAST' TRUDA
>   Organ Ufimskogo gubkoma RKP(b) i gub. Gorispolkoma
sovetov rab. krest'. i kr.-arm. deputatov. [Organ of the Ufa
Provincial Committee of the Russian Communist Party (of Bolsheviks)
and of the Provincial Executive Committee.]
>   Ufa, 1922, daily

1922:   Mar. 12 (No. 26)
>   Ref: LC, p. 173

VLAST' TRUDA
>   Organ Vladikavkazskogo i Sunzhenskogo okruzhkomov VKP(b),
Okrispolkomov i Sovetov profsoiuzov.
>   Vladikavkaz, 1925

1928:   Apr. 8 (No. 84(1089))

VO IMIA SVOBODY
>   Odnodnevnaia gazeta Soiuza deiatelei iskusstva. [Published
by the Artists' Union.]
>   Petrograd, 1917, one day's newspaper

1917:   May 25 (8 p.)
>   Ref: LC, p. 80

VOENNYI SOIUZ
>   Organ severnago organizatsionnago komiteta Ofitserskago
soiuza.

(Continued on next page)

VOENNYI SOIUZ   (Continued)
>   Continued as a journal Narodnaia Armiia.
>   Monthly

>   1906:   Nov. - Dec. 2 (Nos. 1-2 and pril. k No. 2)
>   Ref: Columbia 639

VOENNYI TELEGRAF
>   Petrograd

>   1914:   Oct. 17 (No. 52)

VOENNYI VESTNIK
>   Gazeta voennaia, obshchestvennaia i literaturnaia.
>   Vladivostok, 1919, twice a week

>   1919:   Aug. 18-29, Sept. 29 (Nos. 1-4, 13)
>   Ref: LC, p. 184

VOINA I MIR
>   Ezhednevnaia voennaia i politicheskaia gazeta.   [Published
> by the Moscow Soviet of Officers' Deputies.]
>   Moscow, daily

>   1917:   June 17 (No. 11)

>   Ref: Columbia 640, LC, p. 128

VOLIA
>   Ezhednevnaia obshchestvenno-politicheskaia gazeta.
>   Ekaterinodar, daily

>   1920:   Feb. 18 (No. 9)

VOLIA
>   Politicheskaia, obshchestvennaia i literaturnaia gazeta.
>   Riga, 1920

>   1920:   Mar. 6-7 (No. 19-20)

VOLIA
>   Organ Dal'nevostochnago biuro vsesibirskago kraevogo
> komiteta partii sotsialistov-revoliutsionerov.   [Organ of the All-
> Siberian Regional Committee of the Party of Social Revolutionaries.]
>   Vladivostok, 1920, daily

(Continued on next page)

VOLIA (Continued)

>Apr. 18, 1920 - Jan. 4, 1921 (Nos. 1-7, 9-14, 16, 19-26, 30-38, 43,
45-46, 52-53, 64-65, 69-73, 75, 82-95, 97-101, 106-113, 115,
120-123, 125, 127-157, 159, 161-163, 176, 178, 184-188, 190-
195, 197-200)
>
>Ref: LC, p. 184

VOLIA I DUMY ZHELEZNODOROZHNIKA
Moscow, 1917

>1918:   Oct. 19-23, Nov. 14-28 (Nos. 70-71, 77-81)
>
>Ref: LC, p. 129

VOLIA NARODA
Organ komiteta osvobozhdeniia narodov Rossii.
Berlin, biweekly

>1944:   Nov. 15 (No. 1)
>1945:   Jan. 31 (No. 10(23))
>
>Ref: Columbia 642

VOLIA NARODA
Literaturno-politicheskaia ezhednevnaia gazeta, izdavaemaia
pod redaktsiei chlenov partii sotsialistov-revoliutsionerov. [Pub-
lished under the editorship of members of the Party of Social
Revolutionaries. Continued as Volia narodnaia.]
Petrograd, 1917, daily
>1917:   Apr. 29 - Dec. 31 (No. 1-150, 153-180, 182-206)
>
>Ref: Columbia 643, LC, p. 80

VOLIA NARODNAIA
Literaturno-politicheskaia ezhednevnaia gazeta, izdavaemaia
pod redaktsiei chlenov partii sotsialistov-revoliutsionerov, E.K.
Breshkovskoi i dr.
Continuation of Volia naroda. Subsequently published as Volia,
Volia vol'naia, Svobodnaia volia, and Volia strany.
Petrograd, 1917, daily

>1917:   Nov. 28 (No. 1)
>
>Ref: LC, p. 80

VOLIA ROSSII
Vykhodit ezhednevno krome ponedel'nikov.
Praga, 1920, daily

(Continued on next page)

VOLIA ROSSII   (Continued)

        Sept. 12, 1920 - Oct. 9, 1921 (Nos. 1-258, 260-327)
                                   Ref: Columbia 644

VOLIA STRANY

        Literaturno-politicheskaia ezhednevnaia gazeta, izdavaemaia
pod redaktsiei chlenov partii sotsialistov-revoliutsionerov. [Published
under the editorship of members of the Party of Social Revolutionaries.
Continuation of Svobodnaia volia which in turn is one of the newspapers
which continued Volia narodnaia.]
        Petrograd, 1917, daily

1918:   Feb. 14 (1) - 19 (6) (Nos. 15-17)
                                   Ref: LC, p. 80

VOLIA TRUDA

        Organ TSentral'nogo komiteta partii revoliutsionnogo kommu-
nizma. Vykhodit ezhednevno, krome dnei posleprazdnichnykh.
[Organ of the Central Committee of the Party of Revolutionary
Communism.]
        Moscow, 1918, daily

1918:   Oct. 20-27, Nov. 3-9, 12-22, 24-30 (Nos. 31-37, 43-46,
        48-57, 59-64)
                                   Ref: LC, p. 128

VOLNA

        Ezhednevnaia gazeta.
        St. Petersburg, 1906, daily

1906:   Apr. 26 - May 24 (Nos. 1-25) (Microfilm)
                         Ref: Columbia 648, Beliaeva 1492

VOLNA BAKU

        Baku

1909:   Nos. 1-2 (Microfilm)

VOL'NAIA LITVA

        Organ nezavisimoi demokraticheskoi mysli. Vykhodit
ezhednevno, krome dnei posleprazdnichnykh. [Organ of Independent
Democratic Thought.]
        Kovno, 1921, daily

1921:   June 5 (101)

                                Ref: Columbia 650, LC, p. 25

VOL'NAIA SIBIR'
>   Politicheskaia, ekonomicheskaia i literaturnaia gazeta.
Osnovana Soiuzom sibiriakov-oblastnikov. [Published by the Union
of Siberian Autonomists.]
>   Petrograd, 1918, weekly, semiweekly

1918:   Jan. 14 - Apr. 20 (No. 1-18)
>   Ref: LC, p. 81

VOL'NOE SLOVO
>   Geneva, daily

1881 - 1883 (Nos. 1-62)

VOL'NOST'
>   Ezhednevnaia politicheskaia i obshchestvenno-literaturnaia i
kazach'ia gazeta.
>   Continued by Nasha vol'nost'.
>   Petrograd, 1917, daily

1917:   Oct. 17 (30), Nov. 8, 12 (25), 17 (30) (Nos. 7, 17, 21, 25)
>   Ref: Columbia 651; LC, p. 81

VOL'NYI GOLOS TRUDA
>   Organ anarkhosindikalistov.
>   Moscow

1917:   Sept. 16(No. 4)
>   Ref: LC, p. 129

VOL'NYI GORETS
>   Organ of Revoliutsionnoi demokratii narodov Severnogo
Kavkaza. Obshchestvenno-politicheskaia i literaturnaia gazeta.
>   Tiflis, 1918, monthly

1919,   Sept. 8 - Dec. 31, 1920 (Nos. 1-68)
>   Ref: Columbia 652; LC, p. 170

VOL'NYI KRONSHTADT
>   Izdanie Kronshtadtskoi organizatsii anarkhistov. [Published
by the Kronshtadt Organization of Anarchists.]
>   Kronshtadt, 1917

1917:   Oct. 12, 23 (Nos. 2, 3)
>   Ref: LC, p. 43

VOL'NYI PAKHAR'
      Organ Uezdnogo komiteta RKPB i uezdnogo ispolnitel'nogo
komiteta. [Organ of the District Committee of the Russian Communist
Party (of Bolsheviks) and of the District Executive Committee.]
      Kargopol

1921:   Nov. 7 (No. 34(144))
                         Ref: LC, p. 24

VOLYNSKOE SLOVO
      Ezhednevnaia obshchestvennaia, literaturnaia i ekonomiches-
kaia gazeta.
      Rovno, 1921, daily

1927:   Jan. - June (Nos. 1082-1086, 1089, 1091-1094, 1097-1100, 1102,
        1104-1109, 1126-1131, 1145)
                         Ref: Columbia 657

VOLZHSKAIA KOMMUNA
      Organ Kuibyshevskogo obkoma i gorkoma VKP(b) oblastnogo i
gorodskogo sovetov deputatov trudiashchikhsia. [Organ of the
Kuibyshev Provincial Committee and the City Committee of the All-
Union Communist Party (of Bolsheviks) and of the Provincial and
City Soviets of Toilers' Deputies.]
      Kuibyshev, daily

1945:   July 3 - Dec. 26 (Nos. 128 - 136, 138, 140 - 141, 143 - 149, 151,
        153, 155 - 156, 160 - 161, 163 - 167, 169 , 171 - 175, 177, 180 -
        188, 191 - 192, 195 - 199, 202, 204, 207, 210, 213- 215, 217 -
        219, 221 - 222, 226, 233 - 236, 238, 240 - 241, 246 - 248,
        250 - 251, 253.
                         Ref: LC, p. 45

VOORUZHENNYI NAROD
      Organ Voennoi sektsii Petrogradskogo Soveta. [Organ of the
Military Section of the Petrograd Soviet.]
      Petrograd, 1918, daily

1918:   July 17 - Sept. 3 (Nos. 1 - 39, 41- 45, 47- 48, 50, 52- 53,
        55 - 59, 61 - 63, 65 - 67, 69 - 110, 112 - 115)
                         Ref: LC, p. 81

VORONEZHSKAIA KOMMUNA
      Organ Gubkoma VKP(b), Gubispolkoma i Gubprofsoveta.
      Voronezh, 1920

1928:   May 29 (No. 123(2559)

VOSKRESENIE
Organ russkoi nezavisimoi mysli.
Kishinev, 1933, weekly

1933:   Oct. 8 - 22 (Nos. 21 - 23)

VOSKRESENIE ROSSII
Golos russkoi monarkhicheskoi mysli pod redaktsiei N. P.
Izmailova.
Stratford, Conn., 1933

1933:   July 17 (No. 2)

Ref: Columbia 659

VOSTOCHNO-SIBIRSKAIA PRAVDA
Organ Irkutskogo oblastnogo i gorodskogo komitetov vsesoiuznoi kommunisticheskoi partii (bol'shevikov) i oblastnogo Soveta
deputatov trudiashchikhsia. [Organ of the Irkutsk Provincial and
City Committees of the All-Union Communist Party (of Bolsheviks)
and of the Provincial Soviet of Toilers' Deputies.]
Irkutsk, 1918, irreg.

1945:   Jan. 14, 22, 25 (Nos. 10, 16 - 18)

Ref: LC, p. 22

VOZROZHDENIE
Bezpartiinaia demokraticheskaia gazeta.   Vykhodit ezhednevno,
krome ponedel'nikov, na russkom i frantsuzskom iaz.
Copenhagen, daily

1919:   June 27, Sept. 23, 24, 26 - Oct. 29, 31 - Nov. 2, 8 (Nos. 19,
69, 70, 72 - 100, 102 - 104, 109)

Ref: Columbia 660

VOZROZHDENIE
Bol'shaia ezhednevnaia politicheskaia i literaturnaia gazeta.
Moscow, 1918, daily

1918:   June 7 (May 25), June 20(7) (Nos. 5, 15)

Ref: LC, p. 129

VOZROZHDENIE
Paris, 1925, daily; from July 18, 1936, weekly

1925,   June 3 - June 7, 1940 (Nos. 1-4239)

(Continued on next page)

VOZROZHDENIE (continued)

Beginning June 21, 1936, this newspaper temporarily ceased publication. On July 18, 1936 it resumed publication as a weekly newspaper. Suspended June 3, 1940-Dec. 1948. In 1949 it resumed publication as a serial under the same title.

Missing numbers:

1925: Nos. 18, 37, 55-56, 61-62, 67, 69-70, 72-77, 79-81, 83-92, 94-97, 99, 101-107, 109-111, 114, 115-119, 121-126, 128-129, 131, 133-144, 146-151, 156-159, 166-171, 173-175, 177-180, 182-189, 191,198, 200-210, 212

1929: Nos. 1491-1583, 1585-1586, 1589-1592, 1594, 1596-1597, 1601, 1608-1610, 1613-1623, 1625, 1627-1629, 1631, 1635, 1636, 1646, 1652, 1655-1659, 1662, 1668-1670

1930: Nos. 1920-1946, 1948, 1950-1951, 1953, 1955, 1957, 1959-1960, 1962, 1965, 1967-1972, 1977-2006, 2008-2010, 2012, 2014 - end of year

1931: Jan. 1 - Apr. 30 (Nos.   - 2097

1939: Nos. 4195 - 4209, 4214 - 4215

1940: Nos. 4221 - 4222

Ref: Columbia 661

VOZROZHDENIE AZII

[Supersedes Golos Azii.]
Tientsin, 1933, daily

1933, Feb. 15-Mar. 13, 1937 (Nos. 1-49, 51-58, 61-131, 133-146, 148-704, 708-755, 757-774, 776-802, 804-816, 818-831, 833-1477)

1937: Apr. 29, Aug. 3 (Nos. 1517, 1597)

1938: Mar. 1, Oct. 9, 11 (Nos. 1773, 1962-1963)

1939: Aug. 4, Dec. 9 (Nos. 2215, 2326)

1941: Oct. 14 (No. 2896)

1942: Oct. 11 (No. 3252)

VOZROZHDENIE SEVERA

Ezhednevnaia oblastnaia obshchesotsialisticheskaia gazeta.
Arkhangelsk, 1918, daily

1919: July 12, Nov. 15, Dec. 2 (Nos. 150(257), 252(358), 265(371)
Ref: LC, p. 5

VPERED

Organ bol'shevikov (Lenin i dr.).
Geneva, 1905

1905: Jan. 4 (Dec. 22, 1904) - May 18 (5)
Ref: Columbia 662

VPERED

Kievskaia Rabochaia Gazeta.
Kiev

1896 - 1898: Nos. 1, 2, 5, 8-9   (Microfilm)

VPERED

Organ Mosk., Spb., Mosk. okr., Kazansk., Kursk. i
Permsk. komitetov R. S. - D. R. P.
Moscow, 1906

1906:   Sept. 23 (No. 2)
1907:   Feb. 7, May 1 - Oct. 8 (Nos. 8, 11-16)
Ref: Columbia 664

VPERED

Sotsial-demokraticheskaia rabochaia gazeta. [Organ of the
Moscow Organization of the Russian Social Democratic Workers'
Party.]
Moscow, 1917, daily; (discontinued in 1918)

1917 - 1918: (Nos. 4-5, 8, 10, 43, 52, 57-102, 105-117, 146-150, 152,
153-192, 195, 198-241, 243-246; 3(249), 62(308), 63(309),
64(310), 66(312) - 72(318), 74(320), 76(322) - 78(324), 80(326))
Ref: LC, p. 129

VPERED

St. Petersburg, 1906, daily

1906:   May 26 - June 14 (Nos. 1-17) (Microfilm)
Ref: Columbia 666, Beliaeva 1622

VRACHEBNAIA ZHIZN'

Ezhenedel'naia gazeta, izdavaemaia Pravleniem Obshchestva
russkikh vrachei v pamiat' N. I. Pirogova. [Published by the Administration of the Russian Medical Association.]
Moscow, 1917, weekly

1917:   Aug. 15 - Oct. 22 (Nos. 1-9)
Ref: LC, p. 127

VREMIA

Berlin, 1919, weekly

1920:   Sept. 13 (No. 115)
1925:   Jan. - June (Nos. 340, 346, 348, 350, 352, 353)
Ref: Columbia 667

VREMIA

Ezhenedel'naia natsional'naia gazeta.
Buenos Aires, 1937, weekly

1937, Oct. 1 - Jan. 8, 1938 (Nos. 1-15)

VREMIA

Vecherniaia gazeta.
Moscow, 1915, daily

1917: Mar. 2(15) - Mar. 5(18), 27(20) - 14(27) (Nos. 880-883, 885-
       888)

Ref: Columbia 668; LC, p. 129

VREMIA

Pod redaktsiei Bor. Suvorina.
Simferopol

1920: Oct. 16(No. 82)

Ref: LC, p. 161

VREMIA

Pod redaktsiei B. A. Suvorina.
Shanghai, daily

1930: Jan. 7 - Dec. 19
1931: Jan. 6 - June 21 (Nos. 131, 138, 140, 145, 148, 151, 156, 158,
       160, 162, 163, 177-178, 184, 195, 197-205, 207, 211-213, 218,
       220-222, 231, 233, 235, 237, 238d- 239, 241-243, 245, 256 d,
       258-259, 261, 265, 268, 271, 274, 277-279, 289, 293, 295,
       298, 397-400, 404, 423, 436, 438, 440, 446-449, 452-456,
       462, 470-471, 474, 477, 480-485, 493-502, 510-513, 519-523,
       531-535, 538-541, 554-571)

VREMIA

Gazeta politicheskaia i literaturnaia.
Tomsk, 1906, daily

1906: Jan. 1-11 (Nos. 1-7)

Ref: Beliaeva 1682

VSE NOVOSTI

Ezhednevnaia, obshchestvennaia, nezavisimaia gazeta.
Continuation of Rassvet. Continued as Nasha rech'.
Chicago, 1941, daily

1941: Jan. 5 - Feb. 20 (Nos. 1-40)

VSEGDA VPERED
>Organ TSentral'nogo i Moskovskogo komitetov RSDRP. [Organ of the Central and Moscow Committees of the Russian Social Democratic Workers' Party.]
>Moscow, 1919, irreg.

>1919:   Nos. 1-2 (Microfilm)
>>Ref: Columbia 671, LC, p. 129

VSEROSSIISKAIA KOCHEGARKA
>Organ Donskogo Gubispolkoma, Gubnarkoma, Gubotdela Vserossiiskogo Soiuza gornorabochikh tsentral'nogo pravleniia kamennougol'noi promyshlennosti (TS RKP). [Organ of the Don Provincial Executive Committee, of the Provincial Department of the All-Russian Union of Miners and of the Coal Mining Industry.]
>Bakhmut, 1921

>1921:   Nov. 7 (No. 369(519))
>1922:   Mar. 12 (No. 52(653))
>>Ref: LC, p. 5

VSEROSSIISKII PECHATNIK
>Moscow

>1920:   No. 6 (June 10)   (Microfilm)

VTOROE POKOLENIE
>Prague, 1931, weekly

>1931:   Apr. 4 - June 13 (Nos. 1-11)
>>Ref: Columbia 674

Z

ZA INDUSTRIALIZATSIIU see CHERNAIA METALLURGIIA

ZA KOMMUNISTICHESKOE PROSVESHCHENIE
        Organ Narkomprosov soiuznykh respublik i TSekprosa SSSR.
[Organ of the People's Commissariats of Education of the Union
Republics and of the Central Committees of the Union Republic School
Employees' Labor Unions.]
        Continued as Uchitel'skaia gazeta as of 1937.
        Moscow, 1924, every other day

1934:   Sept. 15-21, Dec. 9-29 (Nos. 213-218, 282-299)
                              Ref: LC, p. 130

ZA MIR I TRUD (Krasnyi Kavallerist)
        Ezhednevnaia krasnoarmeiskaia gazeta Politicheskogo
Upravleniia Severo-Kavkazskogo voennogo okruga.
        Novocherkassk, 1920, daily

1929:   June 12 (No. 131(2628))

ZA NARODNOE DELO
        Organ Komiteta gruppy sotsialistov-revoliutsionerov.
        Continuation of Narodnoe Delo. With No. 57 the newspaper
ceased publication.
        Revel, 1921, daily

1921:   Mar. 15 - May 28 (Nos. 1-13, 15-57)

ZA NOVUIU ROSSIIU see ZA ROSSIIU

ZA PARTIIU
        Izd. Plekhanovskoi gruppy.
        Paris

1912, Apr. 16(20) - Feb. 14 (Nos. 1-5)

ZA RODINU see ZA ROSSIIU

ZA RODINU

 Krasnoarmeiskaia gazeta N-skogo pogranpolka.
 Moscow

 1942: May 17 (No. 62(347)

ZA ROSSIIU

 Gazeta Severnoi oblasti.
 Arkhangel'sk

 1919: Oct. 2(Sept. 19) (No. 19)
          Ref: LC, p. 5

ZA ROSSIIU

 Organ Natsional'nogo Soiuza Novogo Pokoleniia.
 Sofia, Belgrade, 1932, monthly, semi-monthly

 1932, Mar. - May 15, 1940: (Nos. 1-100, 4 (101)-5 (102), 7 (104)-
   8 (105)
   Nos. 44-96 were published in Sofia; No. 97 - in Belgrade.
   Title varies: Mar. 1935 - Mar. 1937, Za novuiu Rossiiu;
 Apr. 1937 - Jan. 15, 1940, Za rodinu; Feb. 1, 1940 - Za Rossiiu.
        Ref: Columbia 685

ZA ROSSIIU

 Organ sotsialistov vsekh partii.
 Helsinki

 1917: Nos. 1, 2 (Microfilm)

ZA RUBEZHOM

 Ezhednevnaia literaturno-politicheskaia gazeta.
 Berlin

 1906: Nos. 7-10, 54, 57 (Microfilm)

ZA SOTSIALDEMOKRATIIU

 Odnodnevnaia gazeta, posviashchennaia nedele sotsialdemokra-
 ticheskoi propagandy v Latvii. Izdanie Rizhskogo komiteta sotsial-
 demokraticheskoi rabochei partii Latvii.
 Riga, 1927, one day's newspaper

ZA SVOBODU
Russkaia demokraticheskaia gazeta v Pol'she.
Warsaw, 1921, daily

1928: June 5 (No. 127(2459))
1929: Nos. 36, 39, 47, 51, 52, 54, 61, 62, 64, 86, 106, 107, 114,
144-146, 148-151, 155-156, 158 (incomp.), 159, 161, 165-167,
171, 172, 175-178, 180, 182-183, 189-191, 194-204, 207, 209,
212-214, 216, 219-220

Ref: Columbia 687

ZA TSARIA I RODINU
Organ soiuza russkago naroda.
Odessa, 1906

1907: Apr. 5 (No. 50)

Ref: Beliaeva 2912

ZA VOZVRASHCHENIE NA RODINU
Izdanie komiteta "Za vozvrashchenie na rodinu".
In 1960 the title changed to Golos Rodiny.
Berlin, twice a week

1956: Feb., Mar. - Dec. (Nos. 6 (22), 9 (25) - 69 (85), 74 (90))
1957: Jan. - Dec. (Nos. 1 (91) - 13 (103), 15 (105) -
101 (191))
1959: Apr. - Dec. (Nos. 29, 32, 34, 37-38, 41, 43, 46, 49, 51, 53,
56-65, 67, 69-72, 74-77, 79-82, 84-85, 87-89, 91-95, 97-99))
1960: Jan. - Dec. (Nos. 2-3, 5-6, 8, 10-11, 13-14, 16-17, 19-20,
22-23, 26, 29-31, 34, 36, 38, 42, 45, 47, 53-54, 56, 58, 60,
67, 69, 75-77, 81, 84, 86, 90, 94-95))
1961: Aug. - Sept. (Nos. 64-65, 73-74)

Ref: Columbia 688

ZABAIKAL'SKII KAZAK
Odnodnevnaia gazeta v pamiat' Voiskovogo prazdnika Zab.
kaz. voiska.
Kharbin, 1933, one day's newspaper

1933: Mar. 30 (8 p.)

ZABAIKAL'SKII RABOCHII
Organ Chitinskogo obkoma, gorkoma VKP(b) i oblastnogo
soveta deputatov trudiashchikhsia. [Organ of the Chita Provincial
Committee, of the City Committee of the All-Union Communist Party
and of the Provincial Soviet of Toilers' Deputies.]

(Continued on next page)

ZABAIKAL'SKII RABOCHII (Continued)
        Chita, 1905, daily

1945:   Sept. 20 (No. 185)
                          Ref: LC, p. 15

ZAKASPIISKOE OBOZRENIE
        Gazeta politicheskaia, obshchestvennaia, torgovo-promyshlen-
naia i literaturnaia s ezhemesiachnymi i'liustrirovannymi prilozheni-
iami.
        Ashkhabad, 1895, daily

1897:   Mar. 20, July 26 (Nos. 58, 153)
                     Ref: Lisovskii 2412, Beliaeva 2948

ZARIA
        Kharbin, 1920, daily

1929, 1932 - 1936
Missing nos.
1929:   Nos. 1-47, 61, 64, 66, 68-69, 75-76, 80-84, 87-88, 92, 97,
        113, 116, 132, 133, 148, 150, 152, 156, 161-162, 164-165, 168 -
        end of year
1932:   Nos. 1-99, 101-105, 107-350
1933:   Nos. 33, 65-67, 75, 89, 130, 169, 248, 280, 306, 322, 355-
        356, 358
1934:   Nos. 6, 19, 59, 153 incomplete, 157-158, 191, 247
1935:   Nos. 33, 129, 131, 243
1936:   No. 56

ZARIA
        Organ Mozhaiskogo uispolkoma s. r. k. i k. d. Uezdkoma RKP
(b-kov) i Uezdnogo otd. Rosta. [Organ of the Mozhaisk District
Executive Committee of the Soviet of Toilers' Deputies, of the
District Committee of the Russian Communist Party (of Bolsheviks)
and of the District Office of the Russian Telegraph Agency.]
        Mozhaisk, 1919, twice a week

1921:   Nov. 6 (No. 73)
                       Ref: LC, p. 132

ZARIA
        Ezhednevnaia obshchestvenno-politicheskaia i literaturnaia
gazeta. [Organ of Vsesibirskii sovet kooperativnykh s''ezdov.]
        Omsk, 1917, daily

1918:   Dec. 13 (No. 144)
                   Ref: Columbia 692, LC, p. 142

ZARIA
> Politicheskaia i literaturnaia vecherniaia gazeta.
> Petrograd

1918:   Jan. 22 (No. 1)
> Ref: LC, p. 81

ZARIA KOMMUNY
> Organ Belozerskogo ukoma RKP(b) Cherepovetskoi gubernii.
> [Organ of the Belozersk District Committee of the Russian Communist
> Party of the Cherepovets Province.]
> Belozersk, 1918, 4 times a week

1921:   Nov. 7 (No. 125)
> Ref: LC, p. 11

ZARIA ROSSII
> Moscow, 1917, daily

1918:   Apr. 19(6), May 14 (1), 24(11) (Nos. 2, 19, 28)
> Ref: LC, p. 131

ZARIA VOSTOKA
> Organ TSentral'nogo i Tbiliskogo komitetov KP(b) Gruzii.
> (Organ of the Central Committee of the Communist Party of Georgia
> and of the Soviets of Toilers' Deputies of the Georgian S. S. R.]
> Tiflis, June 20, 1922, daily

1927:   June 23 - Dec. 21 (Nos. 1581, 1583)
1945:   Nos. 124-125, 131-135, 137, 139-142, 145-146, 148-159, 161, 163,
        165, 169-174, 176-181, 185-186, 190-193, 195, 197-198, 200, 204,
        209, 211-213, 215-216, 219-224, 226-227, 229-232, 235-246,
        249, 251
> Ref: Columbia 696, LC, p. 170

ZARIA ZAPADA
> Ezhednevnaia gazeta Vitebskogo okruzhkoma K. P. (b)B. ,
> Okrispolkoma i Okrprofsoveta.
> Vitebsk, daily

1928:   May 29 (No. 124)

ZASHCHITA
Ezhednevnaia gazeta, izdavaemaia v Moskve pri blizhaishem
uchastii A. A. Evdokimova i kn. D. I. Shakhosvkogo.
Moscow, 1914, daily

1914:   Sept. 1 - Nov. 11 (Nos. 1 - 53)
                                Ref: Beliaeva 3199

ZAVETNAIA MYSL'
Krest'ianskaia i rabochaia gazeta.
St. Petersburg, 1913, twice a week

1913:   Sept. 28 - Oct. 18 (Nos. 1-7)
                                Ref: Beliaeva 2926; Columbia 697

ZAVOD I PASHNIA
Gazeta Saranskago i Ruzaevskogo ukomov VKP(b), Uispolkomov,
Uprofbiuro 4 i Raipotrebsoiuza.
Saransk, Penzenskoi gub., 1918, twice a week

1928:   Jan. 4, 11-25, Feb. 8-15, Mar. 17, 24, Apr. 4-7, 14, 21, 25,
        May 5, 9, 12-30 (Nos. 1(1029), 3(1029)-7(1033), 11(1037)-
        13(1039), 22(1048), 24(1050), 27(1053)-28(1054), 30(1056),
        32(1058)-42(1068))

ZEMLEDELETS I RABOCHII
Organ Orlovskogo gubkoma RKP(b) i Gubispolkoma. [Organ
of the Orel Provincial Committee of the Russian Communist Party
and of the Provincial Executive Committee.]
Orel, 1919, daily

1922:   Mar. 12 (No. 59)
                                Ref: LC, p. 142

ZEMLIA
Petrograd, 1917

1917:   July 1(14), 4(17), 5(18), Aug. 31((Sept. 13) (Nos. 10, 12, 13, 61)
                                Ref: LC, p. 81

ZEMLIA
Krest'ianskaia gazeta.
Simferopol, 1920, 3 times a week

1920:   May 1 (No. 10)
                                Ref: LC, p. 161

ZEMLIA I VOLIA
>   Krest'ianskaia gazeta Partii sotsialistov-revoliutsionerov.
>   [Published by the Party of Social Revolutionaries.]
>   Moscow, 1917, irreg.

1917:   June 22(July 5) (No. 75)

Ref: LC, p. 131

ZEMLIA I VOLIA
>   Ezhednevnaia Narodnaia gazeta. Izdanie Petrogradskago
>   Oblastnogo Komiteta partii sotsialistov-revoliutsionerov. [Published
>   by the Petrograd Provincial Committee of the Party of Social
>   Revolutionaries.]
>   Petrograd, Est. Mar. 21, 1917, daily

1917:   No. 130   (Aug. 1954)

Ref: Columbia 698, LC, p. 82

ZEMSHCHINA
>   Politicheskaia, obshchestvennaia i literaturnaia gazeta.
>   Petrograd, 1909, daily

1916:   Apr. 30, May 1, Dec. 15, 18-31 (Nos. 2341, 2342, 2550)
1917:   Jan. 1-3 Nos. 2553-2566

Ref: Beliaeva 3172, Columbia 700
LC, p. 82

ZHELEZNODOROZHNAIA GAZETA
>   Organ Moskovskogo i St. Peterburgskogo komitetov RSDRP.
>   St. Petersburg

1906:   No. 1 (Microfilm)

Ref: Columbia 701

ZHELEZNODOROZHNAIA ZHIZN'
>   Moscow, 1906, weekly

1906:   Nos. 1-2   (Microfilm)

Ref: Beliaeva 2670

ZHIVAIA MYSL'
>   Krest'ianskaia i rabochaia gazeta.
>   St. Petersburg, 1913, twice a week

1913:   Aug. 17 - Sept. 6 (Nos. 1-7)

Ref: Beliaeva 2707, Columbia 702

ZHIVAIA MYSL' TRUDA
>Krest'ianskaia i rabochaia gazeta.
>St. Petersburg, 1914, three times a week

>1914:   June 11 - July 22 (Nos. 1, 3, 4, 6)
>>Ref: Beliaeva 2708, Columbia 703

ZHIVAIA ZHIZN'
>Gazeta men'shevikov-likvidatorov.
>St. Petersburg, 1913, daily

>1913:   Nos. 1-19   (Microfilm)
>>Ref: Columbia 704, Beliaeva 2704

ZHIVOE DELO
>St. Petersburg, 1912, weekly

>1912:   Nos. 1-16   (Jan. - April) (Microfilm)
>>Ref: Columbia 704(a), Beliaeva 2711

ZHIVOE SLOVO
>Petrograd, 1916, daily

>1917:   Mar. 8(21), 15(28), July 5-9, Sept. 12 (Nos. 1(354), 3(356),
>7(360), 51(404)-55(408), 96(450))
>>Ref: Columbia 705, LC, p. 82

ZHIZN'
>Politicheskaia, obshchestvennaia i literaturnaia gazeta
>(vykhodit ezhednevno krome ponedel'nika)
>Geneva-Paris, 1915, daily

>1915:   Mar. 21 - Aug. 22 (Nos. 1-69, 71, 72, 88)
>1916:   No. 89
>>Ref: Columbia 708

ZHIZN'
>Organ Kamenskogo uezdnogo partiinogo komiteta i uezdnogo
>ispolnitel'nogo komiteta.   [Organ of the Kamen District Party
>Committee and of the District Executive Committee.]
>Kamen, twice a week

>1922:   Mar. 12 (No. 20(239))
>>Ref: LC, p. 24

ZHIZN'
>
Ezhednevnaia politicheskaia, literaturnaia i obshchestvennaia
gazeta.
>
Petrograd, 1917, daily

1917: Nov. 19 (Dec. 2) (No. 1)

Ref: LC, p. 82

ZHIZN'
>
Ezhednevnaia demokraticheskaia gazeta.
Revel, 1920, daily (6 times a week)

1920: Feb. 19 - Mar. 30 (Nos. 2, 3, 5, 6, 8, 10, 12-14, 16-22, 25,
27, 28, 31, 32)

Ref: LC, p. 166

ZHIZN'
>
Ezhednevnaia gazeta, obshchestvenno-politicheskaia i
literaturnaia.
Rostov-on-Don, daily

1919: July 20(Aug. 2), Aug. 20(Sept. 2), Aug. 21(Sept. 31),
24(Sept. 6), 28(Sept. 10), 31(Sept. 13), Sept. 1(14) - 5(18),
Oct. 8(21), Nov. 7(20), 13(26), Dec. 1(14) (Nos. 73, 97-98,
101, 104, 106-110, 136, 161, 166, 180)

Ref: Columbia 709, LC, p. 152

ZHIZN' I SVOBODA
>
Ezhenedel'naia politicheskaia, obshchestvennaia i literaturnaia
gazeta.
Moscow, 1906, weekly

1906: Nos. 1-23 (Microfilm)

Ref: Columbia 710, Beliaeva 2770

ZHIZN' ISKUSSTVA
>
Izdanie Otdela teatrov i zrelishch Narodnogo komissariata
prosveshcheniia Soiuza kommun Severnoi oblasti.
Petrograd, daily

1919: Jan. 14, Aug. 8, Dec. 14 (Nos. 58, 210, 316-317)

ZHIZN' NA VOSTOCHNOI OKRAINE
        Obshchedostupnaia sel'sko-khoziaistvennaia, torgovo-pro-
myshlennaia, literaturnaia i politiko-ekonomicheskaia gazeta na
russkom i mongolo-buriatskom iazykakh. (Bez predvaritel'noi
tsenzury)
        Chita, 1895, 5 times a week

    1896:   Apr. 2, June 29 (Nos. 59, 112)
                                    Ref: Lisovskii 2483

ZHIZN' NATSIONAL'NOSTEI
        Ezhenedel'nyi organ narkomnatsa. [Organ of the People's
Commissariat for Nationalities.]
        In Jan. 1923, superseded by journal of same title, which was
discontinued in Jan. 1924.
        Moscow, weekly

    1918,   Nov. 9 - Sept. 11, 1922
    1923,   Jan. - Jan. 1924 (Journal) (Microfilm)

ZNAMIA
        Rabochaia gazeta.
        New York, daily

    1889:   (Nos. 1-10, 13-16)
    1890:   (Nos. 1-6)
                                    Ref: Columbia 713

ZNAMIA BOR'BY
        Ezhednevnaia politicheskaia i literaturnaia gazeta. Organ
Petrogradskago i Oblastnogo Komiteta partii levykh sotsialistov-
revoliutsionerov. [Organ of the Petrograd and Provincial Committees of the Party of Left-Wing Social Revolutionaries.]
        Petrograd, 1918, daily

    1918:   Mar. 19 - June 13 (Nos. 2, 3-31, 33-36, 38-71)
                                    Ref: Columbia 715, LC, p. 82

ZNAMIA KOMMUNY
        Ezhednevnaia gazeta Novocherkasskogo gorkoma VKP(b),
Gorsoveta i Gorsovprofa.
        Novocherkassk, daily

    1936:   July 21, Aug. 30 (Nos. 163(1873), 194(1904)

ZNAMIA REVOLIUTSII

Organ Sovetov rabochikh, krest'ianskikh i krasnoarmeiskikh deputatov g. Kazani i gubernii i Kazanskogo gubernskogo komiteta RKP (bol'shevikov). [Organ of the Soviets (of Toilers' Deputies) of the City of Kazan' and of the Province, and of the Kazan' Provincial Committee of the Russian Communist Party.]
Kazan , 1917, daily

1919:   Nov. 7 (No. 253)

Ref: Columbia 716, LC, p. 26

ZNAMIA REVOLIUTSII

Organ Saratovskago komiteta partii levykh sots. -rev. (inter-natsionalistov). Bol'shaia ezhednevnaia politicheskaia i literaturnaia gazeta. [Organ of the Saratov Committee of the Party of Left-Wing Social Revolutionaries (Internationalists).]
Saratov,1918, daily

1918:   June 6(May 24) (No. 4)

Ref: LC, p. 154

ZNAMIA TRUDA

Ezhednevnaia rabochaia gazeta, izdavaemaia Petrogradskim komitetom Partii sotsialistov-revoliutsionerov. [Published by the Petrograd Committee of the Party of Social Revolutionaries.]
Petrograd, 1917, daily

1917:   Oct. 31 (No. 58)

Ref: Columbia 717, LC, p. 82

ZNAMIA TRUDA

Organ TSentral'nago Komiteta Partii Levykh Sotsialistov-Revoliutsionerov.
Petrograd, daily

1918:   Jan. 9 - June 13 (Nos. 114, 143-146, 148-153, 159-177, 179-226)

ZNAMIA TRUDOVOI KOMMUNY

Organ TSentral'nogo biuro narodnikov-kommunistov. [Organ of the Central Bureau of the Narodniki . (Populists).]
Moscow, 1918, daily

1918:   Oct. 20-26, Nov. 3-12 (Nos. 50(71) - 55(76), 62(83) - 67(88))
Ref: LC, p. 132

ZRENIE

Ezhenedel'nik.
St. Petersburg, 1907, weekly

1907:   Jan. 25 - Feb. 4 (Nos. 1-2)
                        Ref: Beliaeva 3227; Columbia 718

ZVENO

Ezhenedel'naia literaturno-politicheskaia gazeta pod redaktsiei
M.M. Vinavera i P.N. Miliukova.
Paris, 1923, weekly

1925:   Jan. 5-26, Feb. 28, June 1, 8, 22, Sept. 21 (Nos. 101 - 104,
        106, 122-123, 125, 128)
        Continued by the journal Zveno, ezhemesiachnyi zhurnal
literatury.

ZVEZDA

Organ Dnepropetrovskogo okrkoma KPBU, Okrispolkoma,
OSPS, Dorprofsozha i Raikoma metallistov.
Dnepropetrovsk, 1918, daily

1928:   Jan. 8 (No. 7(1641))
                        Ref: LC, p. 134

ZVEZDA

Ezhednevnyi organ Novogorodskogo gubispolkoma i Gubkoma
RKP. [Organ of the Novgorod Provincial Executive Committee and
of the Provincial Committee of the Russian Communist Party.]
Novgorod, 1918, daily

1919:   Nov. 7 (No. 264)
                        Ref: LC, p. 134

ZVEZDA

Ezhenedel'naia gazeta.
St. Petersburg, 1910, weekly
Continued as Nevskaia zvezda.

1910, Dec. 29(16) - May 5(Apr. 22), 1912 (Nos. 1-69)
                        Ref: Beliaeva 3106